GREAT RELIGIONS OF MODERN MAN

# Buddhism

GREAT RELIGIONS OF MODERN MAN

Richard A. Gard, *General Editor*

BUDDHISM

*Edited by* Richard A. Gard

CHRISTIANITY: CATHOLICISM

*Edited by* George Brantl

CHRISTIANITY: PROTESTANTISM

*Edited by* J. Leslie Dunstan

HINDUISM

*Edited by* Louis Renou

ISLAM

*Edited by* John Alden Williams

JUDAISM

*Edited by* Arthur Hertzberg

# Buddhism

EDITED BY

Richard A. Gard

GEORGE BRAZILLER

NEW YORK 1962

For information address the publisher
George Braziller, Inc.
215 Park Avenue South
New York 3

*Library of Congress Catalog Card Number: 61-15499*

First Printing, October 1961
Second Printing, December 1961

*Printed in the United States of America*

# Acknowledgments

The editor wishes to thank the following for permission to reprint the material included in this volume:

GEORGE ALLEN and UNWIN LTD.—for selection from T. R. V. Murti, *The Central Philosophy of Buddhism.*

BANARAS HINDU UNIVERSITY—for selections from Franklin Edgerton, *Buddhist Hybrid Sanskrit Language and Literature.*

E. J. BRILL, N. V. BOEKHANDEL—for selection from M. W. de Visser, *Ancient Buddhism in Japan.*

TRUSTEES OF THE BRITISH MUSEUM—for selection from Lionel Giles, *Descriptive Catalogue of the Chinese Manuscripts from Tunhuang in the British Museum.*

BRUNO CASSIRER (PUBLISHERS) LTD.—for selection from Edward Conze, *Buddhist Texts Through the Ages.*

THE CLARENDON PRESS, OXFORD—for selections from T. W. Rhys Davids, *Dialogues of the Buddha;*—and for selections from T. W. and C. A. F. Rhys Davids, *Dialogues of the Buddha.*

NALINAKSHA DUTT—for selection from his *Early Monastic Buddhism,* 1941.

JACOB ENSINK—for selection from his *The Question of Rastrapala.*

GORDON FRASER—for selections from Walpola Rahula, *What the Buddha Taught.*

HUTCHINSON PUBLISHING GROUP—for selections from Herbert V. Guenther, *Jewel Ornament of Liberation,* by permission of Rider & Company.

KITABISTAN—for selections from Anagarika B. Govinda, *Some Aspects of Stupa Symbolism.*

LUZAC & COMPANY LTD.—for selections from A. M. Hocart, *The Temple of the Tooth in Kandy* (Memoirs of the Archaeological Survey of Ceylon, Vol. IV);—and for selections from Sukumar Dutt, *The Buddha and Five After-Centuries.*

MOUTON & COMPANY—for selection from Edward Conze, *The Prajñāpāramitā Literature.*

FIRMA K. L. MUKHOPADHYAY—for selections from Benoytosh Bhattacharyya, *The Indian Buddhist Iconography.*

JOHN MURRAY and GROVE PRESS, INC.—for selections from Richard Robinson, *Chinese Buddhist Verse* (Wisdom of the East Series).

PALI TEXT SOCIETY—for selections from T. W. Rhys Davids & William Stede, *The Pali Text Society's Pali-English Dictionary;*—for selections from E. M. Hare, *The Book of Gradual Sayings;*—for selections from I. B. Horner, *The Collection of the Middle Length Sayings;*—for selections from Mrs. Rhys Davids and F. H. Woodward, *The Book of Kindred Sayings,* Part II;—for selections from F. L. Woodward, *The Book of Kindred Sayings,* Part V;—for selection from T. W. and C. A. F. Rhys Davids, *Dialogues of the Buddha,* Part II;—for selection from Rhys Davids, *Dialogues of the Buddha,* Part III;—for selections from Mrs. Rhys Davids, *Psalms of the Early Buddhists;*—for selections from I. B. Horner, *The Book of the Discipline;*—for selections from F. L. Woodward, *The Book of the Gradual Sayings,* or *More-Numbered Suttas;*—for selections from C. A. F. Rhys Davids, *The Minor Anthologies of the Pali Canon;*—for selections from J. J. Jones, *The Mahāvastu;*—for selection from G. P. Malalasekera, *Dictionary of Pāli Proper Names.*

G. P. PUTNAM'S SONS—for selection from T. W. Rhys Davids, *Buddhism: Its History and Literature.*

ROUTLEDGE & KEGAN PAUL LTD.—for selections from Har Dayal, *The Bodhisattva Doctrine in Buddhist Sanskrit Literature.*

ROYAL ASIATIC SOCIETY—for selections from Th. Stcherbatsky, *The Central Conception of Buddhism and the Meaning of the Word "Dharma"*.

R. SEMAGE—for selections from Bhikku Ñāṇamoli, *The Path of Purification (Visuddhimagga)*.

DAISETZ TEITARO SUZUKI—for selections from his *The Training of the Zen Buddhist Monk.*

UNION BUDDHA SĀSANA COUNCIL—for selections from *Dīgha Nikāya: Sīlakkhandha.*

UNIVERSITY OF CALCUTTA—for selections from Shashi Bhushan Dasgupta, *An Introduction to Tāntric Buddhism.*

TO

MY TEACHERS, STUDENTS, AND FRIENDS
IN BUDDHIST ASIA
AND TO ALL OTHERS INTERESTED
IN THEIR WAY OF LIFE

# Contents

CHAPTER ONE

# Introduction

## 1. *The Buddhist Point of View*

Conceived in Asia, Buddhism is an historic expression of a universal human ideal. It offers any individual or society a voluntary way of thought and conduct, based upon an analysis of conditioned existence, dependent upon supreme human effort, and directed toward the realization of freedom in perfect existence.

As a way of life, Buddhism has been variously understood, followed, and expounded by its adherents, and variously studied, interpreted, and described by non-Buddhists. Ethnic traits and social customs, subjective interests and partial knowledge, and many other factors have influenced the development of Buddhist beliefs and practices and thus condition an understanding of the nature of Buddhism by all concerned.

In its historical development and geographical expansion—in twenty-five centuries, over thirty Asian countries, and some twenty-two Asian languages—Buddhism has been designated in several ways. The Theravāda Buddhists in South and Southeast Asia traditionally speak of, and live in, the Buddha Sāsana. The Pāli term *sāsana* (cf. Sanskrit *śāsana*) means "teaching, doctrine, discipline, religion" and "is perhaps the nearest equivalent of the modern expression, Buddhism. In its developed sense, it denotes a System. It has a socio-religious content and is used as a term of delimitation, with a touch perhaps of communal consciousness too,—'within the *sāsana*' meaning 'within the Buddhist system of faith and its rule of living.' "[1]* Hence, the Theravāda conception of Buddhism connotes an emphasis upon community spirit and order in life. The Mahāyāna Buddhists in East Asia and elsewhere customarily refer to the Buddha Dharma in Sanskrit (cf. Buddha Dhamma in Pāli, also used by the Theravādins), Fo-chiao in Chinese, Bukkyō in Japanese, Pulgyo in Korean, or Phật-Giáo in Vietnamese, all meaning "the Teaching of the Buddha," while Chös in Tibetan signifies the Dharma or simply "the religion." Thus the Mahāyāna conception of Buddhism embodies an emphasis on doctrinal guidance in the conduct of life.

On the other hand, most Westerners or non-Buddhists tend to view and define Buddhism as a philosophy, noting its humanistic concern with right action being based upon right knowledge, or as a religion, perceiving the frequent incorporation of folk religious beliefs and practices in its institutional development. But "philosophy" and "religion" are primarily Western concepts which have had various meanings in the course of Western thought; although they have been transposed and translated into Asian terms (for example, *chê-hsüeh* and *tsung-chiao* in Chinese, *tetsugaku* and *shūkyō* in Japanese) they should not be used contradistinguishably to dichotomize the essential unity of Buddhist thought and practice. In other respects, however, Buddhism may be described as a philosophic interpretation and religious expression of a way of life, Asian in origin but intended to be universally human in outlook.

* For numbered footnotes, see References, pp. 245 ff.

The simple definition of the Buddha as "the Enlightened One" in both epistemological and metaphysical or existential respects and the meaning of Bodhi as supreme "Enlightenment" remind us that Buddhism, however conceived, is primarily experiential in nature and purpose. It concerns the life, here and now, of each sentient being and thus interrelatedly of all existence.

Where, then, should our exposition of Buddhism begin? The Buddhist, living within the circle of the Buddha Sāsana/Śāsana* and following the Buddha Dhamma/Dharma, would suggest that we start from where we stand in life: our perspective normally develops from our present, conditioned state of being; how could we begin from where we are not? Similarly, the non-Buddhist, living outside the circle and facing it from any direction, might well begin where he is, reaching out and touching the circle at his special point of interest. In any case, whether in study or in practice, Buddhism invites and accepts us as we are and is characteristically tolerant of

* Pāli words (and their versions in Burmese, Cambodian, Lao, Môn, Sinhalese, and Thai) are customarily used by the Theravāda tradition, whereas Sanskrit and especially Buddhist Hybrid Sanskrit words (and their translation into Chinese, Tibetan, and other languages with corresponding versions in Japanese, Korean, Vietnamese, Mongolian, etc.) are used by the Mahāyāna and Vajrayāna traditions. Hence the particular use of a Pāli, Sanskrit, or other Asian-language word in this book will indicate the relevant Buddhist tradition or ethnic context of that word. For example, Dhamma is the Pāli term used in the Theravāda tradition, whereas Dharma is the Sanskrit term used in the Mahāyāna and Vajrayāna traditions; Ch'an-tsung refers to a particular school in Chinese Buddhism, while Zen-shū refers to its Japanese development. In the case of a twofold Pāli-Sanskrit word, the slash mark / will be used when the Pāli and Sanskrit, or Buddhist Hybrid Sanskrit, words are spelled differently; but a single word will be used when the spelling is identical: for example, the Dhamma/Dharma, Nibbāna/Nirvāṇa, whereas the Buddha, Bodhi.

those views and ethnocentric mores which typify us. To start in Buddhism we need no doctrinal assumptions but simply an awareness of the conditioned existence of ourselves and all others.

This concern with conditioned existence and one's immediate perception and subsequent study of it, this tolerance of all right-minded inquiry and stress on right action guided by right understanding, this philosophical-religious way of life for any individual or society, this reliance upon supreme human effort and the possibility of experiencing freedom in perfect existence—these principles characterize Buddhism and express its point of view in life. In short, freedom in thought is a prerequisite for freedom in existence.

The Buddhist spirit of reasoned inquiry is exemplified in numerous accounts of the Buddha's own conduct and advice to others. Two examples from early Pāli texts may be cited here:

> And the Bhagavā [the Buddha] said: "Monks, if others speak against me, or against the Dhamma [the Teachings] or the Sangha [the Order], you should not on that account either have a grudge against them or suffer heart-burning or feel ill-will. If you, on that account could be angry and hurt, that would become a danger to your own selves. If, when others speak ill of me, or of the Dhamma or the Sangha, you feel angry at that, and displeased, would you then be able to judge how far that speech is good or bad?"
>
> "That would not be so, Lord."
>
> "But when others speak ill of me, or of the Dhamma or of the Sangha, you should rebut their statement by saying: 'For this or that reason, this is not the fact, that is not so, such a thing does not exist among us, is not in us.'
>
> "But also monks, if others should speak in praise of me, in praise of the Dhamma, in praise of the Sangha, you should

not on that account be filled with pleasure and gladness, or be lifted up in mind.

"Monks, if others should speak in praise of me, in praise of the Dhamma, in praise of the Sangha, and you, on that account, be filled with pleasure or gladness, or be lifted up in mind, that also would become a danger to your own selves.

"Monks, when others speak in praise of me, or of the Dhamma or the Sangha, you should admit the fact as right, saying: 'For this or that reason this is the fact, that is so, such a thing exists among us, is in us.' "[2]

Now the Kālāmas of Kesaputta heard it said that Gotama the recluse, the Sakyans' son who went forth as a wanderer from the Sakyan clan, had reached Kesaputta. . . . So the Kālāmas of Kesaputta came to see the Exalted One [Bhagavā]. On reaching him, some saluted the Exalted One and sat down at one side: some greeted the Exalted One courteously, and after the exchange of greetings and courtesies sat down at one side: some raising their joined palms to the Exalted One sat down at one side: some proclaimed their name and clan and did likewise; while others without saying anything just sat down at one side. Then as they thus sat the Kālāmas of Kesaputta said this to the Exalted One:

"Sir, certain recluses and brāhmins come to Kesaputta. As to their own view, they proclaim and expound it in full: but as to the view of others, they abuse it, revile it, depreciate and cripple it [lit., deprive it of its wings]. Moreover, sir, other recluses and brāhmins, on coming to Kesaputta, do likewise. When we listen to them, sir, we have doubt and wavering as to which of these worthies is speaking truth and which speaks falsehood."

"Yes, Kālāmas, you may well doubt, you may well waver. In a doubtful matter wavering does arise. Now look you, Kālāmas. Be ye not misled by report or tradition or hearsay. Be not misled by proficiency in the collections [citing the authority of religious texts], nor by mere logic or inference, nor after considering reasons, nor after reflection on and approval of some theory [taking delight in speculative opinions], nor because it fits becoming [has seeming possibilities], nor out of respect for a recluse (who holds it). But, Kālāmas, when you know for yourselves: These things are unprofitable, these things are blameworthy, these things are censured by the intelligent; these things, when performed and undertaken, conduce to loss and sorrow,—then indeed do ye reject them, Kālāmas. . . .

"But if at any time ye know of yourselves: These things are profitable, they are blameless, they are praised by the intelligent: these things, when performed and undertaken, conduce to profit and happiness,—then, Kālāmas, do ye, having undertaken them, abide therein."[3]

Similarly, the Buddhist spirit of tolerance is related in the *Upāla-sutta* of the Pāli Majjhima-Nikāya and has been summarized by the Venerable Dr. Walpola Rahula:

Once in Nālandā a prominent and wealthy householder named Upāli, a well-known lay disciple of Nigaṇṭha Nātaputta (Jaina Mahāvīra), was expressly sent by Mahāvīra himself to meet the Buddha and defeat him in argument on certain points in the theory of Karma, because the Buddha's views on the subject were different from those of Mahāvīra. Quite contrary to expectations, Upāli, at the end of the discussion, was convinced that the views of the Buddha were right and those of his master were wrong. So he begged the Buddha to accept him as one of his lay disciples (*Upāsaka*). But the Buddha asked him to reconsider it, and not to be in a hurry, for "considering carefully is good for well-known men like you." When Upāli expressed his desire again, the Buddha requested him to continue to respect and support his old religious teachers as he used to.

In the third century B.C., the great Buddhist Emperor Asoka of India, following this noble example of tolerance and understanding, honoured and supported all other religions in his vast empire. In one of his Edicts carved on rock [No. XII], the original of which one may read even today, the Emperor declared:

"One should not honour only one's own religion and condemn the religions of others, but one should honour others' religions for this or that reason. So doing, one helps one's own religion to grow and renders service to the religions of others too. In acting otherwise one digs the grave of one's own religion and also does harm to other religions. Whosoever honours his own religion and condemns other religions, does so indeed through devotion to his own religion, thinking 'I will glorify my own religion.' But on the contrary, in so doing he injures his own religion more gravely. So concord is good: Let all listen, and be willing to listen to the doctrines professed by others.' "[4]

The Buddhist principle of tolerance for everyone is experientially based, and expressed, in the belief and practice that all beings can attain freedom in perfect existence: Nibbāna (Pāli term) in the Theravāda tradition and Nirvāṇa (Sanskrit term) in the Mahāyāna and Vajrayāna traditions. Such an ideal gives a profound meaning and direction to life for those who seek, find, and follow the Buddha-view as the Buddhist way. Here, the teaching of sGam.po.pa (1079-1153 A.D.), the Tibetan philosopher-saint, is particularly relevant:

He is convinced that every sentient being is capable of attaining enlightenment which is not so much a change from one extreme, Saṃsāra, to another, Nirvāṇa, but the ineffable experience in which both have ceased to dominate the thought of man so that he begins to live his life as transformed by pure transcendence.

Saṃsāra and Nirvāṇa are not entities, but interpretations of our experiences, and as such are both Śūnyatā, which again is an operational term, not an ontological concept. Although all sentient beings may attain enlightenment by their own efforts, because each is a potential Buddha, human existence is the most suitable occasion for such striving. It is not something self-evident, although we can only act as human beings. We must always be aware of human dignity and so respect others as equally worthy beings. By this awareness we gain confidence in being able to realize a thoroughly human and humane goal, and find the meaning of life. In this striving we are in need of spiritual friends. They may be found at any level, because, if Saṃsāra and Nirvāṇa as interpretations have their common root in transcendence, which from the ordinary point of view is just nothing (Śūnyatā), whatever and whomsoever we meet serves as a symbol and guide to transcendence. Since all our experiences, from the most sordid aspects of life to the most lofty ideals, are of a transitory nature, it is important for us always to be aware of this fact and not to build on them as a solid foundation which will only obscure our mind and expose us to unending sorrow. In this awareness the transitory does not lead us into despair, but serves as a lamp to the everlasting which no words can express and which pervades everything temporal. . . .

Thus in whatever we do we are in duty bound to be aware of being human beings and of our task which must not be allowed to glide into a betrayal of human dignity but must be expressive of this dignity in benevolence and compassion.[5]

## 2. *Buddhist Historical Developments*

Since the sixth century B.C., Buddhist beliefs and practices, literature, and institutions have been spreading, developing, and adjusting to diverse societal environments in more than thirty countries in Asia and, in turn, influencing their cultures and religious ways of life. Since the nineteenth century, Buddhist ideas have also been of interest to Western philosophy, literature, music-drama, and other cultural arts.

In these and other respects, Buddhist historical developments are so complex and ramified that it is difficult to view them comprehensively. In fact, most present histories of Buddhism relate only a few of its regional or topical developments, since the subject cannot be surveyed in its entirety until more source materials have been collected, evaluated, and interpreted, further political-social-cultural histories of Buddhist areas have been written and consulted for reference purposes, and the principles of accretion and concurrent growth in the nature of Buddhist expansion have been better determined and studied. In short, Buddhist historical research and writing need to be much increased before the subject can be properly understood. Nevertheless, an attempt will be made here to indicate some of the significant Buddhist developments within periods of five centuries each.

During the sixth to first centuries B.C., the Buddha was regarded as a Teacher (Satthā/Śāstar) and conceived as a Great Man (Mahāpurisa/Mahāpuruṣa) and Universal Ruler (Cakkavattin/Cakravartin); popular veneration of him developed into a Buddha-cult (Buddha-pūjā), which expressed and facilitated belief in him as the Exalted One (Bhagavā or Bhagavant). The Buddha Dhamma/Dharma was developed in doctrinal statement and scholastic interpretation and textually begun in Pāli, Sanskrit, and Buddhist Hybrid Sanskrit. Several Buddhist Councils or Conferences (Saṅgīti) are traditionally believed to have been held in India: the First Council at Rājagaha/Rājagṛha (Rājgir) shortly after the Buddha's demise [its nature has been questioned by scholars]; the Second Council at Vesāli/Vaiśāli (Besarh) some 100 or 110 years later; and, according to Theravāda accounts, a Third Council at Pāṭaliputta/Pāṭaliputra (Patna) allegedly convened by Emperor Aśoka of the Maurya Dynasty sometime in the third century B.C. [its historicity or nature has been questioned]; a Vinaya recital in the Thūpārāma at Anurādhapura in Ceylon (then called Siṅhala[dvīpa] or Laṅkā) in the mid-second century B.C.

and a Fourth Council in the Aluvihāra at Mātale in Ceylon in the late first century B.C. [these Ceylonese councils are recognized only by the Theravāda tradition]. Accordingly, various Buddhist schools arose, coalesced, disappeared, or developed—totaling more than eighteen—among which the Theravāda, Mahāsaṅghika, Sarvāstivāda, and Sautrāntika became the most influential. The Theravāda tradition was widespread but established itself permanently in Ceylon; the Mahāsaṅghika fostered dissension from the Theravāda which, together with other factors, eventually resulted in the rise of the Mahāyāna tradition; the Sarvāstivāda tradition likewise spread, particularly in north-central and northwest India and probably also in Suvaṇṇabhūmi/Suvarṇabhūmi (cf. lower Burma, Thailand, and possibly Cambodia); and the Prajñāpāramitā doctrinal literature and related Mahāyāna tradition began to evolve. Buddhist followers as wanderers (*pabbajakas/parivrājakas* or *pabbajitas/pravrājitas*) and mendicants (*bhikkhus/bhikṣus* = monks, *bhikkhunīs/bhikṣunīs* = nuns) settled in residences (at first as *āvāsas* during the Vassa or rainy season retreat, later established as *vihāras* including *pariveṇas;* in the next period as *saṅghārāmas*), became communities (*saṅghas*), and thus established Buddhist monasticism. Buddhist architecture, sculpture, and literary arts also developed, and the Buddha Sāsana/Śāsana was identified with political and social welfare in various countries in India and Ceylon.

During the first to fifth centuries A.D., Buddhism spread rapidly from India eastward to Bengal during the Gupta Dynasty rule (320?-533/4 A.D.); southeastward to Suvaṇṇabhūmi/Suvarṇabhūmi including Fu-nan (Cambodia) and Champa (Việt-nam), and to Suvarṇadvīpa

(Malay Peninsula in Indonesia); northwestward to Kāśmīra (Kāshmīr), Gandhāra, Bactria (capital Balkh), Parthia, and Sogdiana (capital Samarkand); thence eastward through Tokharistan to Central Asia (Tarim or Taklamakan Desert): Kāshgar, Yarkand, Karghalik, Khotan, Niya, Tukhara (Endere), Calmadana (Cherchen), and Kroraina (later Loulan, now Shan-shan in the Lobnor region) on the southern route and Kāshgar, Yarkand, Bharuka (Uch-Turfan), Kucī (Kucha), Agni (Karasahr), Turfan, and Hami on the northern route, and Tun-huang, An-hsi, and Yu-mên-kuan at the east end; to China principally from Central Asia but also from Southeast Asia by sea (also by land?); and from China northeastward to Koguryŏ, Paekche, and Silla (Samguk in Korea). During 399–414 A.D., the Chinese Buddhist pilgrim Fahsien visited Central Asia, India, Ceylon, and Java (dvīpa). In northwest India, a Buddhist Council or Conference was convened, either in Kāśmīra or in Gandhāra at Puruṣapura (cf. Peshawar) by King Kaniṣka of the Kuṣāṇa Dynasty sometime during the first century A.D. which strengthened the Sarvāstivāda tradition; its authority is not recognized by the Theravādins but is generally regarded by others as the Fourth Council (or the Third for the Sarvāstivādins). The Theravāda tradition developed principally in Ceylon but was also known in northern India; the Sarvāstivāda tradition (under several School names, and finally as the Vaibhāṣika) appears to have prevailed in Suvarṇabhūmi, Suvarṇadvīpa, Kāśmīra, Gandhāra, and Central Asia and was known elsewhere in India, China, and Korea. The Prajñāpāramitā literature and related Mahāyāna tradition developed mainly in the Buddhist areas of India, Central Asia, China, and Korea; this movement was in two general directions, the Mādhyamika School and the Yogācāra School, each with varying subschools. Conceptions of the Buddha further developed into the Bodhisattva doctrine and numerous idealized Buddhas in the Mahāyāna tradition, while the Buddha-cult was aided by Hindu Bhakti devotional practices and acquired variant ethnic forms as it was being adopted by different peoples. The Dhamma in Pāli accumulated scholarly commentaries and treatises, for example, those by Buddhaghosa in the fifth century, and the Dharma in Buddhist Hybrid Sanskrit expanded into the canonical literatures of various non-Theravāda and Mahāyāna Schools through translations, commentaries, and original compositions in many languages. Buddhist monasticism became institutionalized as Saṅghas (Communities) or Nikāyas (Groups) in various countries, usually in close cooperation with kingship which was the prevailing form of political authority. Also in this period, Buddhist cultural pursuits made remarkable progress and established their traditional place in the heritage of Asian art.

During the sixth to tenth centuries A.D., Buddhism continued to spread, principally from Korea and China to Japan, and from India to Nepal and thence to Tibet. Foreign travel by Buddhist pilgrims and scholars increased: notably, Sung-yün and Hui-sang during 518–*ca.* 521 to Central Asia, Tokharistan, (Sogdiana?), Udyāna, and Gandhāra; Hsüan-tsang (or Yüan-chuang, 596–664) during 629–645 to Central Asia and India; I-ching (or I-tsing, 635–713) during 671–695 to Sumatra and India; Chien-chên (Japanese: Ganjin, 688–763); during 724–754 to Japan, Hainan, and China; and the Japanese Ennin (Jikaku Daishi, 793–864) three times during 838–847 to China. The Theravāda tradition grew in Ceylon whereas the Sarvāstivāda was still prominent in Central Asia and respected in Tibet but declined elsewhere; the Mahāyāna tradition generally prevailed, often concurrently with non-Buddhist beliefs and practices, in China, India, Japan, Korea, Nepal, Śrīvijaya, and Tibet and at times in Ceylon (Anurādhapura), Champa (Việt-Nam), Chen-la (Cambodia), and Pagān or Pukām (north-central Burma); the Vajrayāna tradition developed principally in northern India, Bengal, Nepal, and Tibet while some of its beliefs and practices were incorporated into the Chinese (Mi-chiao), Korean (Milgyo), and Japanese (Mikkyō) esoteric forms of the Mahāyāna tradition and apparently were also known in Pagān, Ceylon, and Southeast Asia (Śrīvijaya especially). Mahāyāna literature continued to be written, translated, and studied, while Vajrayāna texts developed in relation to it and the Tantras in India. The Buddha-concept and Buddha-cult culminated in the Buddhist pantheons and elaborate rituals in the Mahāyāna and Vajrayāna traditions. In every Buddhist country or area, the Saṅgha progressed or declined according to favorable or unfavorable royal and public support, societal conditions, and its own observance or negligence of monastic discipline. In architecture, painting, sculpture, literature, and the handicrafts, Buddhism everywhere made historic contributions to the cultural arts of Asia. In many ways this period was perhaps the most remarkable and significant in the history of Buddhism.

During the eleventh to fifteenth centuries A.D., Buddhist institutions declined, disappeared, or were supplanted by Hinduism or Islam in most of India and Central Asia; they were established in Lang Chang (Laos), Mongolia, various Siamese states, and presumably in Bhutan and Sikkim; they progressed in Cambodia, Ceylon, and Japan but not notably in China, Korea, or Nepal. By the end of the period, the Theravāda tradition had supplanted any remaining Mahāyāna elements in Burma, Cambodia, Laos, and Siam, whereas a reformed Vajrayāna predominated in Tibetan cultural areas. The Buddha concepts, cults, and pantheons expanded in doctrine, practice, and art forms; Buddhist literature continued to be written, studied, and edited as canonical collections; and in all areas, Saṅgha institutions were subjected to occasional persecutions, societal strife, and monastic reforms. The Buddhist cultural arts presented remarkable achievements in Burma (Pagān), Cambodia (Angkor Thom), Ceylon (Polonnaruva), Japan (Kamakura), and elsewhere.

During the sixteenth to twentieth centuries A.D., the most significant changes in Buddhist traditional beliefs, practices, and institutions occurred in their varied responses to the challenges presented by European colonialism, Westernized ideas and values, modern technology, and educational reforms. Henceforth, conceptions and cults of the Buddha are questioned from non-Buddhist viewpoints, the Buddha Dhamma/Dharma is reinterpreted by nontraditional scholarship, and the Saṅgha is conditioned by relatively new forms of political and public interest. Adherents of the Theravāda, Mahāyāna, and Vajrayāna are beginning to study each other's traditions as components of their common heritage, and are attempting to determine, describe, and support the role of the Buddha Sāsana/Śāsana in the present-day world. Asian Buddhists are making pilgrimages and visits to each other's country on an unprecedented scale; they are conferring with each other more frequently and internationally, as in the case of the Sixth Great Council (Chaṭṭha Sangāyanā) in Rangoon during May, 1954–May, 1956 [the Fifth Burmese Council was convened by King Min-don-min at Mandalay in 1871], the Buddha Jayanti celebrations in Asia during May, 1956–November, 1957, and the World Fellowship of Buddhists Conferences of 1950 (Colombo), 1952 (Tōkyō), 1954 (Rangoon), 1956 (Kathmandu), 1958 (Bangkok), and planned for 1961 (Phnom-Penh). The reorganization of monastic education in the form of Westernized or modern Buddhist schools, colleges, and universities; the exchange of Buddhist publications among the laity and between scholars; the increasing social consciousness of the Saṅgha and public welfare activity by Buddhist lay organizations; and the ideological and material exploitation of Buddhist beliefs, personnel, and facilities by Communist governments—these new factors may become significant in the future development of Buddhism.

### 3. *Traditional Buddhist Ways, Schools, and Paths*

In the historical development of Buddhism, various ways (*yāna*), schools (*vāda* and *vādin*), and paths (*magga/mārga*) have been devised and instituted as *means* for the realization of the Buddhist way of life and attainment of Enlightenment (Bodhi). These have naturally acquired varying ethnic-cultural expressions and characteristics and have often induced proponents of a particular approach to differentiate their own means from those of others, but usually there is considerable unity among them.

With regard to major Buddhist ways, the word *yāna* in Pāli, Sanskrit, and Buddhist Hybrid Sanskrit signifies "the way, method, or means by which one may attain Enlightenment." Chinese-oriented Mahāyānists, perhaps precedented by the views of the early Mahāsaṅghika/Mahāsāṅghika School, customarily distinguish two kinds of *yānas:* Mahāyāna, meaning the Expansive Way, Means, Career or the Great Method; and Hīnayāna, meaning the Exclusive Way, Means, Career or the Lesser Method. (These terms are often misleadingly translated literally as the Great Vehicle and the Small Vehicle.) In Buddhist Hybrid Sanskrit texts, three *yānas* are ordinarily distinguished: the Śrāvaka-yāna for Śrāvakas (Pāli: Sāvakas; disciples who become Arahants/Arhats through hearing the Teachings of the Buddha and are unconcerned about the possible Enlightenment of others); the Pratyekabuddha-yāna or Pratyeka-yāna for Pratyeka-buddhas (Pāli: Pacceka-buddhas; those who attain Enlightenment by themselves and are unconcerned about the Enlightenment of others); and the Bodhisattva-yāna for Bodhisattvas (in this sense not quite comparable to Pāli: Bodhisatta, a being destined to become Enlightened; those who qualify as Buddhas but postpone their Enlightenment in order to help all sentient beings) or sometimes called the Buddha-yāna. In these respects, they equate the Śrāvaka-yāna and Pratyekabuddha-yāna with the so-called Hīnayāna and the Bodhisattva-yāna with the Mahāyāna. To this threefold classification of Buddhist ways, Tantric Buddhists add their own way, the Vajrayāna.

In general, Mahāyāna and Vajrayāna proponents do not disavow the Hīnayāna, or Śrāvaka-yāna and Pratyeka-buddha-yāna, as the basis of their way but regard it historically as having been incorporated into their own system. However, this view is not acceptable to adherents of the Theravāda, which is the earliest Buddhist tradition continuing today. Instead, they regard the Theravāda as the Teaching of the Theras (senior bhikkhus) which transmits the orthodox Dhamma of the Buddha and thus is to be distinguished from other Buddhist schools. In such cases, Bhikṣu Sangharakṣita has proposed that followers of the major Buddhist ways mutually understand each other's practices through a historical-sociological, comparative study of rituals in the Sarvāstivāda, Mahāyāna, and Vajrayāna traditions.[6]

With regard to the principal Buddhist schools which implement the major Buddhist ways, the suffixes *-vāda* and *-vādin* are often used in their Pāli/Sanskrit names to connote "doctrine, theory put forth, creed, belief, school, sect" and its "proponents, adherents, followers." As mentioned in the preceding Section 2, numerous Buddhist schools evolved primarily from the Buddhist Councils, or from their resultant conditions for the well-being and spread of the Buddha Sāsana/Śāsana. They have been established in many countries according to societal and monastic requirements, have assumed certain ethnic-cultural expressions and characteristics, and have either survived as traditional Buddhist institutions or succumbed to external and internal disintegrating forces. Here only the most influential schools in Buddhist historical developments can be mentioned.

The so-called Hīnayāna movement once comprised many schools, totaling more than eighteen, of which there are various lists. Among these the most important were:

1. The Theravāda (Sanskrit: Sthaviravāda; the Teaching of the Elders, senior bhikkhus) which has continued as the orthodox Pāli form of Buddhism in

Burma, Cambodia, Ceylon, Laos, Thailand, and certain Buddhist communities elsewhere in South and Southeast Asia.

2. The Mahāsaṅghika (Sanskrit: Mahāsāṅghika; cf. Mahāsaṅgīti as the Great Assembly, hence "the majority") which is believed to have dissented from the Theravāda at the Second Council at Vesāli/Vaiśāli and fostered views which later culminated in the Mahāyāna.

3. The Sarvāstivāda (Pāli: Sabbathavāda; the Teaching or Doctrine that All *dharmas* [elements] Exist; also later called in some areas Mula-Sarvāstivāda or Abhidharma [variously defined, e.g. Special Dharma, Higher Religion, for the attainment of Enlightenment] and finally Vaibhāṣika because of its dependence upon commentaries, *vibhāṣā*) which was once widespread in Suvarṇabhūmi and Suvarṇadvīpa, Gandhāra, Kāśmīra, and elsewhere in India, Central Asia, Nepal, Tibet, China (as the P'i-t'an-tsung and Chü-shê-tsung), Korea (textual study only?), and Japan (Kusha-shu, later Kusha-shū; cf. Chü-shê-tsung). The Buddhist Council convened by King Kaniṣka of the Kuṣāṇa Dynasty was essentially a Sarvāstivāda Conference. Among the notable Sarvāstivāda writers (dates often unknown or problematic) may be mentioned: Ārya Kātyāyanīputra, Mahākauṣṭhila, Sthavira Vasumitra, Sthavira Devaśarmā, Pūrṇa, Ārya Śāriputra, Ārya Maudgalyāyana, Vasubandhu (*ca.* 320–400 A.D.; later a Yogācāra writer), Saṅghabhadra, Dharmottara, Dharmatrāta, Yaśomitra, and others.

4. Several transitional schools between the Sarvāstivāda and the Mahāyāna, such as the Vātsīputriya (Pāli: Vajjiputtaka, Vajjiputtiya), which held the doctrine of *pudgala* (*puggala;* the individual is neither the same nor

different from the five *skandhas/khandhas*, compounding elements of being or agglomerations comprising "personality": *rūpa* [material qualities], *vedanā* [feeling], *saṃjñā* [*saññā, perception*], *saṃskāra* [*sankhāra*, coefficients of consciousness], and *vijñāna* [*viññāṇa*, consciousness] and challenged the adequacy of the *dharma* exposition by the Sarvāstivādins; and the Sautrāntika or Sūtravāda (Pāli: Suttavāda; the reliance upon original texts, *sūtrānta* or *sūtra*), also called Saṅkrāntivāda (the view that the *skandhas* transmigrate from the former world to the later world), which developed the doctrines of conceptual construction (*vikalpa*) and representative perception (*bāhyānumeya-vāda* or *jñānākāra* as *viṣaya-sārūpya*). Later, *Sautrāntika* ideas coalesced with, or influenced, Mahāyāna doctrines to help form the Sautrāntika-Yogācara system and especially the Sautrāntika-Mādhyamika-Svātantrika School. Another important development was the Ch'êng-shih-tsung (Satyasiddhi? or Tattvasiddhi? School) in China, the Syŏng-sil-jong (cf. Ch'êng-shih-tsung) in Korea, and Jōjitsu-shu (in the mid-eighth century renamed Jōjitsu-shū; cf. Syŏng-sil-jong and Ch'êng-shih-tsung) in Japan. The principal text of this movement was the *Ch'êng-shih-lun* in Chinese translation by Kumārajīva (344–413 A.D.) from a now lost work (*Satyasiddhī-śāstra? Tattvasiddhi-śāstra?*), attributed to Harivarman (in India *ca.* third century A.D.), which may have been an attempt to synthesize the Vaibhāṣika and early Mahāyāna doctrines. It should be noted that in Japan, Sautrāntika studies (cf. Jōjitshu-shu, later Jōjitsu-shū) were affiliated with Mādhyamika studies (cf. Sanron-shu, later Sanron-shū).

Similarly, the so-called Mahāyāna movement has comprised various developments which are too numerous to be listed here by country. In general, however, the Mahāyāna may be viewed according to the following major schools or textual aspects.

1. The Prajñāpāramitā literature was a doctrinal development rather than a school, although a Pan-jo-tsung (Prajñā School) existed in China from the early fifth to about the seventh centuries A.D. "The composition of Prajñāpāramitā texts extended over about 1,000 years. Roughly speaking, four phases can be distinguished: 1. The elaboration of a basic text (*ca.* 100 B.C. to 100 A.D.), which constitutes the original impulse; 2. the expansion of that text (*ca.* 100 A.D. to 300); then, as the third, we get the re-statement of the doctrine in 3a. short Sūtras and in 3b. versified Summaries (*ca.* 300 to 500); and 4. the period of Tantric influence and of absorption into magic (600 to 1200)."[7] These texts were basically in Buddhist Hybrid Sanskrit with translations and commentaries in Central Asian languages or scripts, Chinese, Japanese, Tibetan, and Mongolian. Prajñāpāramitā doctrines stimulated the development and spread of the Mahāyāna in India, Central Asia, China, Korea, Japan, Nepal, Tibet, and Mongolia and were partly known in Cambodia (Khmer period), the Siamese and Indochinese states, Indonesia (Śrīvijaya period), and probably also in Burma (Pagān period) and Ceylon (Anurādhapura period).

2. The Mādhyamika, a formative school of Mahāyāna thought which expounds the main doctrines contained in the Prajñāpāramitā literature, signifies a doctrinal position: those who adhere to the middle view (*madhya*) devoid of duality or implied contradictions (*śūnya*), and thereby avoid all possible extremes (*madhyamā prati-*

*pad*) in attaining transcendent comprehension and understanding (*prajñā*) for Enlightenment (Bodhi). The name Mādhyamika is formed from the Sanskrit word *madhyama* (superlative of *madhya* meaning "middle, neutral, non-dual") and the *taddhita* suffix *ika*. As an exposition of the Buddha Dharma from the Prajñāpāramitā viewpoint, the Mādhyamika is also sometimes called Madhyamaka Darśana (the Middle View) or Śūnyavāda (the Teaching or Doctrine of Śūnyatā). The Mādhyamika in India was established by Nāgārjuna (*ca.* 150–250 A.D.) possibly at Nāgārjunikoṇḍa in Āndhradēśa in the south and at Nālandā in Magadha in the north, and was continued by his disciple Āryadeva (*ca.* 170–270 A.D.) in Āndhradēśa as well as at Nālandā, Pāṭaliputra, and elsewhere, and by Nāgabodhi (third century A.D.) and Rāhula(bhadra) (third century A.D.). The School later became divided into two main lines: the Mādhyamika-Prāsaṅgika School (fifth to eighth centuries A.D.), founded by Buddhapālita (*ca.* 470–540) at Dantapurī and continued especially by Candrakīrti (*ca.* 600–650) at Nālandā, by Śāntideva (*ca.* 691–743) at Nālandā, and by Dīpaṁkara Śrījñāna (Ācārya Atīśa, 980–1053) at Vikramaśīla; and the Mādhyamika-Svātantrika School (sixth to eleventh or later centuries), founded by Bhāvaviveka or Bhavya (*ca.* 490–570) near Dhānyakaṭaka which subdivided into the Sautrāntika-Mādhyamika-Svātantrika led by Bhāvaviveka and apparently continued by Divākara (613–687) in China during 676/680–687, and the Yogācāra-Mādhyamika-Svātantrika led by Śāntarakṣita (*ca.* 705–762) at Nālandā and continued by Śrīgupta (early eighth century) and his disciple Jñānagarbha (early eighth century), Kamalaśīla (*ca.* 713–763), Vimuktasena (dates?), Haribhadra

(9th? century) and his disciple Buddhajñānapāda (dates?). Concurrently, the Mādhyamika School developed in other areas under different names and, with the exception of Tibet and possibly Central Asia, according to a different group of texts now mostly extant only in their Chinese translations by Kumārajīva (344–413) and others. These area developments of the Mādhyamika outside India are: (a) in Central Asia (mid-fourth? to ninth? centuries) called the Chung-tsung (Middle School, cf. Mādhyamika?) by the Chinese, and introduced from India; (b) in China (early fifth to eighth? centuries) called the San-lun-tsung (Three [Mādhyamika] Treatises School) and other names, and introduced from Central Asia; (c) in Korea (early sixth to seventh or later centuries) known as Sam-non (cf. San-lun; Three [Mādhyamika] Treatises) studies [also a school?], and introduced from China; (d) in Japan (early seventh to fourteenth or later centuries) called the Sanron-shu (cf. Sam-non studies; Three [Mādhyamika] Treatises Study Group) and after the mid-eighth century the Sanron-shū (cf. San-lun-tsung; Three [Mādhyamika] Treatises School), and introduced first from Korea and then from China; and (e) in Tibet (mid-eighth to eleventh or later centuries) called Dbu-ma-pa (Mādhyamika), introduced from India via Nepal and still studied there in its Mādhyamika-Prāsaṅgika and Mādhyamika-Svātantrika forms.

3. The Yogācāra School (which emphasized ethical and meditative practices), with its epistemological-metaphysical development, the Vijñānavāda (the Teaching or Doctrine [*vāda*] that only "discriminating consciousness" [*vijñāna*] exists), was concurrent with the Mādhyamika School as a formative movement in Mahāyāna thought

and generally has predominated, particularly in its Chinese expression and extension in Japan, Korea, and Việt-Nam. It was established in India by Ārya Maitreya(nātha) (*ca.* 270–350 A.D.), the reputed author of the *Mahāyāna-sūtrālaṃkāra(-nāma-kārikā)*, the *Madhyānta-vibhaṅga(-kārikā)*, the *Dharma-dharmatā-vibhaṅga*, the *Ratnagotra-vibhāga Mahāyānottaratantra-śāstra* or simply *Uttaratantra* (attributed to him by the Tibetan tradition, but probably by Sāramati [*ca.* 350–450 A.D.]; later valued from the Mādhyamika-Prāsaṅgika standpoint), and the *Abhisamayālaṃkāra(-kārikā)* or *Abhisamayālaṃkāra-nāma Prajñāpāramitā-upadeśa-śastra* (later valued from the Yogācāra-Mādhyamika-Svātantrika standpoint). He was followed by Ārya Asaṅga (*ca.* 310–390), author of the *Mahāyāna-saṃgraha*, the *Mahāyāna-samuccaya*, and other works; the *Yogācāra-bhūmi-śāstra* (containing the *Bodhisattva-bhūmi*) is attributed to him by the Tibetan tradition but to Maitreya(nātha) by the Chinese tradition. In turn, Asaṅga converted his brother Vasubandhu (*ca.* 320–400) from Sarvāstivāda views; Vasubandhu wrote numerous commentaries and various works among which his *Vijñaptimātratā-siddhi: viṃśika* and *triṃśika* are particularly well known. Thereafter, the philosophical Vijñānavāda developed, especially by the logicians Dignāga (or Diṅnāga, *ca.* 400–480) and Dharmakīti (late seventh-early eighth centuries) and the commentators Dharmapāla (*ca.* 530–561) and Sthiramati (*ca.* 470–500). The Yogācāra School and especially its Vijñānavāda development spread to East Asia and is still studied in China (Wei-shih = Vijñaptimātratā) and Japan (Yuishiki = Wei-shih, Vijñaptimātratā) as well as in Tibet. The Ch'an-tsung (Dhyāna School) in China and its developments and modifications in Korea

(T'an-jong), Japan (Zen-shū), Việt-Nam and elsewhere may have been considerably influenced in *yoga* practi and *vijñāna* doctrine by the Yogācāra School.

4. A so-called Sukhāvatī ("Land of Bliss = Pure Land") movement, centering around a Buddha-pūjā veneration of Amitābha ("of Infinite Light") or Amitāyus ("of Infinite Life"), apparently in the early centurie A.D. arose in India, developed in Central Asia, and became established as various schools in China, Korea, Japan, and Việt-Nam; for example, in China the Ching-t'u-tsung (Pure Land School) in four transmissions among which Hui-yüan (333–416), T'an-luan (476–542), Tao-ch'o (562–645), and Shan-tao (613–681) are usually regarded as important exponents, and in Japan the Yūzū-nembutsu-shū of Ryōnin Shōnin (1071–1132), the Jōdo-shū (cf. Ching-t'u-tsung) of Hōnen Shōnin (1133–1212), the Jōdo-Shin-shū development of Shinran Shōnin (1173–1262), and the Ji-shū of Ippen Shōnin (1238–1289; precedented by Kūya, 903–972). The basic texts are the *Sukhāvatī-vyūha* in large and abridged versions and the *Amitāyur-dhyāna-sūtra.*

5. Numerous texts, besides those already mentioned, influenced the foregoing developments and, in certain cases, engendered particular Mahāyāna schools devoted to their study and veneration (cf. sūtra-*pūjā*). For example, the *Laṅkāvatāra* or *Saddharma-Laṅkāvatāra-sūtra* (especially important for Ch'an-tsung/Zen-shū doctrine), the *Saddharma-puṇḍarīka-sūtra* (basic for the Fa-hua-tsung or T'ien-t'ai-tsung/Tendai-shū and Nichiren-shū and influential elsewhere), the *Mahāyāna-śraddhotpāda* ("The Awakening of Faith in the Mahāyāna," attributed to an Aśvaghosa different from the author of the *Buddhacarita*), the *Saṃdhinirmocana-sūtra* (funda-

mental for Yogācāra studies), the *Avataṁsaka-sūtra* or *Buddhāvataṁsaka-sūtra* (last section extant in Buddhist Hybrid Sanskrit as the *Gaṇḍavyūha;* the basis for the Hua-yen-tsung/Kegon-shū), the *Nirvāṇa-sūtra* (the basis for the Nieh-p'an-tsung), the *Ratnagotra-vibhāga Mahāyānottaratantra-śāstra* or *Uttaratantra* probably by Sāramati (*ca.* 350–450 A.D.), the *Suvarṇaprabhāsa* or *Suvarṇabhāsottama-sūtra,* the *Samādhirāja* or *Candrapradīpa-sūtra,* the *Kāraṇḍa-vyūha,* the *Rāṣṭrapālaparipṛcchā,* the *Daśabhūmika-sūtra,* and numerous other works in Sanskrit, especially Buddhist Hybrid Sanskrit, and other Asian language versions or original compositions.

The Vajrayāna (the Way of the Vajra), as a major Buddhist *means* for attaining Enlightenment, bases its monastic order on the Sarvāstivāda Vinaya and derives many of its metaphysical doctrines from Mahāyāna texts (perhaps more from the Yogācāra than the Mādhyamika) with certain Vedāntic and Tantric influences. In addition, it characteristically employs advanced meditative practices and special, esoteric media for rituals: equipped with *abhiṣeka* (empowerment to perform, received from the teacher), instructed by *tantra* (special directions), and often through the *maṇḍala* (diagramed sphere of power), one may integrate personality in Body with *mudrā* (special hand-gesture), Speech with *mantra* (special spell) and *dhāraṇī* (special formula), and Mind with *dhyāna* (concentrated thought). Hence, as a composite system, the Vajrayāna is sometimes called Buddhist Tantra to distinguish it from Hindu Tantra (although both were probably influenced by a common, general source) or Tantra-yāna or Mantra-yāna or Kālacakra-yāna (the Means of Protection against the

Wheel of Time [Destruction]), but all these are actually aspects or phases of its development. The historical rise and spread of the Vajrayāna was briefly described above in Section 2, but four principal Indian/Tibetan kinds of Vajrayāna may be listed here: (1) Kriyā-tantra-yāna/Byavhi-rGyud-kyi-theg-pa, (2) Caryā-tantra-yāna or Upāya-tantra-yāna/Spyod-pahi-rGyud-kyi-theg-pa, (3) Yoga-tantra-yāna/rNal-hbyor-kyi-theg-pa, (4) Anuttara-yoga-tantra-yāna/Blamed-rGyud-kyi-theg-pa; cf. the Sahaja-yāna or Buddhist Sahajiyā development in Bengal.

Just as the major Buddhist ways (*yāna*) of thought and practice for the attainment of Enlightenment have been diversified in numerous schools (*vāda* and *vādin*), so these schools may be grouped and classified according to the nature of their functional approach or method for attaining Enlightenment. In this respect, five Buddhist paths (*magga/mārga*) may be briefly noted of which one or more may typify a particular Buddhist school and all, in varying degrees, implement the principal Buddhist ways. These paths are correlated with the Threefold Training (Ti-sikkhā/Tri-śikṣā), which will be described below in Chapter IV, Section 2; when fundamentally integrated, they comprise but one path or One Way.

1. *Sīla-magga/Śīla-mārga* is the path of discipline and virtuous conduct (cf. Adhisīla-sikkhā/Adhiśīla): followed by the Theravāda in its Vinaya (especially the Dasa-sikkhāpadāni, Dasa-sīla, Pañca-sīla, and the *Pāṭimokkha*), the Sarvāstivāda in its Vinaya (especially the *Prātimokṣa*) now largely preserved in the Mahāyāna and Vajrayāna traditions, the Mahāyāna (especially the six, later ten, Prajñāpāramitās and Bodhisattva-śīla practiced by the Mādhyamika, Yogācāra, and other schools), and the Vajrayāna (especially the six Pāramitās and the

*samaya* regarding every *abhiṣeka*). For school examples in Eastern Asia, note the Lü-tsung (Vinaya School) in China and the related Ritsu-shu (later called Ritsu-shū) in Japan.

2. *Jhāna-magga/Dhyāna-mārga* is the path of meditative concentration (*jhāna/dhyāna*) consisting of mindfulness (*sati/smṛti*), concentrative absorption (*samādhi*), and attentive concentration (*bhāvanā*) in two aspects of tranquillity and fixedness of mind = concentration (*samatha/śamatha-bhāvanā*) and introspection and intuition = transcendent analysis or insight (*vipasannā/vipaśyanā-bhāvanā*) (cf. Adhicitta-sikkhā/Adhicitta) leading to transcendent comprehension and understanding (*paññā/prajñā*) for Enlightenment (Bodhi): followed by the Theravāda (especially active today in Burma), the Mahāyāna (various schools, less so in the Sukhāvatī movement), and the Vajrayāna (as stressed in Tibetan cultural areas). For Mahāyāna school examples, note the Ch'an-tsung in China, the related Zen-shū in Japan, and remaining elements in Korea and Việt-Nam.

3. *Paññā-magga/Prajñā-mārga* is the path of transcendent comprehension and understanding for Enlightenment (Bodhi) (cf. Adhipaññā-sikkhā/Adhiprajñā) in which three kinds of *paññā/prajñā* may be distinguished: *sutamayā-paññā/śrutamayī-prajñā* (that transcendent comprehension, understanding, knowledge gained from oral tradition), *cintāmayā-paññā/cintāmayī-prajñā* (that . . . gained from pure thought, cf. *samādhi*), and *bhāvanāmayā-paññā/bhāvanāmayī-prajñā* (*that* . . . gained from cultured thought, cf. *bhāvanā*). This path is followed by the Theravāda (especially its analysis of the relational structure of existence, or study of the *Paṭṭhāna*

in the Abhidhamma Piṭaka), the Sarvāstivāda (previously in its Abhidharma), the Mahāyāna (especially by the Mādhyamika, Yogācāra and other Schools), and the Vajrayāna (as practiced in Tibetan cultural areas). For Mahāyāna (doctrinal examples, note the vast Prajñāpāramitā literature.

4. *Bhatti-magga/Bhakti-mārga* is the path of devotional practice, with some expectation of spiritual aid in return, centering around the veneration (*pūjā*) of the Buddha in various forms or manifestations (cf. Buddha-*pūjā and* thūpa/stūpa-*pūjā*), eminent School founders, and the Buddha Dhamma/Dharma (cf. sutta/sūtra-*pūjā*) —not found in the Ti-sikkhā/Tri-śikṣā and probably a result of the influence of Hindu Bhakti cults on the development of popular Buddhist beliefs and practices. This path is followed by the Theravāda (especially its thūpa-*pūjā*), the Mahāyāna (especially in its veneration of School founders and certain texts: Buddha-*pūjā* and sūtra-*pūjā*), and the Vajrayāna (especially in its esoteric rituals).

5. *Buddhānusmṛti-mārga* is the path of complete reliance upon the efficacy of Karuṇā (cf. "Saving Grace") as manifested and offered by the Amitābha Buddha (A-mi-t'o-fu in Chinese, Amida-butsu in Japanese) who is thus comparable to the Bodhisattva Avalokiteśvara. The idea (practice also?) is embryonic in the Theravāda tradition as Buddhānussati (Pāli term) or "mindfulness of the Buddha" but in the Mahāyāna as Buddhānusmṛti (Buddhist Hybrid Sanskrit term) this means is the culmination of the Sukhāvatī trend in the Bhakti-mārga. It begins with a profound pietism and recollection of the Buddha-object (often orally) and is fulfilled through

utter faith by the devotee. In short, the devotion (*pūjā*) of the Amitābha devotee becomes total piety which is realized as the complete, universal saving-compassion (*karuṇā*) of Amitābha expressed to/through/in that devotee (*pariṇāmana*). In the T'ien-t'ai/Tendai Schools and the Chên-yen/Shingon Schools, this path is esoteric (cf. Mi-chiao/Mikkyō) with Amitābha identified with the Mahāvairocana (the Great Sun Buddha) in the maṇḍala; in the Ching-t'u/Jōdo Schools, the path is based upon the vows or resolutions (*praṇidhāna*) of the Bodhisattva Dharmakāra as expressed or stated in the Sukhāvatī texts; in the Jōdo-Shin School, the path is centered on the eighteenth vow of the Bodhisattva Dharmakāra declared in the larger *Sukhāvatī-vyūha.*

The foregoing classification of five Buddhist paths, or rather a fivefold Buddhist path providing the means for attaining Enlightenment, is admittedly arbitrary and has been compositely formed from a survey of Buddhist principles and practices. An earlier, traditional Mahāyāna conception of the Buddhist path in five degrees or phases is given in the *Abhisamayālaṃkāra*(*-kārikā*), or *Abhisamayālaṃkāra-nāma Prajñāpāramitā-upadeśa-śāstra,* by Ārya Maitreya(nātha), (*ca.* 270–350 A.D.) which "is considered by the learned Tibetan tradition to be the most important [of the five treatises by him] as 1) a summary of the *Prajñā-pāramitā-sūtras,* and 2) as the text containing the special theory of the *mārga* or the Path to the attainment of Nirvāṇa according to the Mahāyānistic standpoint."[8] The following selection is from the analysis by E. Obermiller.

Now, what is this "Path," and in what sense is it to be understood? First of all we have to mention the tradition which takes into consideration 3 kinds of individuals, viz. the lowest (*skyes-bu-chuṅ-ṅu* = *adhama-puruṣa*), the intermediate (*skyes-bu-ḥbriṅ-pa* = *madhya-puruṣa*) and the highest (*skyes-bu-chen-po* = *mahā-puruṣa*). The first is the ordinary worldly being who cares only for worldly matters, and the highest aim he can pursue can be only a blissful existence in a future life. For the individual of the intermediate and the highest kinds, i.e. the Hīnayānist (Śrāvaka and Pratyekabuddha) and the Mahāyānist Bodhisattva, respectively, the Phenomenal World represents nothing but an object of disgust and sorrow. Such individuals accordingly search for a path to attaining a position in which one is no more disturbed by worldly turmoil. It is through constant meditation on the true aspect of existence and the full cognition of it that the deliverance from Phenomenal Existence can be secured. Accordingly, the general definition of the Path for the individuals of both the intermediate and the highest order is "the intuition (*abhisamaya*) of the Truth which is conducive to the attainment of Enlightenment, Nirvāṇa, and the liberation from the bonds of Phenomenal Existence." Its synonyms are "the way to Final Deliverance," "the process of the cognition of Truth," "the Vehicle" (*yāna* = *theg-pa*),—&c. It has five principal degrees which are:—

1) The Path of Accumulating Merit (*sambhāra-mārga* = *tshogs-lam*).

2) The Path of Training (*prayoga-mārga* = *sbyor-lam*).

3) The Path of Illumination (*darśana-mārga* = *mthoṅ-lam*).

4) The Path of Concentrated Contemplation (*bhāvanā-mārga* = *sgom-lam*).

5) The Final Path, where one is no more subjected to training (*aśaikṣa-mārga* = *mi-slob-lam*).

The last three represent "the Path of the Saint" (*ārya-mārga*), whereas the first two are regarded as subservient degrees.

Such are the degrees of the Path in general. But in regard to the various individuals, progressing on this fivefold Path, there is another threefold division, viz. the Path of the

Śrāvaka, the Path of the Pratyekabuddha, and the Path of the Bodhisattva (or the Mahāyānistic Path). These 3 different forms correspond to the 3 varieties of the faculty of cognition of the Truth [note: *śrāvaka-yāna-abhisamaya-gotra, pratyeka-buddha yāna-abhisamaya-gotra* and *tathāgata-yāna-abhisamaya-gotra.*] The Śrāvaka's cognition is that of the unreality of the Ego or individual as an independent whole [*pudgala-nairātmya*]. The Pratyekabuddha comes to the intuition of the objective unreality of the external world, without becoming free from the imputation concerning the reality of the subject that perceives. Finally, the Bodhisattva on his Path cognizes the unreality of all the separate elements of existence [*dharma-nairātmya*], which are intuited by him as merged in the unique undifferentiated Absolute.

The first 2 varieties are characterized as having only an egoistic aim, the liberation of the stream of elements [*saṃtāna*] constituting one's own personality from the bonds of the Phenomenal World. In that sense the Path of "the intermediate individual" is defined as "the mental activity characterized by the aversion towards Phenomenal Existence and the desire of attaining salvation exclusively for one's own self." The path of the Bodhisattva is on the contrary regarded as essentially altruistic; it has for its aim the attainment of Buddhahood in order to bring deliverance for other living beings.—

The principal constituent members of this process of meditation and intuition, the chief factors for the realization of the Path, are two in number, viz. the perfect quiescence of the mind (*śamatha* = *źi-gnas*) and transcendental analysis (*vipaśyanā* = *lhag-mthoṅ*). All the merits and achievements of the Hīnayānist and Mahāyānist Saints on their Paths, the mundane [*laukika*] as well as the super-mundane [*lokottara*], are regarded as the result of these 2 cooperating factors, the latter being the most essential part, the foundation, of every kind of transic meditation. We have accordingly to speak of the Path as conditioned by the joint agency of the said 2 elements. Therefore all the Yogins, all the meditators, *eo ipso* all the Saints on their Paths, must at all times take recourse to mental quiescence and transcendental analysis.[9]

## 4. *The Nature of Buddhist Literature*

A satisfactory presentation of the nature of Buddhist literature would require a historical survey of Buddhist languages and literary forms, councils and school developments, monastic practices and scholarship. Such a description with suitable quoted illustrations is manifestly impossible here, but certain characteristic features may be noted for general interest and as a guide for further study.

The various spoken languages and dialects in which the Buddha Dhamma/Dharma has been expounded since the sixth century B.C. are too numerous to be listed, but it should be mentioned that the Teachings were first stated and transmitted orally (as still emphasized by the Chinese Ch'an and Japanese Zen Schools) and that recitation of texts, usually from memory, is still customary in monastic ceremonies (such as the Pāṭimokkha on alternate Uposatha days in Thailand), in scholastic examinations (such as those held annually in Burma for the Tipiṭakadhara Grade), and in debates (as in Vajrayāna monasteries where argumentation may be enhanced by the ready citation of relevant texts).

Written Buddhist literature may be briefly described here according to language, script, and canon of the major Buddhist traditions.

The Tipiṭaka ("three baskets = containers = collections") of the Theravāda tradition was presented in Pāli from oral accounts, then recorded into early Sinhalese script (by stenciling *ōla* leaves with a stylus and treating them with *dummālā* oil) and is preserved in various editions in Burmese script (several editions and a Burmese translation in progress), Cambodian or Khmer script (an edition and Cambodian translation in progress), canonical Lao or *nang su tham* script (manuscripts, edition suspended), Môn script (manuscripts), Sinhalese script (several incomplete editions, one in progress, and a Sinhalese translation; largely the basis for the Pāli Text Society's edition in roman letters), and Thai script (several editions, and a Thai translation).

The several Tripiṭaka (cf. Tipiṭaka) canons of the Sarvāstivāda, Mahāyāna, and Vajrayāna traditions were originally written in Middle Indic dialects, of which Buddhist Hybrid Sanskrit was developed particularly for this use, in various scripts notably Brāhmī, Kharoṣṭhī, Gupta (especially Central Asian Slanting Gupta and Cursive Gupta), Devanāgarī, and sometimes Siddhamātṛkā (commonly called Hsi-t'an in Chinese, Shittan in Japanese, Siddham in English) and Kavi (Old Javanese). Translations from certain Pāli, Sanskrit, and especially Buddhist Hybrid Sanskrit texts were made into various languages and from these versions further translations were made into other languages in addition to new texts being composed in all these languages; for example, from Buddhist Hybrid Sanskrit into Khotanese (or Khotanī Śaka; in Khotanese script), Sogdian (in Sogdian script), and Turkic (in Uigur script) in Central Asia; from Central Asian languages or scripts as well as from Buddhist Hybrid Sanskrit, and some Pāli and Sanskrit, into Chinese (with terms transliterated and later translated); from Chinese into Korean (in Chinese characters, or *hanmun*, with Korean pronunciation and later in several scripts, principally *ŏnmun* which has been revised as *hangŭl* and used together with *hanmun* as *kuhanmun;* now *hangŭl* is exclusively official), Japanese (in Chinese characters, or *kanji*, with Japanese pronunciation as *go-on* and occasionally *tō-on* and later in *hiragana* script added to *kanji* or used exclusively), and Vietnamese (Vietnamese adaptations of Chinese characters with Vietnamese pronunciation now officially romanized); from Buddhist Hybrid Sanskrit and some Central Asian and Chinese languages into Tibetan (in *dbu-chan* script) and therefrom into Mongolian (especially in *ka-lekka* and *'p'ags-pa* or Pa-sse-pa scripts; cf. former Tibetan script and later Uigur script) and therefrom into Manchu (in Manchu script; cf. Mongolian script).

The Buddha commanded his disciples to use only popular dialects in reciting his teachings. They followed his instructions for a time. Many dialects all over North India were thus used by local schools of Buddhists. One such dialect, perhaps originally spoken at Ujjain [in Central Province; formerly Ujjenī/Ujjayinī, the ancient capital of Avantī/Avanti], was Pali, which was carried to Ceylon, Burma, etc., and became the canonical language of Southern Buddhism. Another such dialect, of unknown original location, began after a time to be modified by the local Buddhists to make it look more like Sanskrit, the socially respected language of their brahman neighbors. This Sanskritization was at first slight and partial. As time went on it increased, but it never became complete. Prakritic forms continued to be used, and many forms were mixed or hybrid, neither genuine Prakrit nor standard Sanskrit. The vocabulary, especially, remained largely Prakritic. Thousands of words were used which are unknown in Sanskrit, or not used there with the same meanings. To this curious language, which became widespread in North India, I have given the name Buddhist Hybrid Sanskrit. . . .

To such localities [where thriving Buddhist centers were established], and there were doubtless many others, came Buddhist monks, who may have been themselves of very different origins, bringing with them a sort of canon: a body of sermons, sayings in prose and verse, narratives of the

Buddha's life and of his previous incarnations, and rules laid down for the conduct of monks and nuns. Many of these canonical works no doubt went back to the earliest times, and were carried everywhere in similar forms; but there is . . . no reason to assume linguistic unity even in the texts as they were thus spread by missionaries; there is no reason to assume *any* single "original language of Buddhism." And whatever the dialects of the missionaries may have been, the sacred texts were soon adapted to the speech native to each locality. Thus various Buddhist "canons," at first loose and fluid, sprang up all over North India. . . .

In some Buddhist Hybrid Sanskrit works, especially the Mahāvastu, the Lalitavistara, the Mahāparinirvāṇa Sūtra, and a few Prātimokṣa and other Vinaya texts, we find passages, in both prose and verse, which correspond more or less closely to passages of the Pali canon. (Many others which no longer exist in Indic are found in Tibetan and Chinese translations.)

In such passages the vocabulary used in Pali and in Buddhist Hybrid Sanskrit is very largely identical, though the phonetic and grammatical forms are different. This is natural, for both were inherited from a common tradition older than either. Neither was translated from the other; each was adapated independently to the dialect of its locality, but used a word-stock that was to a considerable extent identical. And such words, common to both, continued to be used in both languages in new compositions dealing with the Buddhist religion, which were composed in the separate monkish communities where Pali and Buddhist Hybrid Sanskrit flourished.

This explains the fact that there is a very extensive agreement in vocabulary between Pali and Buddhist Hybrid Sanskrit. They have a great many words in common, and many of these words are not used, at least with the same meanings, in Sanskrit, or often even in other Middle Indic dialects. They are words inherited from the dialects in which the oldest Buddhist traditions were handed down. Nor are they by any means limited to technical terms of the Buddhist religion. Equally common are words which belonged to ordinary secular language.[10]

The components and forms of Buddhist literature are naturally varied and may be suggested here by the following list of definitions. In Pāli usage, *gāthā* is "a verse, stanza, line of poetry"; *nikāya* means "a collection, group, division, or section of a literary work," and *nipāta* similarly is "a group or section composed of chapters"; *sutta* (cf. *suttanta*) is "a chapter or text, especially in the sense of a dialogue, discourse," and *vagga* is "a chapter or section in a book." In Sanskrit and Buddhist Hybrid Sanskrit usage, *gāthā* is "a verse or stanza, the metrical part of a *sūtra*," *kārikā* is "a concise statement in verse (especially of philosophical and grammatical) doctrines"; *sūtra* (cf. *sūtrānta*, Pāli: *sutta*) means "basic teaching, text," whereas *śāstra* signifies "commentary, teaching, treatise (often re a *sūtra* or *kārikā*)," and *stotra* is "an ode or hymn of praise, verses to be sung (in contradistinction to *śāstra* which is recited)"; *bhāṣya* is "an exposition or commentary (especially re a technical *sūtra*)," whereas *ṭīkā* is "a commentary (especially on another commentary)." The term *āgama* in Pāli, Sanskrit, and Buddhist Hybrid Sanskrit means "traditional or canonical text" and, in the Mahāyāna usage, is applied particularly to the Four (out of Five) Nikāyas of the Sutta/Sūtra Piṭaka: Dīgha-Nikāya/Dīrghāgama, Majjhima-Nikāya/Madhyamāgama, Saṃyutta-Nikāya/Saṃyuktāgama, Aṅguttara-Nikāya/Ekottarāgama or Ekottarika.

With regard to the nature of Buddhist manuscripts, the following description of Chinese manuscripts recovered from Tunhuang must suffice.

> The manuscripts described in this Catalogue once formed part of a huge collection which was discovered about fifty years ago in a walled-up chamber adjoining one of the "Caves of the Thousand Buddhas" (*Ch'ien Fo Tung*) a few miles

south-east of the Tunhuang oasis on the border of Kansu. Hollowed out in irregular tiers along the face of a steep cliff, these cave-temples were known in the T'ang dynasty [618-906/7 A.D.] as *Mo Kao K'u*, or "Grottos of Surpassing Height." They are said to have owed their origin to a saintly monk, one Lo-tsun, who began the work of excavation in A.D. 366. An account of him is given in an inscription of 698, and his name occurs again in a topographical fragment some 200 years later. . . . The manuscripts, mostly in the shape of long paper rolls, together with a large number of religious paintings, would appear to have been removed from different monasteries in the neighbourhood and hurriedly stowed away here for safety on the approach of an invading tribe, probably the Hsi Hsia, early in the eleventh century. And here they lay, apparently undisturbed and forgotten, for a space of nearly 900 years. . . .

A prominent feature in the Buddhist sections is the tail-piece or "colophon" (as it is here somewhat loosely termed) which is sometimes appended to the copy of a sūtra or some other holy text. Its main purpose is to make known the person who has acquired "merit" by having the copy made at his own expense, and the beneficiary (usually deceased) in whose direction he wishes the merit to flow. An exact date is generally included. Many of these colophons run to a few words only, while others are long and elaborate compositions with a pronounced literary flavour about them. . . . Another occasional appendage to Buddhist sūtras, occurring for some reason with special frequency in copies of the *Chin kuang ming tsui shêng wang ching* (N. 126), is what I have ventured to call a phonetic glossary. This consists of just a few words selected from the preceding text, with their *fan-ch'ieh* (initial *plus* final) pronunciation.

. . . paper was still quite unknown in Europe during the whole period covered by the Tunhuang MSS. . . . Broadly, it may be said that even the earliest fifth-century papers known to us are of remarkably good quality: they are generally a dull or brownish buff in hue, for the application of colouring matter does not appear to have been practised much before A.D. 500. . . . An agreeable lemon-yellow is characteristic of the earlier part of the sixth century. . . . Then, a little later on, a beautiful golden-yellow paper, thin and crisp, makes its first appearance. More uncommon shades of colour are orange-yellow, slate-blue, greenish-buff, pink or pinkish, sulphur-yellow, etc. . . . And one roll (no. 1262) is actually composed of twelve variously coloured sheets. The staining fluid was evidently of an oily nature; sometimes it has been applied on both sides of the paper, but usually on one only. During the seventh century and part of the eighth, the texture of the paper used in the monasteries continues to be fine and smooth, and its colour a bright or brownish-yellow; but after the An Lu-shan rebellion [c. 757 A.D.] a marked deterioration sets in, and most of it now becomes coarse and drab-coloured.

The handwriting of the copyists also passes through a series of changes which are similarly useful in furnishing a rough clue to the date. Throughout the fifth century and perhaps even later, a stubby kind of brush seems to have been in common use which was incapable of producing the fine, delicate strokes that are characteristic of Chinese calligraphy at its best. It was during the Sui dynasty [581/9-618 A.D.] that the art of handwriting appears to have reached its zenith—at any rate, as far as the present Collection is concerned. . . . Only the most carefully trained scribes were entrusted with the task of copying sūtras (supposed to be the pronouncements of the Buddha himself), as opposed to Vinaya and Abhidharma texts, commentaries, and the like; and that is probably the main reason why we find the production of sūtras suddenly diminished almost to vanishing point after the disastrous upheaval mentioned above, which must have affected every monastery in the country.

A new departure of another kind also begins to be noticeable during the tenth century at Tunhuang. Ever since the invention of paper by Ts'ai Lun eight hundred years before, books had been written and circulated in the form of long paper rolls; hence the use, down to the present day, of *chüan*, the word for "roll," to designate a section or chapter. By far the greater part of the Stein Collection consists of such rolls; they are made up of a number of sheets, each about 1½ feet in length, very neatly and efficiently fastened together with glue. The earliest dated roll, a Vinaya text of A.D. 406 (no. 4523), is 23 feet long, which is slightly less than the average length of ordinary sūtra rolls. The longest of all the rolls are to be found among the commentaries, of which nos. 5587 (99 feet), 5597 (90 feet), 5287 (86 feet), and 5523 (80¾ feet) head the list in this respect. The handling of such rolls, or even those of more moderate length, cannot but be awkward for the reader, who has to be constantly unrolling and rolling up again as he goes along, and any reference to a required passage may involve serious loss of time. It is surprising, therefore, that the invention of some more convenient device for the construction of books should have been so long delayed.

The first step in advance was taken when, instead of being rolled up, the paper was folded into leaves of a reasonable size thus forming a volume that could be quickly opened at any point and shut up after consultation. A fairly good specimen, containing as many as 211 leaves, is no. 5591 in the Catalogue. The next innovation was the stitching of all the leaves together at one side, so that they should no longer fly apart in a long chain. This is the style in which Chinese books are still produced. It has the disadvantage, however, of leaving one side of the paper unused; and as scarcity of paper was becoming a problem in the Tunhuang region, booklets were generally made up of small separate sheets, intended for writing on both sides, as with us in the West. Of these there are several hundred specimens, varying greatly in size, in the Stein Collection; but it is fairly clear that even by the end of the tenth century they were far from having superseded the roll, for of the last fifty dated manuscripts only two are in booklet form.

About 70 of our MSS. may be confidently assigned to the fifth century, and for the next 200 years or so the output continues steadily to increase. The great majority of these early MSS. are copies of Buddhist sūtras that happened to be in particular favour at the time. During the following period, when the Tunhuang district passed temporarily under Tibetan rule, the flow of Buddhist literature rapidly dried up, and never returned to anything like its earlier level. . . .

A small but very precious part of the Collection consists of 20 early specimens of block-printing, one of which, a complete and remarkably well-preserved copy of the Diamond Sūtra [*Vajracchedikā Prajñāpāramitā-sūtra*], bears a date corresponding to the 11th May, A.D. 868. Among the other printed documents are two calendars of A.D. 877 and 882, several prayer-sheets from the middle of the tenth century, and a very well printed set of Buddhist verses on the 24 examples of filial piety.[11]

### 5. *The Three Valued Components of Buddhism*

Buddhist beliefs and practices are fundamentally centered in, and traditionally guided by, three valued components called Ti-ratana in Pāli by the Theravāda tradition and Tri-ratna in Sanskrit and Buddhist Hybrid Sanskrit by the Mahāyāna and Vajrayāna traditions, or as a triad Ratana-ttaya/Ratna-traya, literally meaning "The Three Treasures, Jewels, Gems, etc." They are the Buddha (the Enlightened One), the Dhamma/Dharma (the Teachings of the Buddha, Doctrine, Truth, Law, Norm), and the Saṅgha [or Saṃgha, often Sangha] (the Buddhist Order, Community, Ecclesia). Definitions, descriptions, and textual examples of the Buddha, the Dhamma/Dharma, and the Saṅgha will be given in Chapters II, III-IV, and V-VI respectively.

These three components of Buddhism are interrelated: the Buddha taught and exemplified the Dhamma/Dharma which was subsequently taught as doctrine and expounded by his followers who together came to comprise the Saṅgha as a monastic organization. Consequently, in their veneration of the Buddha, his followers, both ecclesia and laity, have tended to idealize him more than remember him historically.

Formal recognition of the Ti-ratana/Tri-ratna has

become the primary, requisite act of veneration in all Buddhist schools and sects. As the most elementary initiation-ritual, it is called Ti-saraṇa-gamana/Tri-śaraṇa-gamana, often rather awkwardly translated as "Taking the Three Refuges." *Saraṇa* may have a literal sense of "protection, shelter, abode, refuge, willed or chosen resort, etc.,"[12] but in the Buddhist context it means "that whereby I will transcend conditioned life and experience freedom in perfect existence and thus attain Nibbāna/Nirvāṇa," for which no single translation-word seems appropriate. *Gamana* has the sense here of "striving for . . . finding shelter in"[13] (cf. *gacchāmi* as "going to," hence "will undertake").

When expressed as a formula (Saraṇattaya/Trīṇi-śaraṇāni), the Ti-saraṇa-gamana/Tri-śaraṇa-gamana becomes at once an act of veneration, resolution, and elementary training. It is stated in Pāli as follows:

*Namo tassa Bhagavato Arahato Sammāsambuddhassa:*
Veneration to the Blessed One, the Enlightened One, the Perfectly Enlightened One:
*Buddhaṃ saraṇaṁ gacchāmi*
To the Buddha, the (chosen) resort, I go.
*Dhammaṃ saraṇaṁ gacchāmi*
To [the] Dhamma, the (chosen) resort, I go.
*Sanghaṃ saraṇaṁ gacchāmi*
To the Sangha, the (chosen) resort, I go.
*Dutiyam pi buddhaṃ saraṇaṁ gacchāmi*
For the second time to the Buddha, the (chosen) resort, I go.
*Dutiyam pi dhammaṃ saraṇaṁ gacchāmi*
For the second time to [the] Dhamma, the (chosen) resort, I go.
*Dutiyam pi sanghaṃ saraṇaṁ gacchāmi*
For the second time to the Sangha, the (chosen) resort, I go.

*Tatiyam pi buddhaṃ saraṇaṁ gacchāmi*
For the third time to the Buddha, the (chosen) resort, I go.
*Tatiyam pi dhammaṃ saraṇaṁ gacchāmi*
For the third time to [the] Dhamma, the (chosen) resort, I go.
*Tatiyam pi sanghaṃ saraṇaṁ gacchāmi*
For the third time to the Sangha, the (chosen) resort, I go.
*Saraṇattayaṃ*[14]

And now I betake myself, Lord, to the Blessed One as my refuge, to the Truth, and to the Order. May the Blessed One accept me as a disciple, as one who, from this day forth, as long as life endures, has taken his refuge in them.[15]

Statements about the Ti-ratana and Saraṇattaya are made in various places in the Sutta Piṭaka of the Pāli Canon, for example,

Whatever spirits have come together here, either belonging to the earth or living in the air, let us worship the perfect (tathâgata) Buddha, revered by gods and men; may there be salvation.
Whatever spirits have come together here, either belonging to the earth or living in the air, let us worship the perfect (tathâgata) Dhamma, revered by gods and men; may there be salvation.
Whatever spirits have come together here, either belonging to the earth or living in the air, let us worship the perfect (tathâgata) Saṅgha, revered by gods and men; may there be salvation.[16]

The complex, ever-developing nature of Buddhism may be comprehended more easily by viewing the Ti-ratana/Tri-ratna as the quintessence of its thought and the Ti-saraṇa-gamana/Tri-śaraṇa-gamana as the fundamental of its practice. As will be noted in the following chapters, in time the Buddha was given various interpretations and cultish veneration by the Saṅgha and lay devotees, the Dhamma/Dharma was much elaborated by various schools, and the Saṅgha was diversified in different areas by historical circumstances. The conception of the Ti-ratana/Tri-ratna as a formula (Saraṇattaya/Trīṇi-śaraṇāni) and ritual (Ti-saraṇa-gamana/Tri-śaraṇa-gamana) was developed especially by the Mahāyāna. For example, the *Uttaratantra* or *Ratnagotra-vibhāga Mahāyānottaratantra-śāstra*, attributed to Ārya Maitreya (nātha) (*ca.* 270–350 A.D.) by the Tibetan tradition but probably by Sāramati (*ca.* 350–450 A.D.), states:

> Now, what aim did the Lord pursue when he established the 3 Refuges [*trīṇi śaraṇāni*]?
> In order to make known the virtues
> Of the Teacher, the Teaching, and the Disciples,
> For the sake of (the adherents of) the 3 Vehicles
> And those devoted to the 3 forms of religious observance,—
> The 3 Refuges have been proclaimed (by the Lord).[17]

The commentator, Ārya Asaṅga (*ca.* 310–390 A.D.), gives the following reasons for the establishment of the Tri-śaraṇa-gamana:

> *In order to show the virtues of the Teacher*, with a view to those individuals who adhere to the Vehicle of the Bodhisattvas and wish to attain the character of a Buddha, as well as those who, (though they have not entered the Path), are devoted to the performance of religious observances which have the Buddha for their object, it has been spoken and ascertained:—the Buddha is the refuge, since he is the Highest of Men [*buddhaṁ śaraṇaṁ gacchāmi dvipadāṇam agryam*].
>
> *In order to make known the virtues of the Doctrine*, for the

sake of those who belong to the Pratyekabuddha Vehicle and start an activity for an independent apprehension of the profound Doctrine of Causality [*pratītya-samutpāda-dharma*], as well as those whose religious fervour is directed toward the Doctrine (exclusively), it has been declared:—The Doctrine is the Refuge, since it is the highest for those who become dispassionate [*dharmaṁ śaraṇaṁ gacchāmi virāgāṇām agryam*].

*In order to show the virtues of the Disciples* [the Arhats and Bodhisattvas], who have embraced the Doctrine of the Teacher, with regard to the individuals who adhere to the Vehicle of the Śrāvakas and proceed on the Path in order to attain (the fruit of Arhatship) on the basis of the instructions heard of others, as well as those who are devoted to the worship of the Congregation, it has been proclaimed:—The Congregation is a refuge, since it is the highest of communities [*saṁghaṁ śaraṇaṁ gacchāmi gaṇānām agryam*].—Thus, in short, for 3 motives, and having in view 6 kinds of individuals, the Lord has proclaimed the 3 Refuges and shown them in their variety. This has been done in order to promote the living beings to the 3 Vehicles respectively, the matter being viewed from the Empirical standpoint [*saṁvṛti*].[18]

The conception and practice of the Tri-śaraṇa-gamana were further developed by sGam.po.pa (1079–1153 A.D.), the Tibetan Vajrayāna Master, who states in his great work, "Jewel Ornament of Liberation":

The mind is purified as the substance of enlightenment in the following manner. Thrice by day and by night, in the desire to attain Buddhahood for the sake of all sentient beings, and once an hour to form an enlightened attitude, we should repeat the following words:

Until I have attained enlightenment I take refuge
In the Buddha, the Dharma, and the noble Sangha.
By performing acts of liberality and other virtues
May I realize Buddhahood for the benefit of the world.[19]

Furthermore, sGam.po.pa devotes a whole chapter to the subject, which has been summarized by his English translator, Herbert V. Guenther:

. . . to attain enlightenment or to realize Buddhahood . . . a special training is needed. It begins with taking refuge in the Three Jewels, the Buddha, the Dharma, and the Sangha, which is of three orders: an outer order in which the Buddha is represented by an image, the Dharma by the Mahāyāna texts, and the Sangha by the Bodhisattvas, those who strive continuously for enlightenment; an inner order, where the Buddha is the patterning of our life, the Dharma the experience of Nirvāṇa and tranquillization, and the Sangha the Bodhisattvas who have reached the highest level of spirituality; and a mystic order, where Buddhahood alone is the refuge, as the foundation, path and goal of our life. Taking refuge in this Mahāyānic sense is always accompanied by the resolution to adopt an attitude which is directed towards enlightenment and the earnest endeavour to develop and cultivate such an attitude.[20]

CHAPTER TWO

# The Buddha: Teacher and Ideal

The Buddha may be viewed in several ways. In belief and practice, he is traditionally remembered and revered as the essential first part of the Three Valued Components of Buddhism (Pāli/Sanskrit: Ti-ratana/Tri-ratna). In literature, his life has been romanticized in folklore and numerous textual accounts in many languages, whereas modern studies usually try to distinguish humanistic aspects from legend. At times, however, personal glimpses of the Buddha appear in the early canonical texts, as for example, in the *Nandaka-sutta* of the Pāli Aṅguttara-Nikāya:

Once, when the Exalted One was staying near Sāvatthī, at Jeta Grove, in Anāthapiṇḍika's Park, the venerable Nandaka [who was chief among those who admonished the monks] gave Dhamma discourse to the monks in the service hall; taught them, roused them, incited them and gladdened them.

Now in the evening the Exalted One rose from seclusion and approached the service hall; and having come, he stood outside the doorway, waiting for the discourse to end. And when he knew that the discourse was ended, he coughed and tapped on the bolt.

Then those monks opened the door to the Exalted One, and he entered the hall and sat down on the appointed seat. When he had seated himself, the Exalted One spoke thus to the venerable Nandaka:

"Surely, Nandaka, this Dhamma discourse, which you preached to the monks, was a long one! My back ached as I stood outside the doorway, waiting for the discourse to end."

When he had thus spoken, the venerable Nandaka, being embarrassed, said to him: "Nay, lord, we knew not that the Exalted One stood outside the door. Had we known, lord, we would not have said so much."

Now the Exalted One knew that the venerable Nandaka was embarrassed, so he said to him: "Well done, well done, Nandaka! This is right for you clansmen, who by faith have gone forth from the home to the homeless life, when you may be seated around for Dhamma discourse! For you assembled, Nandaka, there are two courses: either discourse on Dhamma or maintain the Ariyan silence."[1]

Consequently, the historically minded student will most likely regard the Buddha as a human being, namely Siddhattha Gotama/Siddhārtha Gautama or the Sākyamuni/Śākyamuni, born in the Lumbinī grove near Kapilavatthu/Kapilavastu, capital of the Sākyan/Śākyan oligarchic republic (*gaṇa, saṅgha*), as son of Suddhodana/Śuddhodana the chief or presiding officer (*rājā/rāja;* not "king" in this case), who attained enlightenment (*bodhi*) and thus became a *buddha,* taught many followers, and at the age of eighty years passed away (*mahā-parinibbāna/parinirvāṇa*) at Kusinārā/Kuṣinagarā, one of the two capitals of the neighboring Mallā/Malla oligarchic republic. His dates are still problematical: the Theravādins in Burma, Ceylon, and India date the Buddha 623–543 B.C. and those in Cambodia, Laos, and Thailand date him 624–544 B.C., hence their Buddha Jayanti celebrations were held in May, 1956, and May, 1957, respectively. On the other hand, the Mahāyānists and most Western scholars date the Buddha variously, *ca.* 566–486 (the preferable date), 563–483, or 558–478 B.C.

In Pāli usage and the Theravāda tradition the Buddha has come to mean generally

> one who has attained enlightenment; a man superior to all other beings, human and divine, by his knowledge of the truth, a Buddha. . . . The word Buddha is an appellative, not a proper name. . . . There are 2 sorts of Buddhas, viz. *Pacceka-buddhas* [cf. Arahants] or Buddhas who attain to complete enlightenment, but do not preach the way of deliverance to the world, and *Sammāsambuddhas,* who are omniscient and endowed with the 10 powers (see bala), and whose mission is to proclaim the saving truth to all beings. In this function the Buddhas are *Satthāro* or teachers, Masters. In his rôle of a pre-eminent man a Buddha is styled *Bhagavā* or Lord. . . . The typical career of a Buddha is illustrated in the life of Gotama and the legends connected with his birth, as they appear in later tradition. . . . The *Epithets* attributed to all the Buddhas are naturally assigned also to Gotama Buddha.[2]
>
> The [Pāli] Commentaries, however, make mention of four classes of Buddha: *Sab*[*b*]*aññu-Buddhā, Pacceka-Buddhā, Catusacca-Buddhā* and *Suta-Buddhā.* All arahants (*khīṇāsavā*) are called *Catusacca-Buddhā* and all learned men *Bahussuta-Buddhā.* A Pacceka-Buddha practises the ten perfections (*pāramitā*) for two asaṅkheyyas and one hundred thousand kappas, a Sabbaññu-Buddha practises it for one hundred thousand kappas and four or eight or sixteen asaṅkheyyas, as the case may be. . . . Seven Sabbaññu-Buddhas are mentioned in the earlier books; these are Vīpassī, Sikhī, Vessabhū, Kakusandha, Koṇāgamana, Kassapa and Gotama. This number is increased in the later books.[3]

In Sanskrit usage and the Mahāyāna and Vajrayāna traditions the Buddha is viewed even more pluralistically: Pratyeka-buddhas (cf. Pāli Pacceka-buddhas; Arhats), Buddhas (cf. Pāli Sammāsambuddhas), Tathāgatas (cf. Pāli Tathāgatas), and Bodhisattvas. The essential features of the Mahāyāna Buddhas have been summarized by Har Dayal:

A Buddha is primarily a fully "enlightened" being. But the characteristic attributes and qualities of a Buddha have been described and enumerated in several definite formulae. . . . A Buddha is one, who has acquired [*a*] the ten *balas* [powers], [*b*] the four *vaiçāradyas* [grounds of self-confidence] and [*c*] the eighteen *āveṇika-dharmas* [special and extraordinary attributes]. No other being possesses these attributes. . . . [*d*] A Buddha is distinguished from other beings by his deep and great pity, love, mercy and compassion for all beings (*karuṇā*). . . . [*e*] a Buddha is noted for his thorough and unblemished purity. His bodily actions, his speech, his thoughts and his very soul are pure; and there is not the slightest impurity in him. On account of this fourfold purity, he need not be on his guard against others. These are his four *Ārakṣyas* (Pāli: *arakkheyyā*). . . . [*f*] A *bodhisattva*, who becomes a Buddha, will not live in solitary grandeur, as the Buddhas are numerous. . . . [*g*] A Buddha has his *buddha-kṣetra* (field), which he guides and "ripens" in spirituality. . . . [*h*] A Buddha, who appears on this earth or in any other world, can never cease to exist. . . . [*i*] The Buddhas are not only numerous and immortal, but they are also superhuman (*lok-ottara*) in all their actions, even during their earthly lives. . . . [*j*] Further, if a Buddha is immortal and superhuman, his physical body cannot represent his real nature. . . . [*k*] If the fragile and limited *rūpa-kāya* [physical body] is not the real Buddha, what and who is the Buddha? In contradistinction to the *rūpa-kāya*, the Mahāyānists speak of a Buddha's *dharma-kāya* (cosmic, spiritual Body). A Buddha is the embodiment of *dharma*, which is his real Body. He is also identified with all the constituents of the universe (form, thought, etc.). This Body, which is also called *sad-dharma-kāya, bodhi-kāya, buddha-kāya, prajña-kāya, svābhāvika-kāya* (essential Body), is invisible and universal. It is imperishable and perfectly pure. All beings "live and move and have their being in it." It is the same as the Absolute Reality (*tathatā*), which is also one and indivisible for the entire Universe. It is immutable and undifferentiated. (*l*) If a Buddha's real body is the cosmic Absolute, then it follows that all Buddhas are spiritually united in the *dharma-kāya*. . . . A Buddha also possesses a Body of Bliss or Enjoyment, which is radiant and glorious, and bears thirty-two special marks and eighty minor signs (*sambhoga-kāya, sāmbhogika-kāya, sāmbhogya-kāya*). It is the result of the Merit, which a Buddha has acquired by his good deeds during many aeons. . . . The *sambhoga-kāya* was added subsequently in order to give the Buddhas something like the celestial bodies of the Hindu *devas*. . . . Thus the conception of Buddhahood was developed to its ultimate conclusion in universal pan-Buddhism (as distinct from Pantheism). The Buddhas were subjected to a sixfold process of evolution: they were multiplied, immortalized, deified, spiritualised, universalised and unified.[4]

In summary: As the primary component of the Tiratana/Tri-ratna, the Buddha has been conceived, described, and venerated singularly and plurally in both humanistic and metaphysical terms. Being the Enlightened One, the Buddha was traditionally regarded by his followers as a Teacher or Master (Satthā or Satthāro/Śāstar), a Victor (Jina), a Great Man (Mahāpurisa/Mahāpuruṣa), a Lord, Blessed One or Exalted One (Bhagavā or Bhagavant), whereas he regarded himself primarily as a Tathāgata [one who has "arrived": experienced and transcended the imperfections (*āsavas*) of life]. In later developments, he was idealized as a Bodhisatta/Bodhisattva [one who manifests Bodhi as a potential Buddha] destined to become a Universal Ruler (Cakkavattin/Cakravartin; cf. Buddha-rājā/rāja) or Savior (cf. the Metteyya/Maitreya Buddha), conceived in metaphysical notions such as the Dharma-kāya, Sambhoga-kāya, and Nirmāṇa-kāya, and finally viewed pluralistically as a pantheon. Thus the Buddha in varying respects has been venerated in simple ceremonies and elaborate cults, represented and symbolized in paintings and sculptures, and depicted in literature and folklore.

## 1. *The Buddha as Teacher*

There can be no doubt that the historical Buddha was a great teacher. Numerous stories about him in the Pāli Sutta Piṭaka illustrate his teaching principles and practices, as, for instance, in the Dīgha-Nikāya where the *Lohicca-sutta* (concerning the ethics of teaching) and the *Pāsādika-sutta* (concerning the perfect and imperfect teacher) particularly describe the subject. Even from the viewpoint of present-day pedagogy, the Buddha's methods are interesting and still applicable in many situations.

The discriminating method of preaching adopted by Buddha combined with dialectics, more stress on ethics than on philosophy, the spirit of good will and love, adoption of popular dialects as the medium of instruction, and the individual care taken of the disciples went also a great way towards the success of the religion.

### *Four Ways of Exposition*

Buddha, it is said, adopted the following four ways for removing the doubts of those who approached him to learn the truth:—

(i) *Paṭipucchāvyākaraṇīya;* (ii) *Ekaṃsavyākaraṇīya;* (iii) *Vibhajjavyākaraṇīya;* and (iv) *Ṭhapanīya.*

In the first method, the doubts of the interlocutor are ascertained at the outset by putting suitable questions and then removed by appropriate answers; in the second, a direct reply is given to an enquirer without entering into a discussion with him; in the third, answers are given separately to the different aspects of the question; and in the fourth, it is pointed out that as the question is untenable, no reply will be given.

Buddha insisted that his disciples should be very discriminating in adopting one of these methods for delivering their discourses.

*Gradual Course*

For the propagation of his teachings, Buddha directed his disciples to conform to the following rules: A good preacher should

(*a*) in ordinary discourses before householders make them gradual i.e. commence with *dānakathaṃ, sīlakathaṃ,* etc.

(*b*) Observe sequence (*pariyāyadassāvī*) in the details composing a theme.

(*c*) Use words of compassion (*anuddayataṃ paṭicca kathaṃ*).

(*d*) Avoid irrelevant matters (*nāmisantaraṃ kathaṃ*).

(*e*) Make his speeches free from caustic remarks against others.

For imparting instructions to householders he directed his disciples to be cautious in not giving out the fundamental principles of Buddhism all at once as that would scare them away. To them only the exoteric side of the teaching should be explained first, that is, the elementary tenets, and practices of Buddhism suitable to householders. To those who intend to take them up should be asked to follow at first the tenets and practices that are suitable to their yet undisciplined and undeveloped powers, and then gradually the difficult ones should be placed before them by stages. To a householder, a Buddhist monk can preach at first the *dānakathaṃ sīlakathaṃ saggakathaṃ kāmānaṃ ādīnavaṃ okāraṃ saṃkilesaṃ nekkhamme ānisaṃsaṃ* (the discourse on alms-giving, moral precepts, the heavens, the danger, corruption and impurity of desire and the blessings of retirement) and when he perceives that his mind has been sufficiently prepared by hearing the discourses, he can preach the higher teachings, viz., *dukkhaṃ samudayaṃ nirodhaṃ maggaṃ* (suffering, origin of suffering, removal of suffering and way to the removal of suffering). These discourses have an appealing force which moves the hearts of the people irrespective of their creeds. The higher and deeper truths of Buddhism were gradually imparted and explained to the initiated or rather to the *sotāpannas*. Thus the Buddhists from the lowest grade to the highest did not feel embarrassed by the weight of doctrines and practices too difficult for their yet limited understanding or their undeveloped powers of fortitude and devotion. In order to create a good impression on the minds of the householders, the bhikkhus were enjoined to be sympathetic to the woes and troubles of their listeners and at the same time they were asked not to indulge in talks which might be regarded as worldly and ill-befitting a recluse.

### *Study of Mental Leanings*

Before delivering a discourse Buddha tried to form an idea of the leaning of the persons by putting to them questions on religious matters or answering the questions that he allowed them to put to himself. In this way he used to select a subject most suited to the occasion and agreeable to the persons composing the audience and delivered a discourse on same. Similes, parables, fables very often drawn from experiences of every day life were interspersed with his speeches along with pithy verses to make his arguments sweet and effective. He attached great importance to the art of preaching and tried to impress upon the minds of his disciples the sense of its importance. The particular features by which his speeches were rendered so very impressive were, first because he utilized his higher knowledge (*abhiññā*), by which he could find out the persons who would benefit by his discourses on a particular day; secondly because the selection of the subjects of his discourses was the result of a correct diagnosis (*sanidāna*) of the mentality of the listeners.

### *Disputation*

Many are of opinion that Buddha himself avoided entering into discussion with others, and discouraged those of his disciples who entered into discussions on religious matters in the course of their preaching and wandering. Such opinion is not wholly correct. There are passages in the Buddhist scriptures which lend colour to the aforesaid view. To cite one or two such passages: He is said to have declared that his dhamma is not to be grasped by mere logic (*atakkāvacara*) and he condemned the Śramaṇas and Brāhmaṇas who took to hair-splitting disputations saying, "Issue has been joined against you, you are defeated, set to work to clear your views, disentangle yourself if you can." . . . From such passages, it is not right to draw the conclusion that Buddha condemned or prohibited the holding of all disputations on religious matters.

It should also be kept in mind that the state of the country at the time of Buddha was not such as could permit a missionary to keep clear of disputation. One of the essential works of a preacher was to convince his audience, and this was hardly possible if argumentation was not given a wide berth. Of this time, accounts are available of brāhmaṇa and non-brāhmaṇa heads of religions, wandering about over the whole of eastern India, sometimes with a large band of disciples, and holding disputations with the heads of the rival sects to assert their influence and increase their following. There were the *paribbājakas* who wandered about with their minds open for the reception of religious light wherever available. The lay people also liked to hear disputations as indicated by their setting up of *kutūhala-sālās* (halls for people in quest of truths) or *paribbājakārāmas* in different places where the wandering teachers might reside and hold controversies with convenience in the midst of a large gathering. The people of a locality felt proud if a good many religious teachers visited their *kutūhalasālās* or *paribbājakārāmas*. References are available in plenty in the Buddhist works showing that it was often stated at the disputations that the defeated teacher with his followers relinquished his own doctrines and embraced those of the winner. These defeats in disputations were a fruitful source for the enlisting of converts to the many doctrines and religions that prevailed in the country at the time, and the teachers vied and struggled with one another for securing the largest following. The discussions of the rival sects indicate that they had to be well-grounded not only in the rules by which the disputation was guided and the argumentation was rendered free from fallacies, but also in the doctrines of the various opponents who had to be faced, over and above their own school or tenets and practices with their philosophical bases, if any.

Buddha is described in several places in the Buddhist works as a master of the tenets and practices of the heretical sects. A large number of his disciples was recruited either as the result of defeats suffered by the opponents or from among the followers of the brāhmanic and the heretical teachers convinced of the superiority of the doctrines propounded by him. . . .

To be a successful disputant, one had to be equipped with all the outfit of specious arguments (*kūṭatarka*) to meet those opponents who made a free use of them whenever needed. It is clear from Buddha's injunctions to the bhikkhus, that he wanted them to use their power of argumentation in the service of truth and truth alone, and not to take to sophistry of their own accord. But a preacher ignorant of the wiles of a specious arguer and unable to use counter-wiles for self-defence would certainly be a weak disputant. . . .

### *Medium of Instruction*

For the proper appreciation of his teaching, Buddha insisted that the medium of instruction should be the popular dialect of a province. His injunction . . . "I allow you, O monk, to learn the word of Buddha each in his own language," and . . . it is pointed out that undue importance should not be attached to the dialect of a particular *janapada,* i.e., a monk should be accommodating to dialectical variations, and not insist upon the use of a particular word, e.g., *pāti* instead of *sarāvaṃ* or *dhāropaṃ*. Buddha's preference for provincial language is also responsible for the growth of *piṭakas* in later days in different languages, the existence of which is no longer a matter of doubt. Buddha made a radical departure from the ancient Indian custom of recording the scriptures in a particular language, and this can well be pointed out as one of the causes of the success of Buddhism.

### *Individual Training*

We have already mentioned that Buddha studied the mental leanings of a person before he delivered a discourse. This was particularly evident in the training of his disciples. He constantly watched their conduct and their mode of performance of spiritual practices, studied their character and predilections, and corrected their weaknesses by suitable advice, admonitions and courses of disciplinary practices. . . .

Sāriputta and Moggallāna were already advanced spiritually before they joined the Saṅgha, hence the training imparted to them was of a higher order. Sāriputta was asked to meditate on *suññatā,* i.e., to look upon all things as devoid of substance and to practice self-introspection in order to remove from his mind the usual hindrances to *vimutti* and acquire the qualities leading to perfection. *Sāriputta,* it is said, took only a fortnight to attain *arhathood,* which stage he reached while listening to a discourse on the origin and decay of *vedanā* delivered by Buddha to Dīghanakha paribbājaka. Moggallāna was given the *dhātus* (elements composing a being) as his subject (*kammaṭṭhāna*) for meditation. While meditating, he became slack in his zeal and so he was taken to task by Buddha. He soon removed his sloth and torpor, became diligent and attained perfection. . . .

The instances can be multiplied but those that have been cited are enough to show how the great teacher used to see through the mental composition of the disciples whom he had occasion to train personally studying their tendencies and mental weaknesses as clearly as if they were reflected on a mirror. This accounts for his great success as a spiritual trainer.[5]

## 2. *The Venerated Buddha*

The early veneration of the Buddha as Teacher, Victor, Great Man, and Lord or Blessed One in India and elsewhere gradually developed into a Buddha-cult which absorbed non-Buddhist ideas and in turn conceived new views about the nature and manifestations of the Buddha.

This process was aided in various ways: by Buddha-legend making in folklore and the composing of texts; by *vandanā* or acts of veneration such as the Ti-saraṇa-gamana/Tri-śaraṇa-gamana described in Chapter I, Section 5; by *dāna* or offering flowers and other symbolic articles to sculptural representations of the Buddha; by *sarīra/śarīra-pūjā* (cf. the Hindu Bhakti cult) or relic-worship of memorial symbols, such as the remains of the Buddha's body after the cremation (*sarīra/śarīra-dhātu*) or something which he had used (*paribhoga-dhātu*) or a representation of him (*uddesika/uddeśaka*) such as an image, which were preserved in reliquaries and placed in tumuli (*cetiya/caitya;* cf. *dhātugabba/dhātugarbha,* Sinhalese *dāgaba* or *dāgoba*). These tumuli and consequent architectural tombs, called *thūpa/stūpa,* were thereupon worshipped (*cetiya/caitya-vadanā* and *thūpa/stūpa-pūjā*) and given, or expressed, symbolic meanings which will be described in Chapter VI, Section 5. They constituted sacred objects for pilgrimages which Buddhists undertook (and still do) in order to profess their faith (*saddhā/śraddhā*) in the Buddha and demonstrate their devotion (*vandanā, pūjā*) to him.

In these ways, various conceptions and venerations of the Buddha, developments in doctrinal interpretations of the Dhamma/Dharma, the evolution of rituals and sculptural and architectural forms, scholarship and folk-beliefs all commingled and were correlated. In turn, they stimulated relatively new movements in the Theravāda and contributed to the rise of the Mahāyāna and subsequent Vajrayāna traditions.

The initial phases in the development of the Buddha-cutl have been described by Sukumar Dutt:

> In the history of Indian religions it is a familiar phenomenon that a cult quickly forms round the person of the founder after his decease within the sect founded by him. Buddhism

was no exception, and it took probably no more than two to three decades after the Lord's decease for a Buddha-cult to come into existence. It was the primitive cult of the Buddhists: it centred not so much in dogma or creed as in a subjective idealised concept of the Lord, his nature and personality.

The cult, a somewhat fluid one, was modified in course of time; it was interpenetrated by a growing spirit of docetism in the religion; it was finally superseded in Buddhist thought by the Mahāyānist developments of a later age. The only school of Buddhism which retains this primitive Buddha-cult is the ancient conservative Theravāda in its Pali canon. The cult shapes largely the Buddha-legends of which that canon is made up.

In these legends, however, the cult-concept of the Founder is not a simple or unitary one. Its composite character may be sensed through the variety of meaningful appellations given to the Lord in the legends,—*Bhagavā, Tathāgata, Buddha, Satthā* and *Jina*. Tradition, devotion and doctrine all enter into their *nuances,* and the great overarching notion in them is that the Lord's life illustrates perfectibility and his "enlightenment" the climax and culmination of the practice of his *Dhamma*. The key to the Buddha-cult which, after the Lord's departure from the earth was the bond of faith of the *Sākyaputtiya Samaṇas* [the first group of Buddhist wanderers] as well as their sectarian distinction within the wanderers' community, lies in these canonical names.

In the legends the plain family name, *Gotama,* for the Lord is put only in the mouths of those outside the rank of his followers. To the devotee he is Bhagavā (literally, "one endowed with great riches"),—an honorific appellation usually given in India even to-day by a disciple or devotee to his spiritual guide. Another name, *Satthā,* by which his followers call him has a more concrete content, but to them it has a significance, as we shall presently observe, deeper than a mere instructor or educator. The foundation of all efforts at the cultivation of one's inner life,—"removing barrenness of heart (*cetokhila*)," as it is put,—is held to be reliance (*saddhā*) on the Teacher (*Satthā*) himself as well as on his system (*Dhamma*), his sect (*Sangha*) and his teachings (*Sikkhā*).

Over against the purely descriptive content of these two names, *Bhagavā* and *Satthā,* a doctrinal element stands out in the pair of correlated names, *Tathāgata* and *Buddha.*

The first one is the name by which the Lord is not only called by others, but most frequently refers to himself. No explanation of the term is offered in the canon and there is no agreement among ancient commentators on the canon over its import. Yet sometimes the context in which it is used throws unexpected light. The well-known *Brahmajāla Suttanta,* for example, contains a lengthy exposition (*veyyākaraṇa*) by the Lord of the doctrines held by contemporary rival sects. As against their dubious and speculative doctrines, is placed the *Dhamma* of the Tathāgata who, it is said, has set it forth, *"having experienced and realised it himself."* This gives the essential note of the Tathāgata concept: the Lord "gone or arrived there" [note: The compound word *Tathāgata* may be broken up as *Tathā* (there) + *Gata* (gone), or as *Tathā* (there) + *Āgata* (arrived).], i.e., having reached and realised the culmination of his own *Dhamma.* The name, *Buddha,* is complementary to it. What remains vague and fluid in the term, *Tathāgata,* is crystallized, defined and brought to a point, identifying the culmination of the *Dhamma* with the supreme enlightenment,—the Saṁbodhi that the Lord himself attained under the legendary Bodhi Tree. . . .

When the Lord is described as *Satthā* in the legends, it hits off an aspect of his personality,—the *Sammā-saṁbuddha* [Buddha for All], as distinguished from the *Buddha* aspcct,— and though his teaching function may be ultimately derived from the human tradition of him that remained in the inseparable background of the legends, the cult conceived this function to be the expression of his *Karuṇā* (compassion for mankind) attribute.

A curious instance, however, of interpenetration of the legends by the human tradition is that, in spite of the cultish conception, the teachings are actually couched in a manner and style in which an individuality distinctly appears. It is so strong indeed that we have to refer it to a common source, for the many makers compiling these discourses could hardly have imparted the individual quality so distinctly and consistently.

The discourse in a legend is not always addressed to acquiescent hearers. Opponents come forward, challenging the Lord with statements of their divergent views and doctrines, and he carries on discussion with them in a fashion eminently characteristic,—putting himself at first apparently in the place of the opponent, setting out from the same point of view, making use of the same expressions, and almost imperceptibly leading him over to the opposite standpoint. The manner is ever the same,—refined, skilful, suave and polite. . . .

But the *Satthā* character of the Lord is functional, not essential. It is only a dynamic expression of his personality. More essentially he is the *Bhagavā,* and from that concept stem those attributes which set him up as a *Mahāpurisa* in his followers' eyes: he bears on his person the marks of a Superman; he emits supernatural radiance from his body; he has foreknowledge of human events, and can with equal penetration see into the past and the future.

What rounds off his personality, however, giving it its final distinction, installing it in a unique category, in his Buddhahood. In the cult it is conceived as attained by him through victory over the imperfections of life (*āsavas*).

A primitive view of the religion, held by the Buddhists, was that it was a process and system of training in perfectibility, of which the culmination was a spiritual status technically termed *Arhatship,* exemplified by the personality of the Lord himself. One must rise to this status by the gradual conquest of what are called *Āsavas* (Imperfections).

The *āsavas* are inherent in all forms of conscious life, earthly or celestial, and are set forth in groups of three and, in later doctrine, of four, viz., addiction to the senses (*kāmāsava*), lust for life (*bhavāsava*), speculative mentality ( *diṭṭhāsava*) and ignorance (*avijjāsava*). For each group, a regimen is prescribed. It is not clear, however, what the term, *āsava,* exactly meant to the Buddhist; it has been variously interpreted and translated; its etymological meaning seems to be "leak," something through which the quality of perfection dribbles to waste, and, by stoppage of the leaks, it is said, one "rolls away all fetters and makes an end of *Dukkha*."

It is there, where "all fetters are rolled away and *Dukkha* is at an end," that the Lord arrived,—he became the Tathāgata ("Arrived or Gone there") by virtue of his conquest of the *āsavas*. Thereby the Lord transcended life, passed out of all categories of being. Hence his alternative name is *Jina* (Conqueror). . . .

It is this *perfect* Buddha, risen superior to all imperfections of life and therefore no longer in the category of beings, earthly or celestial,—neither god nor man, nor Gandharva, nor Yakṣa,—but a unique personality whose only description can be that he is *Buddha*, the Enlightened,—that was the object of the primitive Buddha-cult. Lotus-like in quality, "born and dwelling in the world, but unstained by the world"—is the figurative summarisation of the outward aspects of his personality.

With the dawn of this Buddha-concept on the devotee's mind, a felt disharmony arose between faith and tradition,—between what the Lord came to be in the eyes of the devotee and the lingering "Gotama-Buddha" tradition of the supremely holy man, the long-lived teacher and founder of a religion. The Man (*Purisa*) had then become the Superman (*Mahāpurisa*) in Buddhist faith.

So it is that the humanity of the Lord, known in all accounts of him in tradition, is consistently subdued in the legends to the colours of Buddhahood. It is the implicit, but prevailing tendency of the legends . . . : the Buddha-doctrine comes first and then its concrete application to the Lord.

Sophistication of this kind may be illustrated by a few simple examples. Thus (i) one marked out as a Superman must have certain physiognomical characteristics, e.g. "a protuberance on the head," "a mole between eye-brows" and "blue eyes," and it is presumed that the Lord had them . . . ; (ii) one, who is destined for Buddhahood, must pass through actual experiences of human misery and sorrow, and they occur to the Lord as signs (*nimitte*) of his future Buddhahood; (iii) one who aims at attainment of the supreme enlightenment must undertake the "Noble Quest" (*ariya pari-*

*yesaṇa*) and so had the Lord done; and, lastly, (iv) his death at Kusinārā was no common mortality, but the doctrinal "Great Decease."

Evidently it is not from the layman's angle, but a doctrinal standpoint, that the makers of the legends contemplate their Lord.

This attitude makes them strangely indifferent to the truth of biography, completely unhistorical in the treatment of tradition. If a doctrine has nothing in tradition to illustrate it, they would not scruple to imagine an incident of the Lord's life and set it down in illustration. It is therefore in the light of the Buddha-cult that we must read and evaluate the legends of the canon.[6]

For the casting of a Buddha-legend, a recognised conventional form seems to have been early invented by monks. It is inherited by all sects and schools of Buddhism and probably dates back within half a century of the Lord's decease when his followers formed a single undivided body. It got stereotyped and, except where a number of legends is consolidated into some sort of continuous narrative, it characterises each particular legend, composed half a century or five centuries after the Lord.

There are three components in the form,—(i) the introductory Formula, "So have I heard," (ii) a Statement of the Time and Occasion (*Nidāna*), and (iii) the Discourse or Dialogue (*Buddha-vacana*). The formula is a link with the supposed origin of the legend in tradition; the *nidanā* supplies verisimilitude, and the discourse is the discharge of the Buddha's function, according to canonical doctrine, of "enlightening" mankind.

It is evident that the pre-legendary tradition, where it was actually drawn upon in the legends, was treated rather as raw material. It celebrated and transmitted the memory of a man now transfigured in the legend-maker's faith. Hence his selective use of the materials to indicate, illustrate and emphasise the Lord's Buddhahood or his Superman character. Doubtlessly there was much infiltration of the traditional memory of the Lord from tradition into legend,—even the manner of discourse in the earlier legends has some individuality and the cultish Buddha-concept individual traits. On the legend-maker's ideation of the Lord, that traditional memory must have exerted a light, perhaps unconscious moulding pressure.

It is only in this superseded pre-legendary "Gotama-Buddha" tradition of Magadha (*circa* 483–433 B.C.) that the foundation for a "real life of the Buddha," could have existed.[7]

Henceforth, conceptions of the Buddha became philosophic and doctrinal, descriptions became poetic and venerable. The Buddha was worshiped in ceremony and praised in literature composed to express more fully the expanding Buddha-concept. Consequently, even the writing and recitation of texts about him became acts of veneration. For example, the following chapter "In Praise of the Buddha" in the *Suvarṇaprabhāsa-*(or *Suvarṇabhāsottama-)sūtra*, a Buddhist Hybrid Sanskrit text (in various versions) of the Mahāyāna tradition, declares:

1. The countenance of the Buddha is like the clear full moon,
Or again, like a thousand suns releasing their splendour.
His eyes are pure, as large and as broad as a blue lotus.
His teeth are white, even and close, as snowy as white jade.
2. The Buddha's virtues resemble the boundless great ocean.
Infinite wonderful jewels are amassed within it.
The calm, virtuous water of wisdom always fills it.
Hundreds and thousands of supreme concentrations throng it.
3. The marks of the wheel beneath his feet are all elegant—
The hub, the rim, and the thousand spokes which are all even.
The webs on his hands and his feet are splendid in all parts—
He is fully endowed with markings like the king of geese.

4. The Buddha-body's radiance is like a golden mountain's;
It is clear, pure, peculiar, without equal or likeness,
And it too has the virtues of beauty and loftiness.
Therefore I bow my head to the Buddha, king of mountains.

5. His marks and signs are as unfathomable as the sky.
And they surpass a thousand suns releasing their splendour.
All like a flame or a phantom are inconceivable.
Thus I bow my head to him whose mind has no attachments.[8]

### 3. *The Manifested Buddha*

As previously described, the veneration of the Buddha led to a Buddha-cult which fostered new conceptions of the Buddha: he was idealized in superhuman terms, conceived in metaphysical forms, and symbolized through the cultural arts. In a word, the man was "doctrinated." Hence, the Buddha came to be expressed in the Buddharājā/rāja concept, the Metteyya/Maitreya Buddha belief, the Bodhisatta/Bodhisattva ideal, and the cosmological Buddha-kāyā doctrine.

In the *Lakkhana-sutta* of the Pāli Dīgha-Nikāya, for example, the Buddha as Superman has a choice of becoming a World Monarch (Cakkavattin) or a Supreme Buddha (Sammā-saṃbuddha):

Thus have I heard:—

The Exalted One was once staying near Sāvatthī, in Anāthapiṇḍika's park, the Jeta-Vana. And there the Exalted One addressed the Brethren, saying Bhikkhus! Yea, lord! they responded. And he said:—There are thirty-two special marks of the Superman, brethren, and for the Superman possessing them two careers lie open, and none other. If he live the life of the House, he becomes Monarch, Turner of the Wheel, a righteous Lord of the Right, Ruler of the four quarters, Conqueror, Guardian of the people's good, Owner of the Seven

Treasures. His do those seven treasures become, to wit, the Wheel treasure, the Elephant treasure, the Horse treasure, the Gem treasure, the Woman treasure, the Housefather treasure, the Adviser treasure making the seventh. More than a thousand sons will be his, heroes, champions, vigorous of frame, crushers of the host of the enemy. He, when he has conquered this earth to its ocean bounds, is established not by the scourge, not by the sword, but by righteousness. But if such a boy go forth from the life of the House into the Homeless State, he becomes Arahant, a Buddha Supreme, rolling back the veil from the world.[9]

In the *Mahāvastu,* a Buddhist Hybrid Sanskrit text of the Mahāsāṅghika School, the Buddha as Siddhārtha Guatama chose the religious life:

King Śuddhodana turned back from the gates of Kapilavastu with all his Śāykan retinue and came and stood in his reception-hall. There King Śuddhodana addressed the Śākyan men and women, saying, "The prince has deprived himself of the lordship of this great domain and taken up the religious life. If the prince had not taken up the religious life, he would be a universal king over the four continents, triumphant, righteous, a king of dharma, possessing the seven treasures. For those seven treasures would be his, namely, the treasure of the wheel, of the elephant, of the horse, of the jewel, of the woman, of the householder and of the counsellor. He would have a full thousand sons, brave, courageous, handsome, vanquishers of their foes. He would reign and exercise his sway over these four great sea-girt continents without turmoil or trouble, without rod or weapons, without violence, but with justice. He would be attended by thousands of kings. This universal rule would mean power for us here. But now that the prince has taken up the religious life we have been deprived of the lordship of this mighty realm."[10]

Accordingly, upon his demise (*mahā-parinibbāna/ mahā-parinirvāṇa*) the Buddha is to be treated by his followers like a king of kings. In the *Mahā-parinibbāna-sutta* of the Pāli Dīgha-Nikāya, the instructions are ascribed to the Buddha himself:

"What should be done, Lord, with the remains of the Tathâgata?"

"As men treat the remains of a king of kings, so, Ânanda, should they treat the remains of a Tathâgata"

"And how, Lord, do they treat the remains of a king of kings [Rājā Cakkavattin]?"

"They wrap the body of a king of kings, Ânanda, in a new cloth. When that is done they wrap it in carded cotton wool. When that is done they wrap it in a new cloth,—and so on till they have wrapped the body in five hundred successive layers of both kinds. Then they place the body in an oil vessel of iron, and cover that close up with another oil vessel of iron. They then build a funeral pile of all kinds of perfumes, and burn the body of the king of kings. And then at the four cross roads they erect a dâgaba [thūpa: a solid mound or tumulus, in the midst of which the bones and ashes are to be placed] to the king of kings. This, Ânanda, is the way in which they treat the remains of a king of kings.

"And as they treat the remains of a king of kings, so, Ânanda, should they treat the remains of the Tathâgata. At the four cross roads a dâgaba should be erected to the Tathâgata. And whosoever shall there place garlands or perfumes or paint, or make salutation there, or become in its presence calm in heart—that shall long be to them for a profit and a joy."[11]

Doctrinally speaking, after his demise the Buddha's followers regarded him as a Bodhisattva and former king who prepares for his future role, as related in the *Jātakamālā* (or *Bodhisattvāvadānamālā*), a Buddhist Hybrid Sanskrit narrative by Āryaśura (sixth? century A.D.):

Long ago the Bodhisattva, it is said, was a king who had obtained his kingdom in the order of hereditary succession.

He had reached this state as the effect of his merit, and ruled his realm in peace, not disturbed by any rival, his sovereignty being universally acknowledged. His country was free from any kind of annoyance, vexation or disaster, both his home relations and those with foreign countries being quiet in every respect; and all his vassals obeyed his commands.

1. This monarch having subdued the passions, his enemies, felt no inclination for such profits as are to be blamed when enjoyed, but was with his whole heart intent on promoting the happiness of his subjects. Holding virtuous practice (dharma) the only purpose of his actions, he behaved liked a Muni.

2. For he knew the nature of mankind, that people set a high value on imitating the behaviour of the highest. For this reason, being desirous of bringing about salvation for his subjects, he was particularly attached to the due performance of his religious duties.

3. He practised almsgiving, kept strictly the precepts of moral conduct (*sîla*), cultivated forbearance, strove for the benefit of the creatures. His mild countenance being in accordance with his thoughts devoted to the happiness of his subjects, he appeared like the embodied Dharma.[12]

Elsewhere, in theory, as in the *Suvarṇaprabhāsa-sūtra,* the king becomes divine, i.e., a Buddha (hence Buddharāja) and in practice, as in Ceylon at times during the Anurādhapura period (third century B.C.–1017 A.D.) and in Cambodia at times during the Khmer Empire (802?–*ca.* 1432 A.D.), the king was occasionally recognized as a Buddha (hence Buddha-rājā/rāja).

In other developments, as a Savior the Buddha became the Bodhisatta Metteyya (= Metteyya Buddha) of the Theravāda tradition and the Bodhisattva Maitreya (= Maitreya Buddha) of the Mahāyāna and later Vajrayāna traditions. The *Cakkavatti-sīhanāda-sutta* of the Pāli Dīgha-Nikāya heralds his coming:

> Thus have I heard: . . . The Exalted One spake thus: . . . At that period, brethren, there will arise in the world an Exalted One named Metteyya, Arahant, Fully Awakened, abounding in wisdom and goodness, happy, with knowledge of the worlds, unsurpassed as a guide to mortals willing to be led, a teacher for gods and men, an Exalted One, a Buddha, even as I am now. He, by himself, will thoroughly know and see, as it were face to face, this universe, with its worlds of the spirits, its Brahmās and its Māras, and its world of recluses and brahmins, of princes and peoples, even as I now, by myself, thoroughly know and see them. The truth [the Norm] lovely in its origin, lovely in its progress, lovely in its consummation, will he proclaim, both in the spirit and in the letter, the higher life will he make known, in all its fulness and in all its purity, even as I do now. He will be accompanied by a congregation of some thousands of brethren, even as I am now accompanied by a congregation of some hundreds of brethren.[13]

Thereafter the Metteyya doctrine developed in the Pāli texts of the Theravāda tradition (probably stimulated by comparable, further developments in Buddhist Hybrid Sanskrit literature), such as the *Pārāyana-vagga* of the Sutta-Nipāta (which mentions Tissa-metteyya and Ajita), the *Anāgatavaṃsa* (a poem on the history of the Future One), and the treatise *Visuddhimagga* by Buddhaghosa (fifth century A.D.). The more developed Maitreya concept became a tradition in various Buddhist Hybrid Sanskrit texts of other so-called Hīnayāna schools, such as in the Avadāna literature (notably the *Avadāna-Śataka,* the *Divyāvadāna* or *Śārdūlakarṇāvadāna, Jātakamālā* or *Bodhisattvāvadānamālā,* and *Dvāviṃśatyavadāna*), the *Mahāvastu,* and especially the *Maitreyavyākaraṇa* which was translated into various Central Asia languages, Chinese several times, and Tibetan. Reference to the Bodhisattva Maitreya is also made in Mahāyāna works, for instance, the *Saddharma-puṇḍarīka-sūtra, Sukhāvatīvyūha, Vimalakīrti-nirdeśa-sūtra,* and *Śāriputraparipṛccha,* and the *Sapta-Buddha-Stotra* of the Vajrayāna tradition. The Metteyya/Maitreya doctrine has not only been a formative part in the development of the Buddha-cult and the Bodhisattva doctrine, it has also had important political connotations (for example in Sanskrit contexts, Cakravartin = Buddha = past Bodhisattva = Future Bodhisattva or Buddha = Maitreya) particularly in Central Asia and West China (reportedly still believed); Metteyya as the Coming Buddha is still envisaged in Theravāda Southeast Asia.

As a potential Buddha, the Bodhisattva is literally "one whose (*tva*) essence (*sat*) is perfect knowledge (*bodhi*)" and greatly resolves (*mahā-praṇidhāna*) to postpone his progression to Nirvāṇa in order to help all other sentient beings with whom he feels interrelated.

The Bodhisatta concept is frequcntly mentioned in the Pāli texts, usually as "the not fully awakened one" (the potential Buddha) or in connection with the Metteyya doctrine described above, but the Bodhisattva doctrine developed in Buddhist Hybrid Sanskrit literature and became a characteristic feature of the Mahāyāna tradition. Har Dayal summarizes this development in his *The Bodhisattva Doctrine in Buddhist Sanskrit Literature:*

> In the course of several centuries (second century B.C. to seventh century A.D.), the *bodhisattva* doctrine was modified in its essential features. The chief lines of development may be indicated as follows:—
>
> (1) In the early Mahāyāna, the *bodhisattvas* are inferior and subordinate to the Buddhas; but they acquire greater importance in course of time till they are at last regarded as equal to the Buddhas in many respects. They are also en-

dowed with ten *balas* [powers], four *vaiçāradyas* [grounds of self-confidence] and eighteen *āveṇika-dharmas* [special and extraordinary attributes]. They are to be worshipped like the Buddhas, or even in preference to them. This gradual exaltation of the *bodhisattvas* at the expense of the Buddhas culminates in the apotheosis of Avalokiteçvara, who is declared to be a kind of "Buddha-maker." He helps others to acquire Buddhahood, while he himself remains the eternal *bodhisattva.*

(2) In the early Mahāyāna, Wisdom [*prajñā*] and Mercy [*karuṇā*] are regarded as equally important, and a *bodhisattva* must possess the double Equipment of Knowledge and Merit (*jñāna-sambhāra, puṇya-sambhāra*). In fact, Wisdom is considered to be somewhat more important than Mercy. Mañjuçrī [Mañjuśrī], who represents Wisdom, is invoked in the opening verses of several treatises, and he is praised in the *Saddharma Puṇḍarīka.* The glorification of Wisdom reaches its climax in the writings of the Mādhyamika school of philosophy, which was founded by Nāgārjuna in the second century A.D. *Prajñā* is extolled *ad nauseam,* while Mercy (*karuṇā*) is not discussed in detail. But the later Mahāyāna emphasises Mercy more than Wisdom. It is emotional rather than argumentative. It sometimes seems to ignore and discard Wisdom altogether, as when it declares that *karuṇā* is the one thing needful for a *bodhisattva.* As this ideal gains ground, the *bodhisattva* Avalokiteçvara increases in importance till he becomes the supreme and unique *bodhisattva.* The Mahāyāna slowly passes from the ascendancy of Mañjuçrī to the reign of Avalokiteçvara.

(3) The early Mahāyāna attaches equal importance to social life and to ascetic retirement from the world. It is, in fact, inclined to exalt the layman-householder and the women in comparison with the solitary recluses. But the later Mahāyāna reverts to the old ideal of celibacy and forest-life. The monk triumphs in the end even in the Mahāyāna, and an inferior position is assigned to family life and to women.

(4) Many practices of *Yoga* are borrowed from external sources by the *Vijñāna-vādin* (or *Yogācāra, Yogācārya*) school of philosophers (fourth century A.D.). A *bodhisattva* is

described as the *yogin* par excellence. The number of *samādhis* (modes of Concentration) is increased, and wonderful properties are ascribed to them. *Yoga*, which is endemic in India, is accepted as an integral part of the *bodhisattva* doctrine.

(5) The quest of *bodhi* (Enlightenment) is relegated to the background, while active Altruism in this world of sin and suffering is regarded as almost sufficient in itself. The early Mahāyāna teaches that altruistic activity is one of the means of attaining Enlightenment, which is the goal. But the later Mahāyāna seems to forget that far-off destination and prefers to loiter on the way. A *bodhisattva* need not be in a hurry to win *bodhi* and become a Buddha, as he can help and succour all living beings more effectively during his mundane career as a *bodhisattva*. This idea also resulted in the subordination of the Buddhas to the *bodhisattvas*. There is a marked tendency to regard Altruism as an end in itself. Avalokiteçvara does not seem to think seriously of becoming a Buddha.

(6) The early Mahāyāna recognises an oligarchy of *bodhisattvas*, and eight are mentioned as a group of equal rank. Perhaps Mañjuçrī is regarded as *primus inter pares*. In the later Mahāyāna, the oligarchy is changed into an absolute monarchy. Avalokiteçvara is first and the rest nowhere. He absorbs all the virtues, powers, functions and prerogatives of the other *bodhisattvas*, because he is the Lord of Mercy. He occupies the supreme position in the Universe and reigns without a rival.

*Karuṇā* (mercy, pity, love, compassion) and its personified symbol, Avalokiteçvara, are all-in-all. This is the last word and the consummation of the Mahāyāna.[14]

The cosmological conception of the Buddha was formulated into the doctrine of Kāyas, essentially an early Mahāyāna view which culminated in the later Mahāyāna and Vajrayāna pantheons. It has been expounded and developed in various Buddhist Hybrid Sanskrit, Chinese, Tibetan and other texts and often described in modern studies. Shashi Bhushan Dasgupta summarizes the Kāya doctrine in his *An Introduction to Tāntric Buddhism:*

> The early Buddhists conceived Buddha is a historical personage in the life and activities of Śākyamuni. But after the demise of Buddha his personality soon became enveloped in a mysterious halo; for, naturally enough, his followers would not be satisfied to confine his extraordinary personality to a particular historical existence; so the belief grew as early as Pali Buddhism that the lord had a double existence, the Rūpa-kāya or the grossly physical existence and the Dharma-kāya, the existence in the external and all-pervading body of law. This tendency of viewing the existence of Buddha in different planes ultimately gave rise to the full-fledged Mahāyānic idea of the three Kāyas. With the Mahāyānists Buddha is no particular historical man,—he is the ultimate principle as the totality of things or as the cosmic unity. But this highest principle has three aspects which are known as the three kāyas of the Buddha. These are,—(i) Dharma-kāya, (ii) Sambhoga-kāya and (iii) Nirmāṇa-kāya. The word Dharma-kāya is often explained as the body of the laws (*dharma*); and it may also be remembered that Buddha is said to have told his disciples that his teachings should be recognised as his own immortal body. But the word *dharma* is generally used in the Mahāyāna texts in the sense of "entity"; and the Dharma-kāya means the "thatness" (*tathatā-rūpa*) of all the entities; it is, in other words, the *dharma-dhātu* or the primordial element underlying all that exists. It has been also termed as the Svabhāva-kāya [also later called Sahaja-kāya, Vajra-kāya, or Mahāsuka-kāya by the Vajrayānists and Sahajiyās as the ultimate stage after the Dharma-kāya], *i.e.*, the body of the ultimate nature. It is described as devoid of all characters, but possessing eternal and innumerable qualities. It is neither the mind, nor matter—nor something different from them both. . . .
>
> The Sambhoga-kāya is generally explained as the "body of bliss" or the refulgent body of the Buddha. It is a very subtle body which manifests itself in the various conditions of bliss in the superhuman beings for preaching the noble

truths and for arousing in the mind of all the Śrāvakas, Pratyeka-Buddhas and the lay Bodhisattvas joy, delight and love for the noble religion (*sad-dharma*). . . .

The Nirmāṇa-kāya is the historical personage of the Buddha or the "Body of Transformation." The historical Buddha is regarded as an incarnation of the eternal Tathāgata or the manifestation in condescension of the Dharma-tathatā. Śākyasiṁha Buddha is only one of the incarnations of Dharma-kāya Buddha and his life and teachings are explained as the "apparent doings of a phantom of the Buddha-kāya," —"a shadow image created to follow the ways of the world" only to convince the ignorant people of the world that it is not beyond the capacity of a man to attain perfection.

The Tri-kāya theory of the Mahāyānists developed cosmological and ontological significance in course of its evolution. Before it developed these cosmological and ontological meanings, the theory as mere Buddhalogy would be explained in the following manner:—

The quintessence of Buddha is Pure Enlightenment (*bodhi*) or perfect Wisdom (*prajñā-pāramitā*), or knowledge of the Law (*dharma*), i.e., the absolute truth. By attaining this knowledge *Nirvāṇa* is also attained; the Dharma-kāya Buddha is the Buddha in *nirvāṇa* (*Samādhi-kāya*). Again, before he is merged into *nirvāṇa* he possesses and enjoys, for his own sake and for others' welfare, the fruit of his charitable behaviour as a Bodhisattva, and this is the Body of Enjoyment or the Beatific Body (Sambhoga-kāya). Again, human beings known as the Buddhas, who are created by the magical contrivances, represent the Created Body (Nirmāṇa-kāya).

But after the Tri-kāya theory acquires a cosmological and an ontological meaning, Dharma-kāya means the unqualified permanent reality underlying the things (*dharma*) or, in other words, the uncharacterised pure consciousness (*vijñapti-mātratā*) according to the Vijñānavādins. Sambhoga-kāya means the Dharma-kāya evolved as Being, Bliss, Charity, Radiance, or the Intellect, embodied as the Bodhisattva. Nirmāṇa-kāya is the Transformation Body, which is the same as consciousness defiled and individualised. Later on, this Buddhalogy, cosmology and ontology were all confusedly mixed up,—and we find the three Kāyas mentioned more often in their composite sense than either as pure Buddhalogy or as pure ontology.

The transformation of the idea of Tri-kāya is found in Tāntric Buddhism in two ways. The idea of Dharma-kāya . . . substantially influenced the Tāntric Buddhists in the moulding of their monistic conception of the Godhead. Secondly the idea of the Kāyas got associated with the various plexuses that were discovered by the Tāntric Sādhakas in the different parts of the human body. These plexuses are said to represent the same principles as the different bodies of the Buddha do.[15]

## 4. *The Buddhist Pantheon*

The process of idealizing and venerating the Buddha in metaphysical forms in the Mahāyāna and especially the Vajrayāna traditions culminated in the Buddhist pantheon. And here Buddhist doctrine, Buddhist practice, and Buddhist art commingled and synthesized into a cosmic meaning of life. The following summarized description is taken from Benoytosh Bhattacharyya's *The Indian Buddhist Iconography:*

The pantheon of the Northern Buddhists revolves round the theory of the five Dhyāni Buddhas [Dharma-kāya manifestations]. The Buddhists believe that the world is composed of five cosmic elements or Skandhas. The five Skandhas are Rūpa (form), Vedanā (sensation), Saṁjñā (name), Saṅskāra (conformation) and Vijñāna (consciousness). These elements are eternal cosmic forces and are without a beginning or an end. These cosmic forces are deified in Vajrayāna as the five Dhyāni Buddhas. In the course of time they were regarded as the five primordial gods responsible for this diversified creation, and thus Vajrayāna took a polytheistic form, although polytheism can hardly apply to a system which considers Śūnya as the One, Indivisible and Ultimate Reality. But so long as form could not be given to Śūnya as an anthropomorphic deity, the system of five Dhyāni Buddhas certainly had the flavour of polytheism. The priests and the Vajrayāna authors were conscious of this shortcoming, especially in view of the fact that all the six Hindu systems of philosophy tended to develop a highly monistic philosophy. They tried at first to cure this defect by the theory of the Kulas (families), and Kuleśas (lord of families) of gods and men, and thus divided everything into five groups. For each group, a particular Dhyāni Buddha becomes the Kuleśa or the primordial lord, all other groups taking their origin from him. Another grand conception of the Vajrayāna Buddhism is the theory of the highest god Vajradhara, also called Ādhibuddha, the primordial monotheistic god who is the embodiment of Śūnya to whom even the Dhyāni Buddhas owe their origin. The theory originated in the Nālandā monastery in about the 10th century. Thereafter, a large number of images of Vajradhara must have been made in the different schools of art. The special Tantra dedicated to Ādhibuddha is the Kālacakra Tantra which appears to be the original Tantra in which the doctrine of Ādhibuddha was for the first time inculcated. The Kālacakra Tantra thus is a product of the 10th century. Vajradhara was particularly popular in Nepal and Tibet where numerous images of this primordial god are to be met with. . . . Homage is paid to Ādhibuddha in the shape of a flame of fire which the priests consider as eternal, self-born and self-existent. It is said in the Svayambhū Purāṇa that Ādhibuddha first manifested himself in Nepal in the form of a flame of fire, and Mañjuśrī erected a temple over it in order to preserve the flame. This ancient temple is known as the Svayambhū Caitya [near present Kathmandu].

The conception of Vajradhara presupposes Ādhibuddha and, therefore, is later than the first half of the 10th century. Vajrasattva, being a regular development of the Bodhisattva Vajrapāṇi emanating from the Dhyāni Buddha Akṣobhya, is a little earlier, although the conception of Vajradhara and Vajrasattva are sometimes inextricably mixed up. In Vajrayāna, Ādhibuddha is regarded as the highest deity of the Buddhist pantheon, the originator even of the five Dhyāni Buddhas. When represented in human form, he begets the name of Vajradhara and is conceived in two forms, single and Yab-yum. When single, he is bedecked in jewels, gaudy ornaments and dress, sits in the Vajraparyaṅka or the attitude of meditation with the two feet locked with soles of the feet turned upwards. He carries the Vajra in the right hand and the Ghaṇṭā (bell) in the left, the two hands being crossed against the chest in what is known as the Vajrahuṅkāra Mundra. The Vajra (thunderbolt) here is the symbol for the ultimate reality called Śūnya while the bell represents Prajñā or wisdom the sounds of which travel far and wide. Sometimes the symbols are shown on a lotus on either side, the Vajra being on the right and the Ghaṇṭā in the left. In Yab-yum, his form remains the same as when single except that here he is locked in close embrace by his Śakti or the female counterpart whose name is . . . Prajñāpāramitā. The Śakti is somewhat smaller in size, is richly dressed and bedecked in ornaments, carrying the Kartri (knife) and the Kapāla (skull cup) in the right and left hands respectively. In these figures the Kartri is the symbol for the destruction of ignorance, the Kapāla stands for oneness absolute, while the double form Yab-yum represents that the distinction between duality and non-duality is unreal, and the two mix themselves into one as salt mixes in water. The deity Vajradhara is an embodiment of the highest reality, Śūnya, while Prajñāpāramitā represents Karuṇā (compassion) and in close embrace they turn into one Śūnya in which Karuṇā merges, and the duality ceases. . . .

But Vajradhara was not universally accepted as the Ādhibuddha or the first creative principle. When the theory of Ādhibuddha was fully established the Buddhists seem to have ranged themselves into so many sects as it were, holding different views regarding specific forms which the Ādhibuddha should take. Some considered one among the five Dhyāni Buddhas as the Ādhibuddha, some acknowledged Vajrasattva as the Ādhibuddha. Many others were content to regard the Bodhisattva such as Samantabhadra or Vajrapāṇi as the Ādhibuddha. Thus the cult of Ādhibuddha was widely distributed amongst the different schools, which gave rise to as many different sects amongst the Tāntric Buddhists.

Vajradhara or the Ādhibuddha is supposed to be the originator of the five Dhyāni Buddhas, the progenitors of the five Kulas or families of Buddhist gods and goddesses. Next to Vajradhara the Dhyāni Buddhas or the Tathāgatas are important in Buddhist iconography. . . . The Guhyasamāja Tantra (Tantra of Secret Communion) was the first to reveal their existence in a Saṅgīti (holy assembly) which is supposed to introduce new ideas into Buddhism. . . . The five Dhyāni Buddhas are the corner stones of Buddhist iconography on which the whole edifice of the Buddhist pantheon is erected. The five Dhyāni Buddhas are the progenitors of the five Kulas or families of deities, and the community worshipping them were known as the Kaulas, and the process of worship was called Kulācāra or family conduct. These Dhyāni Buddhas further split themselves up in the form of Bodhisattva[s] and their female principles who are responsible for creating everything found in existence. The forms of deities are nothing but the gross forms of the different sounds, and thus the connection of the mantra with the deity is established.

The five Dhyāni Buddhas who are the embodiments of the five Skandhas or primordial elements are the progenitors of the five families of deities constituting the whole of the Buddhist pantheon. The emanated deities of these Dhyāni Buddhas, as a rule, hold the miniature figure of the parental Dhyāni Buddha on their heads and are usually of the same colour as that of the Dhyāni Buddha and are placed in the same direction as is assigned to their sires. This very plan is followed most scrupulously in almost all the Maṇḍalas or magic circles as described in the remarkable work, Niṣpannayogāvalī of Mahāpaṇḍita Abhayākara Gupta.

The names, colours and the symbols of the five Dhyāni Buddhas are stated briefly in the following verse occuring in the Sādhanamālā:

. . . "The Jinas (victorious ones) are Vairocana, Ratnasambhava, Amitābha, Amoghasiddhi and Akṣobhya. Their colours are white, yellow, red, green and blue, and they exhibit the Bodhyaṅgī (teaching), Varada (boon), Dhyāna (meditation), Abhaya (protection), and Bhūṣparśa (earth-touching) attitudes of hands respectively."

The Dhyāni Buddhas are a peculiar kind of Buddhas who are not required to pass through the stage of a Bodhisattva. They were never anything less than a Buddha. They are always engaged in peaceful meditation, and they voluntarily abstain themselves from the act of creation. To create is the work of their emanations, the Divine Bodhisattvas. As has been said already, the Dhyāni Buddhas are five in number to which a sixth Vajrasattva is sometimes added. The Guhyasamāja Tantra makes it clear that all the five Dhyāni Buddhas along with their female counterparts and the guardians of gates were known in circa 300 A.D. the time of the introduction of this new Tantra. That the five Dhyāni Buddhas might have owed their origin to the theory of the eternity of the five senses, seems to be borne out by a passage in the Cittavisuddhiprakaraṇa of the Tāntric Āryadeva. But it may also be possible that the five Mudrās which Buddha Śākyasiṁha made sacred by using on memorable occasions and which were constantly depicted in the Buddhistic figures of the different schools of art, gave rise to the five Dhyāni Buddhas. Advayavajra who flourished in the 11th century, has written in one of his short works that the five Dhyāni Buddhas took their origin from the theory of the eternity of the five Skandhas (elements), that is to say, that the Dhyāni Buddhas represented the five primordial cosmic forces which are responsible for creation. Vajrasattva, the sixth Dhyāni Buddha, who is generally regarded as the priest of the five Dhyāni Buddhas and is usually represented with the priestly symbols, the Vajra and the Ghaṇṭā, is an embodiment of the five Skandhas collectively, and undoubtedly a later addition to the pantheon of the Northern Buddhists.

The Dhyāni Buddhas are always represented as seated on a full blown lotus, and in the meditative pose with legs crossed, the right foot crossing over and in front of the left, with the soles of both feet turned upwards. The hand that rests on the lap is sometimes empty, but in most cases holds the bowl. The head is bare, the thick clustering curls radiate effulgence like a flame of fire. The eyes are half-closed in meditation showing the mind completely drawn inwards in perfect introspection. The dress consists of an undergarment reaching from the chest to the knee, and secured by a scarf. The body is loosely covered by the habit of a monk, leaving only the right arm bare.

The Dhyāni Buddhas are generally represented on the four sides of a Stūpa which is the symbol of the Buddhist Universe, facing the four cardinal points. Vairocana is the deity of the inner shrine and is, therefore, generally unrepresented. But exceptions to this rule are by no means rare. He is occasionally assigned a place between Ratnasambhava in the South and Akṣobhya in the East. Independent shrines are also dedicated to each of the Buddhas.

[Description follows concerning 6 Dhyāni Buddhas, including the colour, mudrā, vehicle, symbol, and spiritual consort or Dhyāni Buddhaśakti for each]:

1. Amitābha: Red, Samādhi, Peacock, Lotus; consort Pāṇḍarā, or Pāṇḍaravāsinī: Red, Lotus; Bodhisattva son Padmapāṇi: Red, Lotus.
2. Akṣobhya: Blue, Bhūṣparśa, Elephant, Vajra; consort Māmakī: Blue, Vajra; Bodhisattva son Vajrapāṇi: Blue, Vajra.
3. Vairocana: White, Dharmacakra, Dragon, Discus; consort Locanā: White, Discus; Bodhisattva son Samantabhadra: White, Cakra.
4. Amoghasiddhi: Green, Abhaya, Garuḍa, Viśvavajra; consort Tārā: Green, Utpala; Bodhisattva son Viśvapāṇi: Green, Viśvavajra.
5. Ratnasambhava: Yellow, Varada, Lion, Jewel; consort Vajradhātviśvari: Yellow, Jewel; Bodhisattva son Ratnapāṇi: Yellow, Jewel.
6. Vajrasattva: White, Vajra and Ghaṇṭā. . . . His worship is always performed in secret and is not open to those who are not initiated into the mysteries of Vajrayāna. . . . Vajrasattva originates from the syllable HŪM. . . . consort Vajrasattvātmikā: White, Kartri and Kapāla; Bodhisattva son Ghaṇṭāpāṇi. . . .

### *Mortal Buddhas*

Both the Mahāyānists and the Hīnayānists hold that a Buddha is one who is endowed with the thirty-two major and eighty minor auspicious marks known as "external characteristics" as enumerated in the Dharmasaṁgraha, attributed to Nāgārjuna. He must have in addition, three kinds of mental characteristics, namely, the ten Balas or forces, eighteen Āveṇika Dharmas or peculiar properties, and the four Vaiśaradyas or points of self-confidence or assurance.

The Hīnayānists, even in their earlier stages, recognised twenty-four bygone Buddhas, each having a peculiar Bodhi tree. The Mahāyānists also give several lists, though not systematically and thirty-two different names have been recovered. The last seven Tathāgatas are well known, and are designated by the Mahāyānists as Mānuṣī or Mortal Buddhas. These are, Vipaśyin, Śikhī, Krakucchanda, Kanakamuni, Kaśyapa and Śākyasiṁha [Śākvamuni or Buddha Vajrāsana]. The historicity of these Buddhas is still uncertain excepting of course that of the last, but there are good grounds for thinking that Kanakamuni and Krakucchanda really were historical personages. . . .

When represented, the last seven Mortal Buddhas appear all alike; they are of one colour and one form, usually sitting cross-legged, with the right hand disposed in the Bhūmiṣparśa Mudrā (earth-touching attitude), which is the Mudrā peculiar to Akṣobhya and as a matter of fact, it is not possible to identify a sculpture of the latter unless it is coloured or if no other identification mark is present. In paintings, the Mortal Buddhas have usually a yellow or golden complexion. The only possible chance of identifying them is when they appear in groups of seven. Sometimes they are represented as standing, in which case they appear under a distinguishing Bodhi Tree and with a distinguishing Mudrā. . . .

Like the Dhyāni Buddhas, the Mortal Buddhas have also their respective Buddhaśaktis through whom they obtained the seven Mortal Bodhisattvas. . . . [Thus]:

Vipaśyī—Vipaśyantī—Mahāmati.
Śikhī—Śikhimālinī—Ratnadhara.
Viśvabhū—Viśvadharā—Ākāśagañja.
Krakucchanda—Kakudvatī—Śakamaṅgala.
Kanakamuni—Kaṇṭhamālinī—Kanakarāja.

Kaśyapa—Mahīdharā—Dharmadhara.
Śākyasiṁha [Śākyamuni or Buddha Vajrāsana, also Durgatipariśodhana]—Yaśodharā—Ānanda.

*Maitreya, the Future Buddha*

It would not be out of place to mention here the name of Maitreya who partakes of the nature of a Mortal Buddha, though he is not a Buddha yet. He is supposed to be passing the life of a Bodhisattva in the Tuṣita heaven, preparatory to his descent to earth in human form. It is said that he will come to earth full 4000 years after the disappearance of Buddha Gautama for the deliverance of all sentient beings. Asaṅga is said to have visited Maitreya in the Tuṣita heaven and to have been initiated by him into the mysteries of Tantra. He is the only Bodhisattva who is worshipped alike by the Hīnayānists and the Mahāyānists and his images can be traced from the Gandhara School down to the present time. . . .

Maitreya may be represented as a standing figure, adorned with rich ornaments and holding in his right hand the stalk of a lotus. He is distinguished from Padmapāṇi mainly by the figure of a small Caitya which he bears on his crown . . . his two characteristic symbols, the vase and the wheel. Maitreya may also be represented seated as a Buddha, with legs either interlocked or dangling down. His colour is yellow, and his images sometimes bear the figures of the five Dhyāni Buddhas, on the aureole behind. The small Caitya on the crown of Maitreya is said to refer to the belief that a Stūpa in the mount Kukkuṭapāda near Bodh-Gaya covers a spot where Kaśyapa Buddha is lying. When Maitreya would descend to earth he would go direct to the spot, which would open by magic, and receive from Kaśyapa the garments of a Buddha.

*The Bodhisattvas*

The term Bodhisattva consists of two words *Bodhi* (enlightenment) and *Sattva* (essence) and they [the Bodhisattvas as Sambhoga-kāya manifestations] represent a class of deities who derive their origin from the five Dhyāni Buddhas representing the five primordial elements. The Bodhisattvas thus connote all the male deities of the Buddhist pantheon, while their female counterparts are known by the generic name of Śaktis. These Śaktis should be distinguished from the Buddhaśaktis who are the queens of the five Dhyāni Buddhas. The Bodhisattvas are sometimes represented in the company of their Śaktis who are seated either beside them or on their laps or in close embrace. . . . Amongst the Bodhisattvas, Avalokiteśvara and Mañjuśrī are the chief and have wide popularity not only in this country [India], but also in other Buddhist countries such as Tibet, China and Japan.

[Description follows concerning 25 Bodhisattvas, including the colour and symbol for each, numbers 1-24 according to the *Niṣpannayogāvalī* of Mahāpaṇḍita Abhayākara Gupta and no. 25 according to the *Sādhanamālā*.]

1. Samantabhadra (Universal Goodness): Yellow and Blue, Jewel. 2. Akṣayamati (Indestructible Mind): Yellow, Sword or Jar. 3. Kṣitigarbha (Matrix of the Earth): Yellow or Green, Kalpa Tree on Jar. 4. Ākāśagarbha (Essence of Ether): Green, Jewel. 5. Gaganagañja: Yellow or Red, Kalpa Tree. 6. Ratnapāṇi (Jewel Bearer): Green, Jewel or the Moon. 7. Sāgaramati (Ocean Mind): White, Sea Wave or Conch. 8. Vajragarbha (Matrix of Thunderbolt): Blue or Bluish White, Daśabhūmika Scripture. 9. Avalokiteśvara (The Watchful Lord): White, Lotus. 10. Mahāsthāmaprāpta (One who has obtained great strength): White or Yellow, Six Lotuses or Sword. 11. Candraparabha (Light of the Moon): White, Moon on Lotus. 12. Jālinīprabha (Light of the Sun): Red, Sun-disc. 13. Amitaprabha (Boundless Light) or Amṛtaprabha (Light of Nectar): White or Red, Jar. 14. Pratibhānakūṭa: Green, Yellow or Red, Whip. 15. Sarvaśokatamonirghātamati: Whitish Yellow, Yellow or Red, Staff. 16. Sarvanivaraṇaviṣkambhin (Effacer of All Sins): White or Blue, Sword and Book. 17. Maitreya (the Future Buddha): Golden Yellow, Nāgakeśara Flower. 18. Mañjuśrī: Golden, Sword and Book. 19. Gandhahasti: Green or Whitish Green, Elephant's Trunk or Conch. 20. Jñānaketu: Yellow or Blue, Flag with Cintāmaṇi Jewel. 21. Bhadrapāla:

Red or White, Jewel. 22. Sarvāpāyañjaha (Remover of All Miseries): White, Act of removing sin or goad. 23. Amoghadarśin: Yellow, Lotus. 24. Suraṅgama: White, Sword. 25. Vajrapāṇi: White, Vajra.

*Bodhisattva Mañjuśrī*

There is no doubt that the place assigned to Mañjuśrī in the Buddhist pantheon is one of the very highest. The Mahāyānists consider him to be one of the greatest Bodhisattvas. They believe that the worship of Mañjuśrī can confer upon them wisdom, retentive memory, intelligence and eloquence, and enables them to master many sacred scriptures. It is no wonder, therefore, that his worship became widely prevalent amongst the Buddhists of the North. They conceived him in various forms and worshipped him with various mantras. Those who could not form any conception of him according to Tāntric rites, attained perfection only by muttering his numerous mantras.

. . . the Buddhists believe that their gods and goddesses affiliate themselves to the families of the five Dhyāni Buddhas, and as such, various attempts were made to assign Mañjuśrī to a particular Dhyāni Buddha. Sometimes in the Sādhanas he is made an offspring of Amitābha of red colour, and sometimes of Akṣobhya with the blue colour. Mañjuśrī also shows several colours showing his allegiance to several Kulas or families. The human origin of Mañjuśrī seems to be responsible for this kind of confusion. Mañjuśrī seems to have been deified in the same manner as Aśvaghoṣa, Nāgārjuna, Āryadeva, Asaṅga and many others were regarded as Bodhisattvas in the time of Hiuen Thsang [Hsüan-tsang, 596-664 A.D.]. . . . In his simplest form Mañjuśrī carries the sword in his right hand and the Prajñāpāramitā manuscript in his left. In representations sometimes the two symbols are placed on lotuses. Sometimes he is accompanied only by Yamāri, sometimes only by his Śakti or female counterpart, sometimes by Sudhanakumāra and Yamāri and sometimes again by the four divinities, Jālinīprabha (also called Sūryyaprabha), Candraprabha, Keśinī and Upakeśinī.

*Bodhisattva Avalokiteśvara*

Avalokiteśvara is famous in the Mahāyāna Pantheon as a Bodhisattva emanating from the Dhyāni Buddha, Amitābha and his Śakti, Pāṇḍarā. As Amitābha and Pāṇḍarā are the presiding Dhyāni Buddha and Buddhaśakti of the present Kalpa (cycle), namely, the Bhadrakalpa, Avalokiteśvara is said to be the Bodhisattva who rules during the period between the disappearance of the Mortal Buddha, Śākyasiṁha, and the advent of the Future Buddha, Maitreya. The Guṇakāraṇḍavyūha gives an account of his character, moral teachings and miracles and from it is learnt that he refused Nirvāṇa, until all created beings should be in possession of the Bodhi knowledge and to that end he is still supposed to work and foster spiritual knowledge amongst his fellow creatures. One of the passages in Kāraṇḍavyūha characterises him as taking the shape of all gods of all religions, nay, even the shape of the father and mother,—in fact, the form of the worshipped of any and every worshipper, to whom he might impart knowledge of Dharma. By a slow and gradual process, first human beings and then animals and other creatures would advance spiritually to obtain salvation. For all these reasons Avalokiteśvara is characterised as the best of the Saṅgha, the Jewel of the Buddhist Church or Saṅgharatna.

*Collective Deities*

. . . in the medieval age [the Buddhists] started an unrelenting process of deification by turning all objects, cosmic principles, literature, letters of the alphabet, the directions and even the desires into gods and goddesses, with forms, colour, poses of sitting, and weapons. In this manner the ten directions, eight kinds of head-dress, the different kinds of protection, the dances, musical instruments, components of the door, four kinds of light, important animals, and various other things were all deified with form, colour and weapons. . . .

The process of deification was applied in Vajrayāna to the four cardinal directions, North, South, East and West, and the four intermediate corners, such as Vāyu, Agni, Īśāna and Nairṛta. With the top and the bottom the quarters numbered ten, and thus the Buddhist Tantras added ten gods of the quarters to the already numerous gods in their pantheon. The deities of the ten quarters are not, however, the monoply of the Buddhists, and it is believed that the Buddhists were indebted to the Hindus for the deification of the quarters. Amongst the Hindus the eight Dikpālas are supposed to guard the ten quarters, and are said to be the presiding deities of these directions, or in other words, they are regarded as the embodiments of these quarters in the form of deities.

The Buddhists improved upon the original ideas of the Hindus and showed in an artistic style their origin in an Assembly of the Faithful where the Highest Lord sits in different Samādhis (meditations), and the rays issuing out of his body condense themselves first into syllables which give rise to the different Guardians of the Gates.[16]

## 5. *The Followers of the Buddha*

No matter how the Buddha may be venerated, metaphysically conceived, or cosmologically doctrinated, his followers have ever sought to emulate his living example. Most textual accounts of the Buddha's personal life are understandably idealistic, as for example, the Pāli *Sumangala Vilāsinī* by Buddhaghosa (fifth century A.D.) which visualizes his daily routine:

For the Blessed One used to rise up early (*i.e.* about 5 A.M.), and, out of consideration for his personal attendant, was wont to wash and dress himself, without calling for any assistance. Then, till it was time to go on his round for alms, he would retire to a solitary place and meditate. When that time arrived he would dress himself completely in the three robes (which every member of the Order wore in public), take his bowl in his hand and, sometimes alone, sometimes attended by his followers, would enter the neighbouring village or town for alms, sometimes in an ordinary way, sometimes wonders happening such as these. As he went towards the village soft breezes would waft before him cleansing the way, drops of rain would fall from the sky to lay the dust, and clouds would hover over him, spreading as it were a canopy protecting him from the sun. Other breezes would waft flowers from the sky to adorn the path; the rough places would be made plain and the crooked straight, so that before his feet the path would become smooth and the tender flowers would receive his footsteps. And betimes a halo of six hues would radiate from his form (as he stood at the threshold of the houses) illuminating with their glory, like trails of yellow gold or streamers of gay cloth, the gables and verandahs round about. The birds and beasts around would, each in his own place, give forth a sweet and gentle sound in welcome to him, and heavenly music was wafted through the air, and the jewellery men wore jingled sweetly of itself. At signs like these the sons of men could know—"To-day it is the Blessed One has come for alms." Then clad in their best and brightest, and bringing garlands and nosegays with them, they would come forth into the street and, offering their flowers to the Blessed One, would vie with one another, saying, "To-day, Sir, take your meal with us; we will make provision for ten, and we for twenty, and we for a hundred of your followers." So saying they would take his bowl, and, spreading mats for him and his attendant followers, would await the moment when the meal was over. Then would the Blessed One, when the meal was done, discourse to them, with due regard to their capacity for spiritual things, in such a way that some would take the layman's vow, and some would enter on the paths, and some would reach the highest fruit thereof. And when he had thus had mercy on the multitude, he would arise from his seat and depart to the place where he had lodged. And when he had come there he would sit in the open verandah, awaiting the time when the rest of his followers should also have finished their meal. And when his attendant announced they had done so, he would enter his private apartment. Thus was he occupied up to the midday meal.

Then afterwards, standing at the door of his chamber, he would give exhortation to the brethren such as this: "Be earnest, my brethren, strenuous in effort. Hard is it to meet with a Buddha in the world. Hard is it to attain to the state of (that is to be born as) a human being. Hard is it to find a fit opportunity. Hard is it to abandon the world. Difficult to attain is the opportunity of hearing the word."

Then would some of them ask him to suggest a subject for meditation suitable to the spiritual capacity of each, and when he had done so they would retire each to the solitary place he was wont to frequent, and meditate on the subject set. Then would the Blessed One retire within the private chamber, perfumed with flowers, and calm and self-possessed would rest awhile during the heat of the day. Then when his body was rested he would arise from the couch and for a space consider the circumstances of the people near that he might do them good. And at the fall of the day the folk from the neighbouring villages or town would gather together at the place where he was lodging, bringing with them offering of flowers. And to them, seated in the lecture hall, would he, in a manner suitable to the occasion, and suitable to their beliefs, discourse of the Truth. Then, seeing that the proper time had come he would dismiss the folk, who, saluting him, would go away. Thus was he occupied in the afternoon.

Then at close of the day should he feel to need the refreshment of a bath he would bathe, the while some brother of the Order attendant on him would prepare the divan in the chamber, perfumed with flowers. And in the evening he would sit awhile alone, still in all his robes, till the brethren returned from their meditations began to assemble. Then some would ask him questions on things that puzzled them, some would speak of their meditations, some would ask for an exposition of the Truth. Thus would the first watch of the night pass, as the Blessed One satisfied the desire of each, and then they would take their leave. And part of the rest of the night would he spend in meditation, walking up and down outside his chamber; and part he would rest lying down, calm and self-possessed, within. And as the day began to dawn, rising from his couch he would seat himself, and calling up before his mind the folk in the world he would consider the aspirations which they, in previous births, had formed, and think over the means by which he could help them to attain thereto.[17]

In teaching the Dhamma/Dharma to his disciples and the laity, the Buddha characteristically welcomed both men and women, the rich and poor alike from all social classes and walks of life. This policy and practice undoubtedly gained him broad support in society and in time enriched the development of his Saṅgha. Henceforth, according to Buddhism, the name Ariyo/Ārya no longer has an ethnic or social connotation but means one who follows the Buddhist way of life as distinct from a Puthujjanā/Pṛthagjana, a secularist, a worldly man. "A common designation of the monastic followers of Gotama was *samaṇā Sakyaputtiyā,* recluses (lit. sons of the) Sakyans, or Sakyan recluses. This was also used of them by the laity . . ."[18]

In the Pāli Theravāda canon (and somewhat comparable views in Buddhist Hybrid Sanskrit texts), various types or grades of persons are identified according to recognized stages of progress toward Enlightenment. In the preliminary stage (Gotrabhū in Pāli/Sanskrit), a Gotrabhū is one " 'become of the lineage'; a technical term used from the end of the [Sutta Piṭaka] Nikāya period to designate one, whether layman or bhikkhu, who, as converted, was no longer of the worldlings (puthujjanā), but of the Ariyas, having Nibbāna as his aim."[19] In the first stage, the way of entering the stream or following the Eightfold Path (Sotaāpatti-magga/ Srotaāpatti-mārga), a Saddhānusārin (Śraddhānusārī) walks according to faith, a Dhammānusārin (Dharmānusārī) lives rightly, and a Sotaāpanna (Srotaāpanna) is "one who has entered [and attained or won] the stream, a convert."[20] In the second stage, the way of once-more-returning (Sakadāgāmi-magga/Sakṛdāgāmin-mārga), a Sakadāgāmin (Sakṛdāgāmin) is one " 'returning once,' one who will not be reborn on earth more than once; one who has attained the second grade of saving wisdom."[21] In the third stage, the way of no-more-returning (Anāgāmi-magga/Anāgāmin-mārga), an Anāgāmin (Anāgāmin) is "one who does not return, a Never-Returner, as technical term designating one who has attained the 3rd stage out of four in the breaking of the bonds (Saṃyojanas) which keep a man back from Arahantship. So near is the Anāgāmin to the goal, that after death he will be reborn in one of the highest heaven[s] and there obtain Arahantship, never returning to rebirth as a man. But in the oldest passages referring to these 4 stages, the description of the third does not use the word anāgāmin . . . and anāgāmin does not mean the breaking of bonds, but the cultivation of certain specified good mental habits . . ."[22] In the fourth and final stage of Enlightenment (Arahatta-magga or Arahant-magga/Arhattva-mārga), the Arahant (Arhat) is a technical term for one who has attained Nibbāna (Nirvāṇa).[23]

With regard to persons called Sāvakas/Śrāvakas, strictly speaking, "only those who heard the law [Dhamma/Dharma] from the Buddha's own lips have the name *śrāvaka*, and of these two, viz. Sāriputta and Mogallāna, were Agra-śrāvakas, 'chief disciples,' while eighty, including Kāśyapa, Upāli, and Ānanda, were Mahārāvakas or 'great disciples.' "[24] In general Mahāyāna usage, Śrāvakas mean so-called Hīnayāna disciples who aspire to become Arahants/Arhats and are unconcerned about the Enlightenment of others.

However, according to the Mahāyāna view, if the

Śrāvaka preliminarily prepares (Gotra-vihāra), nobly and resolutely aspires (Adhimukticaryā-vihāra), undertakes supreme worship (Anuttara-pūjā) as described above in Section 2, and makes a profound resolution (Praṇidhāna or Praṇidhi) which becomes a prediction (Vyākaraṇa or Vyākṛti) of his success, then he is ready to undertake the production of the thought of Enlightenment (Bodhi-citt-otpāda) which is requisite for a Bodhisattva (*tva* one whose *sat* essence is *bodhi* perfect knowledge). This requires training in four parts (*caryā*)—later graded in seven, ten, or more stages (*bhūmi*)—which will be described in Chapter IV, Section 4.

The composition of the Saṅgha will be indicated in Chapter V, but here some characterization of the bhikkhu/bhikṣu (monk) and bhikkunī/bhikṣunī (nun) may be given. The following textual passages are idealistic and yet very human.

*Monk* means: he is a monk because he is a beggar for alms, a monk because he submits to wandering for alms, a monk because he is one who wears the patch-work cloth, a monk by the designation (of others), a monk on account of his acknowledgment; a monk is called "Come, monk," a monk is endowed with going to the three refuges [Ti-ratana: the Buddha, the Dhamma, the Saṅgha], a monk is auspicious, a monk is the essential, a monk is a learner, a monk is an adept, a monk means one who is endowed with harmony for the Order [Saṅgha], with the resolution at which the motion is put three times and then followed by the decision, with actions (in accordance with dhamma and the discipline), with steadfastness, with the attributes of a man perfected. Whatever monk is endowed with harmony for the Order, with the resolution at which the motion is put three times, and then followed by the decision, with actions (in accordance with dhamma and the discipline), with steadfastness and the attributes of a man perfected, this one is a *monk* as understood in this meaning.[25]

It may be likened to a worldly man.
When he washes and bathes his body clean,
Anointing it with good and fragrant oils,
Adorning his head with a flowered headdress
And clothing his body in white garments,
He is called the son of a noble clan.
It is even so with thc homeless monk.
For ever pure in conduct and virtue,
Being clothed in the garments of the Law,
Perfect in deportment and appearance,
He is called the true son of the Buddha.[26]

Determined to leave his parents, what does he want to accomplish?
He is a Buddhist, a homeless monk now, and no more a man of the world;
His mind is ever intent on the mastery of the Dharma.
His conduct is to be as transparent as ice or crystal,
He is not to seek fame and wealth,
But to rid himself of all defilements.
There is no other way open to him but to wander about and inquire;
Let him be trained in mind and body by crossing mountains and fording rivers;
Let him befriend wise men in the Dharma and pay them respect wherever he may meet them;
Let him brave the snow and tread the frosty roads, not minding the severity of the weather;
Let him cross the waves and penetrate the clouds, chasing away dragons and evil spirits.
His iron staff accompanies him wherever he travels and his copper pitcher is well filled,
Let him not then be annoyed with the ups and downs of worldly affairs,
His friends are those in the monastery with whom he may weigh the Dharma,

Trimming off once for all the four propositions and one hundred negations.

Beware of being led astray by others to no purpose;
Now that you are in the monastery your task is to walk the great path,
And not to get attached to the world, but to be devoid of all trivialities;
Holding fast to the ultimate truth, do not refuse hard work in any form;
Keeping yourself away from noise and crowds, stop all toiling and craving.
Thinking of the one who threw himself down the precipice, and the other who stood all night in the snow, gather up all your fortitude,
So that you may keep the glory of your Dharma-king always manifested;
Be ever studious in the pursuit of the Truth, be ever reverent towards the Elders;
You are asked to stand the cold, heat and privations,
Because you have not yet come to the abode of peace;
Cherish no envious thoughts for worldly prosperity, be not depressed just because you are slighted;
But endeavor to see directly into your own nature, not depending on others.
Over the five lakes and the four seas you go on pilgrimage from monastery to monastery;
To walk thousands of miles over hundreds of mountains is indeed no easy task;
May you finally meet the master for interview in the Dharma and be led to see into your own nature.
Then you will no longer mistake weeds for medicinal plants.[27]

O woman well set free! how free am I,
How thoroughly free from kitchen drudgery!
Me stained and squalid 'mong my cooking-pots
My brutal husband ranked as even less
Than the sunshades he sits and weaves alway.
Purged now of all my former lust and hate,

I dwell, musing at ease beneath the shade
Of spreading bough—O, but 'tis well with me![28]

Though I be suffering and weak, and all
My youthful spring be gone, yet have I climbed,
Leaning upon my staff, the mountain crest.
Thrown from my shoulder hangs my cloak, o'er-turned
My little bowl. So 'gainst the rock I lean
And prop this self of me, and break away
The wildering gloom that long had closed me in.[29]

With ploughshares ploughing up the fields, with seed
Sown in the breast of earth, men win their crops,
Enjoy their gains and nourish wife and child.
Why cannot I, whose life is pure, who seek
To do the Master's will, no sluggard am,
Nor puffed up, win to Nibbana's bliss?
One day, bathing my feet, I sit and watch
The water as it trickles down the slope.
Thereby I set my heart in steadfastness,
As one doth train a horse of noble breed.
Then going to my cell, I take my lamp,
And seated on my couch I watch the flame.
Grasping the pin, I pull the wick right down
Into the oil . . .
Lo! the Nibbana of the little lamp!
Emancipation dawns! My heart is free![30]

CHAPTER THREE

# The Dhamma/Dharma: Buddhist Principles

In traditional Indian thought, the Sanskrit term *dharma* (cf. *ṛta*) has a variety of ethical, legal-political, metaphysical, and religious meanings which are often interrelated: norm of ethical conduct, universal righteousness, cosmic order and elements, and teaching or doctrine.

As the second part of the Three Valued Components of Buddhism (Pāli/Sanskrit: Ti-ratana/Tri-ratna), the Dhamma/Dharma is the Buddhist Doctrine as distinguished from, but related to, the Buddha and the Saṅgha. In a textual sense, it connotes the Teachings of the Buddha, compiled by his followers as the Sutta/Sūtra Piṭaka (Collection of Teachings) distinct from the Vinaya Piṭaka (Collection of Disciplinary Rules) and subsequent Abhidhamma/Abhidharma Piṭaka (Collection of Higher Dhamma/Dharma)—the three together form the Tipiṭaka/Tripiṭaka (the Three Collections).

This book will present the Dhamma/Dharma in two interrelated aspects as (a) *principles* and (b) *practices*, derived from the Buddha who exemplified them and amplified by his followers to whom he bequeathed his Way as their guide upon his demise.

### 1. *The Basic Problem of Life and the Four Principles in Buddhism*

Since the Buddhist point of view begins with "the here and now," Buddhist thought fundamentally concerns the nature of existence. A person begins to think Buddhistically when he becomes aware, physically and mentally, of himself in his natural and social environment. He experiences something because he "is there in relationship." This "something" is life, conditioned, ever-changing, and not yet fully known. However, in Buddhism life is meant to be rightly comprehended and fully realized as freedom in perfect existence.

For this purpose, the Buddha taught four essential principles according to his own experience and insight. They are characteristic of the Buddhist way but not peculiar to it and are in common with many other approaches to life. These Four Principles in Buddhism are collectively called Cattarī-ariya-saccāni/Catvāri-ārya-satyāni:

1. Dukkha-ariya-sacca/Duḥkha-ārya-satya = *Dukkha-sacca/Duḥkha-satya* (concerning the nature of imperfect existence);
2. Dukkha-samudaya-ariya-sacca/Duḥkha-samudaya-ārya-satya = *Samudaya-sacca/satya* (concerning the nature of causation affecting imperfect existence);
3. Dukkha-nirodha-ariya-sacca/Duḥkha-nirodha-ārya-satya = *Nirodha-sacca/satya* (concerning the removal of causal factors, the disappearance of imperfect existence, and the realization of ultimate freedom in perfect existence as Nibbāna/Nirvāṇa); and
4. Dukkha-nirodha-gāmiṇī-paṭipadā-ariya-sacca/Duḥkha-nirodha-gāminī-pratipad-ārya-satya *or* Magga/Mārga or Ariya-magga/Ārya-mārga = *Magga-sacca/Mārga-satya* (concerning the way to know and accomplish this transformation of existence, the way of supreme life).

In essence, these Four Principles in Buddhism are stages of progress in the realization of the Buddhist way of life (the epistemological-psychical aspect) and states of existence in the attainment of ultimate freedom (the metaphysical-existential aspect).

The Cattarī-ariya-saccāni/Catvāri-ārya-satyāni has frequently been translated into English as "the Four Noble Truths," but this rendering is inadequate because the term *sacca/satya* in the formula has a twofold epistemological-metaphysical meaning comparable to that of the Western concept of *principle* as "a fundamental truth; a primary or basic law, doctrine" and "an essential or characteristic constituent; that which gives a substance its essential properties." In short, when the four Sacca/Satya are experienced, they are recognized as comprising "truth" and realized as constituting "reality." Thus, for example, through them Siddhattha Gotama/Siddhārtha Gautama became Enlightened (Bodhi) as the Buddha: his transcendent comprehension and understanding (*paññā/prajñā*) actualized his Enlightenment and he epistemologically realized and metaphysically attained ultimate freedom in Perfect Existence (Nibbāna/Nirvāṇa). Otherwise, this transformation of being could not have happened if *sacca/satya* meant only "truth" and not also "existence" at the same time, from the beginning of basic awareness of Dukkha/Duḥkha to the culmination of the highest experience. Consequently, the term *ariya/ārya* in the formula assumes a Buddhist connotation of a universal exaltation, accomplishment, realization of being "Arahant/Arhat or supremely human" and no longer denotes an ethnic status of being "Ariya/Ārya" or social recognition of "noble."

The major Buddhist ways and their implemental

schools have numerous textual expositions, with variant doctrinal interpretations, of these Four Principles in Buddhism. In any comparative study of them, they should be understood according to the context of their School-system: for example, the Theravāda method of Magga-sacca is intended for the Theravāda conception of Nirodha-sacca which is pertinent to the Theravāda notion of Samudaya-sacca which concerns the Theravāda view of Dukkha-sacca; similarly, the Sarvāstivāda, Mādhyamika, and Yogācāra views of Mārga re Nirodha re Samudaya re Duḥkha.

An adequate statement of the Four Principles with representative textual quotations would therefore comprise several volumes of sizable proportions and cannot be undertaken within the present available space. Instead, some of the salient features of the First, Second, and Third Principles relating to doctrine will be mentioned in the following Sections 2, 3, and 4 and the Fourth Principle relating to practice will be summarized in Section 1 of Chapter IV.

## 2. *The First Principle: The Nature of Existence*

The First Principle in Buddhism (Dukkha-sacca/Duḥkha-satya) concerns the nature of existence, initially perceived and experienced as Dukkha/Duḥkha. This term has frequently been translated into English as "Suffering, Pain, Ill, Anguish, etc." but such renderings are subjective attributes of imperfect existence and fail to distinguish three aspects or states (*-tā*): (1) *dukkha-dukkhatā/duḥkha-duḥkhatā* as that state of quasi physical pain and mental anguish = ordinary suffering (*dukkha/duḥkha-vedanā*); (2) *(vi)pariṇāma-dukkhatā/duḥkhatā* as that state caused by change (for the worse); and (3) *sankhāra-dukkhatā/saṃskāra-duḥkhatā* as that state of conditionedness (not being free).

Thus Dukkhatā/Duḥkhatā as phenomenal existence is imperfect and to be transcended. It has three, interdependent characteristics (Ti-lakkhaṇa/Tri-lakṣaṇa): (1) *anicca/anitya* = impermanent, (2) *dukkha/duḥkha* = imperfect, and (3) *anatta/anātman* = essentially unsubstantial, nonindependent. These features also apply to sentient beings which function psychologically as individuals and coexist collectively as groups or societies; they consist of five aggregates of being (*pañca-khandha/skandha*): *rūpa* (material qualities), *vedanā* (feeling), *saññā/saṃjñā* (perception), *sankhāra/saṃskāra* (coefficients of consciousness), and *viññāṇa/vijñāna* (consciousness).

More fundamentally considered, all animate and inanimate phenomena are composites of interrelated elements called *dhamma/dharma* which are characterized by *anicca/anitya, dukkha/duḥkha,* and *anatta/anātman.* The Buddhist schools view these elements variously. For example, the Sarvāstivāda regard the *dharma* as existing momentarily: they were real in the past and will be in the future just as they exist noticeably in the present, but do not subsist from one period to another. The Mādhyamika especially views the relational nature (*śūnyatā*) of all *dharma,* and the Yogācāra views their ideational nature (*vijñaptimātratā*). The conception of *dharma* according to the Sarvāstivāda or Abhidharma School has been summarized by Th. Stcherbatsky:

> The conception of a *dharma* is the central point of the Buddhist doctrine. In the light of this conception Buddhism discloses itself as a metaphysical theory developed out of one

fundamental principle, viz. the idea that existence is an interplay of a plurality of subtle, ultimate, not further analysable elements of Matter, Mind, and Forces. These elements are technically called *dharmas*, a meaning which this word has in this system alone. Buddhism, accordingly, can be characterized as a system of Radical Pluralism (*sanghāta-vāda*): the elements alone are realities, every combination of them is a mere name covering a plurality of separate elements. The moral teaching of a path towards Final Deliverance is not something additional or extraneous to this ontological doctrine, it is most intimately connected with it and, in fact, identical with it.

The connotation of the term *dharma* implies that—

1. Every element is a separate (*pṛthak*) entity or force.

2. There is no inherence of one element in another, hence no substance apart from its qualities, no Matter beyond the separate sense-data, and no Soul beyond the separate mental data (*dharma* = *anātman* = *nirjīva*).

3. Elements have no duration, every moment represents a separate element; thought is evanescent, there are no moving bodies, but consecutive appearances, flashings, of new elements in new places (*kṣaṇikatva*).

4. The elements cooperate with one another (*saṃskṛta*).

5. This co-operating activity is controlled by the laws of causation (*pratītya-samutpāda*).

6. The world-process is thus a process of co-operation between seventy-two kinds of subtle, evanescent elements, and such is the nature of *dharmas* that they proceed from causes (*hetu-prabhava*) and steer towards extinction (*nirodha*).

7. Influenced (*sāsrava*) by the element *avidyā* [basic ignorance], the process is in full swing. Influenced by the element *prajñā* [transcendent comprehension and understanding], it has a tendency towards appeasement and final extinction. In the first case streams (*santāna*) of combining elements are produced which correspond to ordinary men (*pṛthag-jana*); in the second the stream represents a saint (*ārya*). The complete stoppage of the process of phenomenal life corresponds to a Buddha.

8. Hence the elements are broadly divided into unrest

(*duḥkha*), cause of unrest (*duḥkha-samudaya* = *avidyā*), extinction (*nirodha*), and cause of extinction (*mārga* = *prajñā*).

9. The final result of the world-process is its suppression, Absolute Calm: all co-operation is extinct and replaced by immutability (*asaṃskṛta* = *nirvāṇa*).

Since all these particular doctrines are logically developed out of one fundamental principle, Buddhism can be resolved in a series of equations:—

*dharmatā* = *nairātmya* = *kṣaṇikatva* = *saṃskṛtatva* = *pratītya-samutpannatva* = . . . *anāsravatva* = . . . *vyavadānatva* = *duḥkha-nirodha* = . . . *nirvāṇa.*

[The *saṃskṛta-dharmas* are divided] from the view-point of the part played by the elements in the process of cognition into six subjective and six objective "bases" (*āyatana*) of cognition. I. Six internal bases (*adhyātma-āyatana*) or receptive faculties (*indriya*): 1. Sense of vision (*cakṣur-indriya-āyatana*), 2. Sense of audition (*çrota-indriya-āyatana*), 3. Sense of smelling (*ghrāṇa-indriya-āyatana*), 4. Sense of taste (*jihvā-indriya-āyatana*), 5. Sense of touch (*kāya-indriya-āyatana*), 6. Faculty of the intellect or consciousness (*mana-indriya-āyatana*). II. Six external bases (*bāhya-āyatana*) or objects (*viṣaya*): 7. Colour and shape (*rūpa-āyatana*), 8. Sound (*çabda-āyatana*), 9. Odour (*gandha-āyatana*), 10. Taste (*rasa-āyatana*), 11. Tangibles (*spraṣṭavya-āyatana*), 12. Non-sensuous objects (*dharma-āyatana* or *dharmāḥ*). In this classification the eleven first items correspond to eleven elements (*dharma*), each including one. The twelfth item contains all the remaining sixty-four elements, and it is therefore called *dharma-āyatana* or simply *dharmāḥ,* i.e. the *remaining* elements.

[A further division of the *saṃskṛta-dharmas* is made] into eighteen classes (*dhātu* = *gotra*) of elements represented in the composition of an individual stream of life (*santāna*) in the different planes of existence. . . . The six *viṣayas* are *viṣaya* [objects] in regard to the six *indriyas* [receptive faculties], but *ālambana* [attributes] in regard to the six *vijñānas* [consciousnesses].[1]

### 3. *The Second Principle: The Nature of Causation*

The Second Principle in Buddhism (Samudaya-sacca/satya) concerns the arising of Dukkha/Duḥkha as the imperfect condition of existence. Why and how does this happen? As previously mentioned, all phenomena are compounded of various elements (*dhamma/dharma*) and characterized threefoldly as *anicca/anitya* (impermanent), *dukkha/duḥkha* (imperfect and not blissful), and *anatta/anātman* (essentially unsubstantial, nonindependently existing).

If such conditioned existence (Dukkha-sacca/Duḥkha-satya = *sankhata-dhamma/saṁskṛta-dharma*) is to be transcended (Nirodha-sacca/satya) and perfect freedom (Nibbāna/Nirvāṇa) to be realized (Bodhi), then the nature of causation must be understood and its operative principle mastered.

Generally speaking, in Buddhism the process of conditioned life is viewed as one of continual phenomenal-change (Saṃsāra) pluralistically caused. For example, a cycle of this process is commonly analyzed and stated in interrelated phases (*nidāna*, usually twelve in number: *dvādasa-anga/dvādaśa-aṅga*).

I. FORMER LIFE

| | |
|---|---|
| 1. *avidyā* | delusion (*caitta-dharma, duḥkha-satya*). |
| 2. *saṃskāra* | (= *karma* [the fact that actions will have consequences affecting future existence]). |

II. PRESENT LIFE

| | |
|---|---|
| 3. *vijñāna* | first moment of a new life, the moment of conception (= *pratisandhi-vijñāna*). |
| 4. *nāma-rūpa* | the five *skandhas* [groups or collections of *dharmas* in space-time] in the embryo before the formation of the sense-organs. |

| | | |
|---|---|---|
| 5. | *ṣaḍ-āyatana* | the formation of the organs. |
| 6. | *sparça* | organs and consciousness begin to co-operate. |
| 7. | *vedanā* | definite sensations. |
| 8. | *tṛṣṇā* | awakening of the sexual instinct, beginning of new *karma*. |
| 9. | *upādāna* | various pursuits in life. |
| 10. | *bhava* | life, i.e. various conscious activities. (= *karma-bhava*). |

III. FUTURE LIFE

| | | |
|---|---|---|
| 11. | *jāti* | rebirth. |
| 12. | *jarā-maraṇa* | new life, decay, and death. |

The five *skandhas* are present during the whole process; the different stages receive their names from the predominant *dharma*. . . . The first two stages indicate the origin of the life-process (*duḥkha-samudaya*). In regard to a future life Nos. 8–10 perform the same function as Nos. 1–2 in regard to the present life. Therefore the series represents an ever revolving "wheel."[2]

This composite life-story of a sentient being has been concisely described by the Venerable Dr. Walpola Rahula.

. . . a being is nothing but a combination of physical and mental forces or energies. What we call death is the total non-functioning of the physical body. Do all these forces and energies stop altogether with the non-functioning of the body? Buddhism says "No." Will, volition, desire, thirst to exist, to continue, to become more and more, is a tremendous force that moves whole lives, whole existences, that even moves the whole world. This is the greatest force, the greatest energy in the world. According to Buddhism, this force does not stop with the non-functioning of the body, which is death; but it continues manifesting itself in another form, producing re-existence which is called rebirth.

Now, another question arises: If there is no permanent, unchanging entity or substance like Self or Soul (*ātman*), what is it that can re-exist or be reborn after death? Before we go on to life after death, let us consider what this life is, and how it continues now. What we call life . . . is the combination of the Five Aggregates [*pañca-khandha/skandha*], a combination of physical and mental energies. These are constantly changing; they do not remain the same for two consecutive moments. Every moment they are born and they die. "When the Aggregates arise, decay and die, O bhikkhu, every moment you are born, decay and die" (*Paramatthajotikā*, PTS ed., p. 78). Thus, even now during this life time, every moment we are born and die, but we continue. If we can understand that in this life we can continue without a permanent, unchanging substance like Self or Soul, why can't we understand that those forces themselves can continue without a Self or a Soul behind them after the non-functioning of the body?

When this physical body is no more capable of functioning, energies do not die with it, but continue to take some other shape or form, which we call another life. In a child all the physical, mental and intellectual faculties are tender and weak, but they have within them the potentiality of producing a full grown man. Physical and mental energies which constitute the so-called being have within themselves the power to take a new form, and grow gradually and gather force to the full.

As there is no permanent, unchanging substance, nothing passes from one moment to the next. So quite obviously, nothing permanent or unchanging can pass or transmigrate from one life to the next. It is a series that continues unbroken, but changes every moment. The series is, really speaking, nothing but movement. It is like a flame that burns through the night: it is not the same flame nor is it another. A child grows up to be a man of sixty. Certainly the man of sixty is not the same as the child of sixty years ago, nor is he another person. Similarly, a person who dies here and is reborn elsewhere is neither the same person, nor another (*na ca so na ca añño*). It is the continuity of the same series. The difference between death and birth is only a thought-moment: the last thought-moment in this life conditions the first thought-moment in the so-called next life, which, in fact, is the continuity of the same series. During this life itself, too, one thought-moment conditions the next thought-moment. So from the Buddhist point of view, the question of life after death is not a great mystery, and a Buddhist is never worried about this problem.

As long as there is this "thirst" to be and to become, the cycle of continuity (*saṃsāra*) goes on. It can stop only when its driving force, this "thirst," is cut off through wisdom which sees Reality, Truth, Nirvāṇa.[3]

A fundamental understanding of this life-process and of the structure and "coming into being" of all conditioned existence requires an explanation of the nature of causation (*paṭicca-samuppāda/pratītya-samutpāda*) and a further analysis of the interrelated nature of all elements (*sarva-dharma* = *śūnya*, hence *dharmatā* = *śūnyatā*).

### *The Doctrine of Causality in the Hīnayāna*

In a previous work [*The Central Conception of Buddhism*] we have characterized Early Buddhism (Hīnayāna) as a system of metaphysics which contained an analysis of existence into its component elements, and established a certain number of ultimate data (*dharma*). Every combination of these data was then declared to represent a nominal, not an ultimate, reality. A substantial Soul was thus transformed into a stream of continuously flowing discrete moments of sensation or pure consciousness( *vijñāna*), accompanied by moments of feeling, of ideation, volition (*vedanā-saṃjñā-saṃskāra*) etc. Matter (*rūpa*) was conceived on the same pattern, as a flow of momentary flashes without any continuant stuff, but characterised by impenetrability, and representing the senses (*āyatana* 1–5) and sense-data (*āyatana* 7–11). The world was thus transformed into a cinema. The categories of substance, quality and motion—for momentary flashes could possess no motion—were denied, but the reality of sense data and of the elements of mind, was admitted. All these elementary data were conceived as obeying causal laws. But the conception of causality was adapted to the character of these entities which could neither move nor change, but could only appear and disappear. Causation was called dependently-coordinated-origination (*pratītya-sam-utpāda* [Pāli: *paṭicca-sam-uppāda*]), or dependent existence. The meaning of it was that every momentary entity sprang into existence, or flashed up, in coordination with other moments. Its formula was "if there is this, there appears that." Causality was thus assumed to exist between moments only, the appearance of every moment being coordinated with the appearance of a number of other moments. Strictly speaking it was no causality at all, no question of one thing *producing* the other. There could be neither a *causa materialis*, since there was no continuant substance, nor could there be any *causa efficiens*, since one momentary entity, disappearing as it did at once, could not influence any other entity. So the formula was supplemented by another one "not from itself (*causa materialis*), not from something foreign (*causa efficiens*), nor a combination of both does an entity spring up," "it is coordinated, it is not really produced." Apart from these momentary entities the system admitted eternal unchanging elements, Space and Nirvāṇa, the latter representing some indefinite essence (*dharma-svabhāva*), of these forces which were active in phenomenal life, but are now extinct and converted into eternal death. Thus both the phenomenal world and this kind of an absolute, both *saṃsāra* and *nirvāṇa*, were conceived as realities, somehow interconnected, linked together in a whole (*sarvam*), but in an ideal whole, having, as a combination of elements, only nominal existence.

### *This Doctrine Modified in Mahāyāna*

Now, the Mādhyamika system started with an entirely different conception of reality. Real was what possessed a reality of its own (*sva-bhāva*), what was not produced by causes (*akṛtaka* = *asaṃskṛta*), what was not dependent upon anything else (*paratra nirapekṣa*). In Hīnayāna the elements, although inter[de]pendent (*saṃskṛta* = *pratītya-samutpanna*), were real (*vastu*). In Mahāyāna all elements, because interdependent, were unreal (*šūnya* = *svabhāva-šūnya*). In Hīnayāna every whole (*rāśi* = *avayavin*) is regarded as a nominal existence (*prajñaptisat*) and only the parts or ultimate elements (*dharma*) are real (vastu). In Mahāyāna all parts or elements are unreal (*šūnya*), and only the whole, i.e., the Whole of the wholes (*dharmatā* = *dharma-kāya*), is real. The definition of reality (*tattva*) in Mahāyāna is the following one —"uncognisable from without, quiescent, undifferentiated in words, unrealisable in concepts, non-plural—this is the essence of reality." A dependent existence is no real existence, just as borrowed money is no real wealth. The theory that all real existence can last only for one moment, since two moments implied already a synthesis, was abandoned, and the conception of a momentary entity (*kṣaṇa*), so characteristic for other schools of Buddhist thought, was given up, as unwarranted (*asiddha*), not capable of resisting critique. In Hīnayāna the individual (*pudgala*), the Self (*ātma*) was resolved in its component elements (*skandha-āyatana-dhātavah* = *anātma*), there were no real personalities (*pudgala-nairātmya*), but a congeries of flashing forces (*saṃskāra-samūha*). In Mahāyāna we have, on the contrary, a denial of real elements (*dharma-nairātmya*), and an assertion of the whole, in the sense of the absolute Whole (*dharma-kāya*). In Hīnayāna, in a word, we have a radical Pluralism, converted in Mahāyāna in as radical a Monism.

### *The Doctrine of Relativity*

In Mahāyāna we are thus faced by a new interpretation of the old Buddhist principle of the dependently-coordinated-existence of the elements (*dharmāṇām pratītya-sam-utpādā*). It is now being declared that whatsoever is dependent or relative cannot be considered as an ultimate reality, and this feature is then pressed to its last extreme. In Hīnayāna existence was bifurcated in conditioned and unconditioned (*samskṛta* and *asamskṛta*), both being realities. Neither of them is now considered as ultimately real, and both are brought under the higher unity of Relativity. The central conception in Early Buddhism is the idea of a plurality of ultimate elements (*dharmas*). The central conception of Mahāyāna is their relativity (*šūnyatā*). The Buddhists themselves contended that the idea of ultimate elements (*skandha-āyatana-dhātavaḥ*), of their interdependence (*pratītya-samutpāda*) and of the "Four Truths of the Saint" are admitted in both Hīnayāna and Mahāyāna. But in the first they are referred to [as] the reality of separate elements, and in the second they are interpreted as meaning their relativity, or non-reality. Since we use the term "relative" to describe the fact that a thing can be identified only by mentioning its relations to something else, and becomes meaningless without these relations, implying at the same time that the thing in question is unreal, we safely, for want of a better solution, can translate the word *šūnya* by relative or contingent, and the term *šūnyatā* by relativity or contingency. This is in any case better than to translate it by "void" which signification the term has in common life, but not as a technical term in philosophy. That the term *šūnya* is in Mahāyāna a synonym of dependent existence (*pratītya-samutpāda*) and means not something void, but something "devoid" of independent reality (*svabhāva-šūnya*), with the implication that nothing short of the whole possesses independent reality, and with the further implication that the whole forbids every formulation by concept or speech (*niṣprapañca*), since they can only bifurcate (*vikalpa*) reality and never directly seize it—this is attested by an overwhelming mass of evidence in all the Mahāyāna literature. That this term never meant a mathematical void or simple non-existence is most emphatically insisted upon. Those who suppose that *šūnya* means void are declared to have misunderstood the term, they have not understood the purpose for which the term has been introduced. "We are Relativists, we are not Negativists!" insists Candrakīrti.[4]

## 4. *The Third Principle: The Ultimate Freedom in Perfect Existence*

The Third Principle in Buddhism (Nirodha-sacca/satya) concerns the cessation of the Samudaya-sacca/satya (the Second Principle) and thus the disappearance of Dukkha-sacca/Duḥkha-satya (the First Principle) whereupon freedom in perfect existence (Nibbāna/Nirvāṇa) may be attained. Nirodha therefore has a twofold meaning: stopping or eliminating causation (*paṭicca-samuppāda/pratītya-samutpāda = nirodha*) and, correlatively, realizing freedom (*nirodha = nibbāna/nirvāṇa*). This twofold task of Nirodha is undertaken by means of Magga-sacca/Mārga-satya (the Fourth Principle).

The first meaning of the Third Principle (*paṭicca-samuppāda/pratītya-samutpāda = nirodha*) is stated in the *Vammīka-sutta* of the Pāli Majjhima-Nikāya where the Buddha declares:

> Although I, monks, am one who speaks thus, who points out thus, there are some recluses and brahmans who misrepresent me untruly, vainly, falsely, not in accordance with fact, saying: "The recluse Gotama is a nihilist, he lays down the cutting off, the destruction, the disappearance of the existent entity." But as this, monks, is just what I am not, as this is just what I do not say, therefore these worthy recluses and brahmans misrepresent me untruly, vainly, falsely, and not in accordance with fact when they say: "The recluse Gotama is a nihilist, he lays down the cutting off, the destruction, the disappearance of the existent entity." Formerly I, monks, as well as now, lay down simply anguish [*dukkha*] and the stopping of anguish [*nirodha*]. If, in regard to this, monks, others revile, abuse, annoy the Tathāgata, there is in the Tathāgata no resentment, no distress, no dissatisfaction of mind concerning them.[5]

The nature of *nirodha* is further explained in the *Mahātaṇhāsaṅkhaya-sutta* of the Majjhima-Nikāya:

> Thus have I heard: . . . Then the Lord addressed the monks, saying: . . . If this, is that comes to be; from the arising of this, that arises, that is to say: conditioned by

ignorance [*avijjā*] are the karma-formations; conditioned by the karma-formations is consciousness; conditioned by consciousness is psycho-physicality; conditioned by psycho-physicality are the six (sensory) spheres; conditioned by the six (sensory) spheres is sensory impingement; conditioned by sensory impingement is feeling; conditioned by feeling is craving; conditioned by craving is grasping; conditioned by grasping is becoming; conditioned by becoming is birth; conditioned by birth, ageing and dying, grief, sorrow, suffering, lamentation and despair come into being. Such is the arising of this entire mass of anguish [*dukkha*]. But from the utter fading away and stopping [*nirodha*] of this very ignorance is the stopping of the karma-formations; from the stopping of the karma-formations the stopping of consciousness; from the stopping of consciousness the stopping of psycho-physicality; from the stopping of psycho-physicality the stopping of the six (sensory) spheres; from the stopping of the six (sensory) spheres the stopping of sensory impingement; from the stopping of sensory impingement the stopping of feeling; from the stopping of feeling the stopping of craving; from the stopping of craving the stopping of grasping; from the stopping of grasping the stopping of becoming; from the stopping of becoming the stopping of birth; from the stopping of birth, old age and dying, grief, sorrow, suffering, lamentation and despair are stopped. Such is the stopping of this entire mass of anguish.[6]

The second, correlative meaning of the Third Principle (*nirodha* = *nibbāna*/*nirvāṇa*) is expressed also in Pāli texts, for example,

The venerable Musīla and the venerable Saviṭṭha . . . were once staying at Kosambī in Ghosita Park. Now the venerable Saviṭṭha said thus to the venerable Musīla: . . .

Apart, friend Musīla, from belief, apart from inclination, hearsay, argument as to method, from reflection on and approval of opinion has the venerable Musīla as his very own the knowledge that—the ceasing of becoming is Nibbāna?

Apart, friend Saviṭṭha, from belief and the rest, this I know, this I see:—The ceasing of becoming is Nibbāna.

Well then, the venerable Musīla is Arahant, for whom the intoxicants are perished.

When this was said the venerable Musīla became silent.[7]

The truth of cessation has the characteristic of peace. Its function is not to die. It is manifested as the signless.*

In other respects of Nirodha = Nibbāna/Nirvāṇa, it should be mentioned that there are various views between and within the principal Buddhist schools; for example, Nibbāna as Peace according to the Theravāda, Nirvāṇa as Śūnyatā (Relativity or the rational view; Absolute or the experiential view), Dharma-kāya (Essence of the Buddha), Tathatā (ultimate Actuality), Dharma-dhātu (ultimate Reality), etc., according to the Mādhyamika and Yogācāra.

Th. Stcherbatsky has summarized "the probable history of the Buddhist conception of the Absolute":

1. In the VI century B.C. there was a great effervescence of philosophical thought among the non-brahmanical classes of India, and a way out of phenomenal life was ardently sought for, the majority of the solutions having a materialistic tinge. Buddha at that time proposed, or accepted, a system denying the existence of an eternal Soul, and reducing phenomenal existence to a congeries of separate elements evolving gradually towards final extinction.

2. To this ideal of a lifeless Nirvāṇa and an extinct Buddha some schools [e.g. Theravāda] alone remained faithful. A tendency to convert Buddha into a superhuman, eternally living, principle manifested itself early among his followers and led to a schism.

* "*Signless*" being secluded from the sign of the five aggregates [*khandhas*], it is taken as having no graspable entity (*aviggaha*) (*Visuddhimagga Atthakathā* (Commentary) 525).[8]

3. This tendency gradually developed until in the I century A.D. it ended in the production of a luxuriant growth of a new kanonical literature. It then adopted, probably borrowing from some Aupaniṣada [non-Upanishad] school, the brahmanical idea of a pantheistic Absolute, of a spiritual and monistic character. After this Buddhistic adaptation of the Vedānta the Buddha was converted into a full blown *brahman* and its personification worshipped under the names of a Cosmical Body (*dharmakāya*), Samantabhadra, Vairocana and others.

4. The philosophical doctrine of the old church [e.g. *Sarvāstivāda*] stuck to the central conception of separate elements of Matter, Mind and Forces, composed lists of them with a view to investigate the method of their gradual extinction in the Absolute.

5. Among the early schools the Mahāsaṃghikas, Vātsīputrīyas and others already assumed a kind of consciousness surviving in Nirvāṇa.

6. They were followed by a school with critical tendencies, the Sautrāntikas, which cut down the list of artificially constructed elements, cut down Nirvāṇa itself as a separate entity and transferred the Absolute into the living world, thus constituting a transition to Mahāyāna.

7. The philosophy of the new religion is an adaptation of the Vedānta system. It forsook the pluralistic principle altogether and became emphatically monistic.

8. It then took a double course. It either assumed the existence of a store-consciousness of which all phenomenal life was but a manifestation. This school [Śūnyavāda or Mādhyamika] in the sequel cultivated logic. The other school [Vijñānavāda or Yogācāra] denied the possibility of cognising the Absolute by logical methods, it declared all plurality to be an illusion, and nothing short of the whole to be the Reality directly cognised in mystic intuition.

9. The transitional school of the Sautrāntikas coalesced in the V century A.D. with the idealistic school [Yogācāra] of the Mahāyāna and produced India's greatest philosophers Dignāga and Dharmakīrti. With regard to Nirvāṇa it assumed the existence of a pure spiritual principle, in which object and

subject coalesced, and, along with it, a force of transcendental illusion (*vāsanā*) producing the phenomenal world.

10. Contemporaneously with this highest development of Buddhist philosophy, in the VII century A.D., the relativist school of early Mahāyāna [Mādhyamika] received a fresh impulse and a revival of popularity. This led to the formation of new hybrid schools.

11. The very high perfection to which philosophy was brought by both the idealistic and relativistic schools of Buddhism could not but influence all philosophical circles of India, and we see in the next period the old Vedānta remodelled and equipped with fresh arguments by an adaptation to it of the methods elaborated in the Vijñānavāda and Śūnyavāda schools of Buddhism.[9]

## 5. *The Correlation of Thought, Conduct, and Being in Buddhism*

In the Buddhist way of life for the attainment of Nibbāna/Nirvāṇa, principles and practices are interdependent: right thought and right conduct are correlated and integrated in right being. This process is the essence of the Buddha Sāsana/Śāsana as evidenced in the manifold meanings of numerous passages in Buddhist texts (when correctly understood) and exemplified in the lives of Buddhist personages. One example must suffice here.

In the Dhamma/Dharma as Buddhist principles, the twofold epistemological-metaphysical meaning of *sacca/satya* as Principle and *bodhi* as Enlightenment was mentioned above in Section 1. Furthermore, *satya*, as expounded especially by the Mādhyamika School and stated here in simplest form, is differentiated in several phases of knowledge/being: *saṁvṛti-satya* as empirical-relative knowledge/relational existence, and *paramārtha-satya* as superrational or transcendent knowledge/absolute existence. The intrinsic epistemological-metaphysical relationship between *saṁvṛti-satya* and *paramārtha-satya* is that of interdependence: the former is transcended/perfected to become the latter, and the latter is expressed/manifested through the former which thereafter is guided by it in the Buddhist way of life. (However, in the study, teaching, and practice of Buddhist thought, it is essential that the *saṁvṛti-satya* concept of knowledge/existence be distinguished from the *paramārtha-satya* concept of knowledge/existence at all times lest seeming inconsistencies of interpretation be attributed to Buddhist doctrinal statements and misunderstandings arise.)

Thus, when *saṁvṛti-satya* has been transcended by means of Prajñā (transcendent comprehension and understanding) for the direct realization (Bodhi) of *paramārtha-satya,* it may be said epistemologically that empirical-relative knowledge has become superrational or transcendent knowledge and metaphysically that relational existence has become absolute existence. In other words, relative-Śūnyatā, formerly viewed rationally, is absolute-Śūnyatā, now experienced existentially. In this process, from the *saṁvṛti* point of view, *saṁvṛti-satya,* Avidyā, Duḥkha, Saṃsāra, etc. are contradistinguished from *paramārtha-satya,* Bodhi or Prajñā, Nirodha, Nirvāṇa, etc.; but from the *paramārtha* point of view, they are not distinguished because the former have been transcended in the process of epistemological/metaphysical Enlightenment. However, after such realization, provisional distinctions must be recognized (cf. *tathya* [true] *saṁvṛti* as distinguished from *mithyā* [false] *saṁvṛti*) by the Bodhisattva in guiding others toward Enlightenment.

This process and its consequences may be expressed by the following equation:

Saṁvṛti-satay = Paramātha-satya = Śūnyatā, Prajñā, Bodhi = Nirvāṇa

*or*

Duḥkhatā (*saṁskṛta-dharma* = *anitya, duḥkha, anātman*) =
Samudaya (*saṁskṛta-dharma* = *pratītya-samutpāda*) and
Saṃsāra (5 *skandha,* 12 *āyatana,* 18 *dhātu*) *become*
Nirodha (*pratītya-samutpāda* = *śūnyatā*) =
Nirvāṇa (*asaṁskṛta-dharma* = *śūnyatā* = *tathatā* = *bhūtatā* or *bhūta-tathatā* = *tathāgata-garbha* = *dharmatā* = *dharma-dhātu* = *dharma-kāya,* etc.)

Consequently, in the Dhamma/Dharma as Buddhist practices, right thought and right conduct are interdependently based in principle and correlated and integrated in right being. This ideal and procedure will be indicated in the following chapters.

CHAPTER FOUR

# The Dhamma/Dharma: Buddhist Practices

## 1. *The Fourth Principle: The Middle Way and the Eightfold Path*

The Fourth Principle of Buddhism is the means whereby The First Principle (Pāli/Sanskrit: Dukkha-sacca/Duḥkha-satya) is recognized and realized, the Second Principle (Samudaya-sacca/satya) is known and understood, and the Third Principle (Nirodha-sacca/satya) is actualized and thereby Nibbāna/Nirvāṇa attained. It is therefore called the Way or Noble Way: Magga or Ariya-magga (cf. Dukkha-nirodha-gāminī-ariya-paṭipadā-sacca) in Pāli texts and Mārga or Ārya-mārga (cf. Duḥkha-nirodha-gāminī-pratipad-satya) in Sanskrit works. As explained above in Chapter III, it may be termed Magga-sacca/Mārga-satya.

This Way by which one may become an Arahant/Arhat or a Buddha is also the Path on which one progresses toward Enlightenment. Hence in principle it is the Middle Way (Majjhimā-paṭipadā/Madhyamā-pratipad) and in practice the Eightfold Path (Aṭṭhangika-magga/Aṣṭāngika-mārga) or sometimes called the Noble Eightfold Path (Ariya-aṭṭhaṅgika-magga/Ārya-aṣṭāngika-mārga).

Historically considered, it may be said that the Middle Way characterizes Buddhist practice especially in the

Theravāda tradition and Buddhist thought especially in the Mahāyāna tradition. The following selections will illustrate this development.

Thus have I heard: Once the Exalted One was dwelling near Benares [then Vārānasī], at Isipatana, in the Deer Park. Then the Exalted One thus spake unto the company of five monks.

"Monks, these two extremes should not be followed by one who has gone forth as a wanderer. What two? Devotion to the pleasures of sense, a low practice of villagers, a practice unworthy, unprofitable, the way of the world (on the one hand); and (on the other) devotion of self-mortification, which is painful, unworthy and unprofitable.

"By avoiding these two extremes the Tathāgata has gained knowledge of that middle path which giveth vision, which giveth knowledge, which causeth calm, special knowledge [of the four truths], enlightenment, Nibbāna.

"And what, monks, is that middle path which giveth vision . . . Nibbāna? Verily it is this Ariyan eightfold way, to wit: Right view, right aim, right speech, right action, right living, right effort, right mindfulness, right concentration. This, monks, is that middle path which giveth vision, which giveth knowledge, which causeth calm, special knowledge, enlightenment, Nibbāna."[1]

The Middle Path is a fundamental tenet of Buddhism, but in early Buddhism it means the middle between materialism and rationalism (*ucchedavāda* and *šāsvata-vāda*); in the Mādhyamika system it means radical relativism or scepticism, nothing to be asserted as ultimate reality; in the Yogācāra system it means the middle way between the Hīnayāna pluralism for which whatsoever is a *dharma* is *eo ipso* real (*sarvam asti* = *samāropa*) and the scepticism of the Mādhyamikas for whom not a single *dharma* is ultimately real, all are only relatively real (*sarvam šūnyam* = *paraspara-āpekṣikam* = *apavāda*).[2]

The essence of the Mādhyamika attitude, his philosophy (the madhyamā pratipad), consists in not allowing oneself to be entangled in views and theories, but just to observe the nature of things without standpoints (bhūta-pratyavekṣā). The *Ratnakūṭa Sūtra* (*Kāśyapaparivarta* pp. 82-87) states the middle position thus:

"The Bodhisattva desiring to adopt the spiritual discipline must cultivate the attitude of unceasing, critical alertness with regard to things (yoniśo dharmaprayuktena bhavitavyam). And what is this alertness? It is the perception of all things in their true form (sarvadharmāṇām bhūtapratyavekṣā). And again, what is the nature of this true perception? Where, Kāśyapa, there is not the viewing of things as atman (substance) etc., that which does not take rūpa, (matter), vedanā, saṁjñā, saṁsksāra, vijñāna as eternal (nitya), or changing (anitya). That things are unchanging (nitya), this, Kāśyapa, is one end (antaḥ); that they are changing is another . . . that reality is substance (ātmeti) is one end; that it is only modal (nairātmyam iti) is another end; the middle between these two extremes of ātman and anirātmya is the intangible, the incomparable, non-appearing, not comprehensible, without any position . . . that verily is the Middle Path—the vision of the Real in its true form."[3]

[*Maitreya* (*nātha*) (*c. 270-350* A.D.) *states:*]

Neither is it asserted
That all (the Elements) are unreal,
Nor are they all realities;
Because there is existence,
And also non-existence,
And (again) existence:
This is the Middle Path!

*Vasubandhu's* [*c. 320–400* A.D.] *Comment*

Neither unreal are (all the Elements of existence), because there are (two items that are real, viz. the eternal, all-embracing) Absolute and the (instantaneous) Constructor of phenomena. Nor are they not-real (i.e. not all are real). Inasmuch as there is separation into two parts (the one grasping the other) there is no (genuine) reality.

"All (the Elements)" means (the two main groups into which the 75 Elements of existence established in the Hīnayāna are divided, viz.) the "caused" ones which are (also) the constructors of phenomena and the "uncaused" ones which is the Absolute. "It is asserted" means it is established. "Because there is existence"—this refers to the real existence of the Constructor of phenomena; "and (also) non-existence," this refers to the division (into an object and a subject); "and (again) existence," this refers to the presence of the Absolute in the Constructor and of the Constructor in the Absolute. "This is the Middle Path," these words intimate that neither are all Elements exclusively unreal nor are they exclusively real. Such an interpretation of the Middle Path agrees with (many) passages from the "Discourse on Transcendent Intuition" and other (scriptural) works where it is stated that "all this is neither unreal, nor is it real." (This means that there are some Elements that are real and others that are unreal.)

### *Sthiramati's* [*c. 470–550* A.D.] *Comment*

With what aim has this stanza been composed? Its aim is to declare that all (the Elements of reality), the caused (or instantaneous) ones and the uncaused (or eternal) ones are (in their ultimate essence) not affected by the division into one part grasping the other. This indeed also appears as the real meaning of the passages from the "Discourse on Transcendent Intuition" which declare that "all this is neither unreal nor is it real." It repudiates the radical (theories of extreme scepticism which declares that not a single Element is real, and of extreme realism which maintains that whatsoever is an Element is *eo ipso* real). Otherwise the first half of this text ("not unreal") would stand in contradiction to the other half ("not real").

(The stanza) moreover has the aim of establishing (the doctrine of) the Middle Path—otherwise either the unreality of the reality (of all Elements) would be onesidedly asserted —and also of making a conclusive statement regarding the repudiation of an exaggerated denial of reality, as well as of an exaggerated assertion of it. (Asserted is as real first of all) the causally interdependent Element, which is the Constructor (or the basis) of phenomena, because it obtains its own realization in strict dependence on causes and conditions. (Asserted is as real) also the Absolute, the uncaused Element, since it does not depend on (causes and possesses an independent, absolute reality of its own). "This is asserted" sc. in the "Discourse on Transcendent Intuition" and similar works.

(The words of the stanza) "because there is existence" refer to (that Element of existence which is) the Constructor of phenomena, (they mean that all Elements cannot be unreal, because admitted must be the reality of the Constructor of the phenomenal worlds). That essence of every causally interrelated Element of existence which is the Constructor of the (corresponding) phenomenon, (it alone) is not unreal, (it is absolutely real as a Thing-in-Itself). But that other essence of this Element which converts it into either an apprehended object or an apprehending subject is (a construction of our productive imagination), it is not ultimately real. (This is expressed in the further words of Vasubandhu) "because there is non-existence," non-existence namely of this duality.

(The repetition in the stanza of the words) "and again because of existence" refers to the presence of the Absolute in the Constructor as being its universal property and (*vice versa*) of the Constructor in the Absolute as being the possessor of that property. Thus it is that the "uncaused" (i.e. the eternal Element or the Absolute) is not unreal, (not relative), inasmuch as it represents the "Elementness" (or absolute totality of all the genuinely real Elements of existence).

When (the Scripture) maintains that it is not real( in saying that it is "neither not devoid nor devoid"), this should be interpreted so that in itself it is essentially devoid, (but devoid only) of the division in two parts, (the one grasping the other).

(It is said in the stanza)—"And this is the Middle Path." Indeed in the Ratnakūṭa [*Kāšyapa-parivarta*] and other (scriptural works) we find the following deliverance: "O, Kāšyapa! It exists" is one extreme, "it does not exist" is another extreme. The intermediate attitude between these two extremes, O, Kāšyapa! is called the Middle Path. It represents the (deepest) intuition of that reality (which is hidden at the bottom) of every Element of Existence. This is the Middle Path. In this manner the Middle Path is made to agree (with our System).

The word "all" (used in the sacred texts in such phrases as "all is real"—*sarvam asti,* and "all is unreal"—*sarvam šūnyam*) refers to (both categories of the Elements of existence as established in the early schools, viz.) the causally dependent (or instantaneous ones—*saṃskṛta*) and the causally independent (or eternal ones—*asaṃskṛta*), The Elements are not all exclusively (relative and) unreal, because there are among them two Elements that are (absolutely) real; they are the (instantaneous) Constructor lying at the bottom of every phenomenon and the (eternal Element) of the (all-embracing) Absolute.

"Nor is it exclusively real," since (their appearance, viz. their division) into two parts (the one grasping the other) does not (in ultimate reality) exist at all.

Whether we assume that all the Elements (into which reality has been analyzed in Buddhism) are real or that all are unreal, in both these cases, we shall have extremes, but not the Middle Path.[4]

The above quoted selections concerning the Middle Way indicate two important points: the Eightfold Path is an amplification, or an exemplification, of the Middle Way, a course of "right doing"; and the Eightfold Path is stressed particularly by the Theravāda Pāli tradition—it has been largely supplanted by the six or ten Pāramitās (Perfections) of the Bodhisattva in the Mahāyāna and Vajrayāna traditions.

The Eightfold Path (Aṭṭhangika-magga/Aṣṭāngika-mārga) consists of eight interdependent categories or aspects of proper Buddhist practice, both mental and physical:

1. Right Understanding (Sammā-diṭṭhi/Samyag-dṛṣṭi)
2. Right Thought (Sammā-saṅkappa/Samyak-saṅkalpa)
3. Right Speech (Sammā-vācā/Samyag-vāk)
4. Right Action (Sammā-kammanta/Samyak-karmānta)
5. Right Livelihood (Sammā-ājīva/Samyag-ājīva)
6. Right Effort (Sammā-vāyāma/Samyag-vyāyāma)
7. Right Mindfulness (Sammā-sati/Samyak-smṛti)
8. Right Concentration (Sammā-samādhi/Samyak-samādhi)

These eight categories have been stated and explained in numerous places in Pāli, Sanskrit, and other texts. The following description is attributed to the Buddha:

And the Exalted One said: . . . what, bhikkhus, is the Aryan Truth concerning the Way that leads to the Cessation of Ill? This is that Aryan Eightfold Path, to wit, right view, right aspiration, right speech, right doing, right livelihood, right effort, right mindfulness, right rapture.

And what, bhikkhus, is right view? Knowledge, bhikkhus, about Ill, knowledge about the coming to be of Ill, knowledge about the cessation of Ill, knowledge about the Way that leads to the cessation of Ill. This is what is called right view.

And what, bhikkhus, is right aspiration? The aspiration towards renunciation, the aspiration towards benevolence, the aspiration towards kindness. This is what is called right aspiration.

And what, bhikkhus, is right speech? Abstaining from lying, slander, abuse and idle talk. This is what is called right speech.

And what, bhikkhus, is right doing? Abstaining from taking life, from taking what is not given, from carnal indulgence. This is what is called right doing.

And what, bhikkhus, is right livelihood? Herein, O bhikkhus, the Aryan disciple having put away wrong livelihood, supports himself by the right livelihood.

And what, bhikkhus, is right effort? Herein, O bhikkhus, a brother makes effort in bringing forth wills that evil and bad states that have not arisen within him may not arise, to that end he stirs up energy, he grips and forces his mind. That he may put away evil and bad states that have arisen within him he puts forth will, he makes effort, he stirs up energy, he grips and forces his mind. That good states which have not arisen may arise he puts forth will, he makes effort, he stirs up energy, he grips and forces his mind. That good states which have arisen may persist, may not grow blurred, may multiply, grow abundant, develop and come to perfection, he puts forth will, he makes effort, he stirs up energy, he grips and forces his mind. This is what is called right effort.

And what, bhikkhus, is right mindfulness? Herein, O bhikkhus, a brother, as to the body, continues so to look upon the body, that he remains ardent, self-possessed and mindful, having overcome both the hankering and the dejection common in the world. And in the same way as to feelings, thoughts and ideas, he so looks upon each, that he remains ardent, self-possessed and mindful, having overcome the hankering and the dejection that is common in the world. This is what is called right mindfulness.

And what, bhikkhus, is right rapture? Herein, O bhikkhus, a brother, aloof from sensuous appetites, aloof from evil ideas, enters into and abides in the First Jhâna, wherein there is cogitation and deliberation, which is born of solitude and is full of joy and ease. Suppressing cogitation and deliberation, he enters into and abides in the Second Jhâna, which is self-evoked, born of concentration, full of joy and ease, in that, set free from cogitation and deliberation, the mind grows calm and sure, dwelling on high. And further, disenchanted with joy, he abides calmly contemplative while, mindful and self-possessed, he feels in his body that ease whereof Aryans declare "He that is calmly contemplative and aware, he dwelleth at ease." So does he enter into and abide in the Third Jhâna. And further, by putting aside ease and by putting aside mal-aise, by the passing away of the happiness and of the melancholy he used to feel, he enters into and abides in the Fourth Jhâna, rapture of utter purity of mindfulness and equanimity, wherein neither ease is felt nor any ill. This is what is called right rapture.

This, bhikkhus, is the Aryan Truth concerning the Way leading to the cessation of Ill.[5]

## 2. *The Threefold Training*

An understanding of the Threefold Training is essential for an understanding of Buddhist principles and practices which form an integrated way of life. Whether directly stated or implied, it is embodied in many Buddhist texts; Buddhaghosa (fifth century A.D.) significantly organized his whole exposition in the Pāli *Visuddhi-magga* (The Path of Purification) in accordance with it. Therefore, the follower of Buddhism must not neglect it, and the student of Buddhism should not overlook it.

The Threefold Training is called Ti-sikkhā in Pāli and Tri-śikṣā (or as a triad, Trīṇi-śikṣāni) in Sanskrit, in which *sikkhā/śikṣā* means "study, instruction, discipline." It comprises: (1) Adhisīla-sikkhā/Adhiśīla: training in *sīla/śīla*, virtuous conduct = higher morality (nos. 3, 4, 5 of the Eightfold Path); (2) Adhicitta-sikkhā/Adhicitta: training in *samādhi/samādhi*, concentrative absorption = higher thought (nos. 6, 7, 8 of the Eightfold Path); and (3) Adhipaññā-sikkhā/Adhiprajñā: training in *paññā/prajñā*, transcendent comprehension and understanding for Enlightenment (Bodhi) = higher insight (nos. 1 and 2 of the Eightfold Path). Thus the Threefold Training provides instruction and guidance for those who would progress toward Enlightenment. In this connection, two compound-forming concepts should be noted: *-khandha/skandha* (as the "group" of factors for progress in the Dhamma/Dharma toward Enlightenment) and *-sampadā/sampad* (as "accomplishment" in the progress . . . ), for example, in the case of Pāli terms:

(1) *sīla-khandha* the group dealing with the practice of morality; (2) *samādhi-khandha* that dealing with the development of concentration; (3) *paññā-khandha* that dealing with the development of true wisdom. They are also known under the terms of *sīla-sampadā, citta-sampadā, paññā-sampadā*. . . . These 3 are completed to a set of 5 by (4) *vimutti-khandha* the group dealing with the attainment of emancipation and (5) *vimutti-ñāṇa-dassana-khandha* the group dealing with the realization of the achievement of emancipation.[6]

*Sampadā* in its pregnant meaning is applied to the accomplishments of the individual in the course of his religious development. Thus it is used with *sīla, citta,* and *paññā*. . . . Here with *sīla-sampadā* the whole of the sīlakkhandha (Dīgha-Nikāya I.63 sq.) is understood; *citta-sampadā* means the cultivation of the heart and attainments of the mind relating to composure, concentration and religious meditation, otherwise called samādhikkhandha. It includes those stages of meditation which are enumerated under samādhi. With *paññā-sampadā* are meant the attainments of higher wisdom and spiritual emancipation, connected with supernormal faculties, culminating in Arahantship and extinction of all causes of rebirth, otherwise called *vijjā*. . . . The same ground as by this 3 fold division is covered by the enumeration of 5 sampadās as *sīla-sampadā, samādhi-sampadā, paññā-sampadā, vimutti-sampadā, vimutti-ñāṇadassana-sampadā*.[7]

The following selections illustrate the purport and use of the Threefold Training (Ti-sikkhā) in the Theravāda Pāli tradition.

Thus have I heard: . . . [And the Exalted One said]:
"Monks, there are these three forms of training. What three? The training in the higher morality, that in the higher thought and that in the higher insight.
"And what, monks, is the training in the higher morality? Herein a monk lives moral and restrained with the restraint of the obligations: following the practice of right conduct he

sees danger in the slightest faults: he takes up and trains himself in the laws of morality. This is called 'the training in the higher morality.'

"And what, monks, is the training in the higher thought? Herein a monk, remote from sensual desires (practises the four musings [*jhāna*]) . . . attaining the fourth musing he abides therein. This is called 'the training in the higher thought.'

"And what, monks, is the training in the higher insight? Herein a monk understands, as it really is, the meaning of This is Ill: This is the arising of Ill: This is the ending of Ill: This is the practice leading to the ending of Ill. This is called 'the training in the higher insight.' These are the three forms of training."[8]

Thus have I heard: . . . [the nun Dhammadinnā, the chief teacher of *dhamma* among the women disciples, said]:

"This, friend Visākha, is the ariyan eightfold Way, that is to say, perfect view, perfect thought, perfect speech, perfect action, perfect way of living, perfect endeavour, perfect mindfulness, perfect concentration."

"But, lady [nun Dhammadinnā], is the ariyan eightfold Way composite [*saṅkhata*] or incomposite?"

"The ariyan eightfold Way, friend Visākha, is composite."

"Now, lady, are the three classes [*ti-sikkhā* = *ti-khandha* = *ti-sampadā*] arranged in accordance with the ariyan eightfold Way or is the ariyan eightfold Way arranged in accordance with the three classes?"

"Friend Visākha, the three classes are not arranged in accordance with the ariyan eightfold Way, but the ariyan eightfold Way is arranged in accordance with the three classes. Whatever, friend Visākha, is perfect speech and whatever is perfect action and whatever is perfect way of living—these things are arranged in the class of Moral Habit. And whatever is perfect endeavour and whatever is perfect mindfulness and whatever is perfect concentration—these things are arranged in the class of Concentration. And whatever is perfect view and whatever is perfect thought—these things are arranged in the class of Intuitive Wisdom."[9]

[The Blessed One, while living at Sāvatthi, said]:

> "When a wise man, established well in Virtue,
> Develops Consciousness and Understanding,
> Then as a bhikkhu ardent and sagacious
> He succeeds in disentangling this tangle."
> (Samyutta-Nikāya, i, 13)

... Here is a brief commentary [on the stanza]. *Established well in virtue:* standing on virtue. It is only one actually fulfilling virtue who is here said to "stand on virtue." So the meaning here is this: being established well in virtue by fulfilling virtue. A *man:* a living being. *Wise:* possessing the kind of understanding that is born of kamma by means of a rebirth-linking with triple root-cause [non-greed, non-hate, non-delusion]. *Develops Consciousness and Understanding:* develops both concentration and insight. For it is concentration that is described here under the heading of "consciousness," and insight under that of "understanding." *Ardent* (*ātāpin*)*:* possessing energy. For it is energy that is called "ardour (*ātāpa*)" in the sense of burning up and consuming (*ātāpana-paritāpana*) defilements. He has that, thus he is ardent. *Sagacious:* it is understanding that is called "sagacity": possessing that, is the meaning. This word shows protective understanding.

For understanding is mentioned three times in the reply to the question. Herein, the first is native understanding, the second is understanding consisting in insight, while the third is the protective understanding that guides all affairs. He sees fear (*bhayam ikkhati*) in the round of rebirths, thus he is a *bhikkhu. He succeeds in disentangling this tangle:* Just as a man standing on the ground and taking up a well-sharpened knife might disentangle a great tangle of bamboos, so too, he —this bhikkhu who possesses the six things, namely, this virtue, and this concentration described under the heading of consciousness, and this threefold understanding, and this ardour—, standing on the ground of virtue and taking up with the hand of protective-understanding exerted by the power of energy the knife of insight-understanding well sharpened on the stone of concentration, might disentangle, cut away and demolish all the tangle of craving that had overgrown his own life's continuity. But it is at the moment of the Path that he is said to be disentangling that tangle: at the moment of fruition he has disentangled the tangle and is worthy of the highest offerings in the world with its deities. That is why the Blessed One said:

> "When a wise man, established well in Virtue,
> Develops Consciousness and Understanding,
> Then as a bhikkhu ardent and sagacious
> He succeeds in disentangling this tangle."

Herein there is nothing for him to do about the [native] understanding on account of which he is called *wise*; for that has been established in him simply by the influence of previous kamma. But the words *ardent and sagacious* mean that by persevering with energy of the kind here described and by acting in full awareness with understanding he should, having become well established in virtue, develop the serenity and insight that are described as *Concentration and Understanding*. This is how the Blessed One shows the path of purification [*visuddhimagga*] under the headings of virtue [*sīla*], concentration [*samādhi*] and understanding [*paññā*] there.

What has been shown so far is the three trainings [*ti-sikkhā*], the dispensation [*Buddha Dhamma*] that is good in three ways [in its beginning, progress, and end], the necessary condition for the threefold clear-vision, etc., the avoidance of the two extremes and the cultivation of the middle way [*majjhima-paṭipadā*], the means to surmounting the states of loss, etc., the abandoning of defilements in three aspects, prevention of transgression, etc., purification from the three kinds of defilements, and the reason for the states of Stream-entry and so on. How?

Here the training of higher virtue [*adhisīla-sikkhā*] is shown by *Virtue;* the training of higher consciousness [*adhicitta-sikkhā*], by *Concentration*; and the training of higher understanding [*adhipaññā-sikkhā*], by Understanding. . . .[10]

Examples of the exposition of the Threefold Training (Tri-śikṣā) in Sanskrit and Buddhist Hybrid Sanskrit texts would be too voluminous for quotation here, but mention may be made of the emphasis which certain Schools in the Mahāyāna and Vajrayāna traditions have placed upon one or more parts of the triad.

Briefly, with reference to the major paths in Buddhism as described in Chapter I, Section 3, the Śīla-mārga group of schools, such as the Lü-tsung in China and related Ritsu-shū in Japan, stresses Adhiśīla; the Dhyāna-mārga group of schools, such as the Ch'an-tsung in China and related Zen-shū in Japan, stresses Adhicitta; the former Prajñā-mārga group of schools, such as the Mādhyamika developments and the Prajñāpāramitā literature, stressed Adhiprajñā; whereas the Buddhānusmṛti-mārga group, such as the Ching-t'u-tsung in China and related Jōdo-shū and Jōdo-Shin-shū in Japan, have developed a different form of Adhicitta in their devotional concentration.

In other respects, it may be said that the Theravāda tradition chiefly practices Adhisīla and Adhicitta, but also Adhipañña in its Abhidhamma studies; the former Sarvāstivāda tradition chiefly practiced Adhiśīla and Adhiprajñā; the former Mādhyamika tradition chiefly practiced Adhiprajñā; the Yogācāra tradition practices all three, Adhiśīla, Adhicitta, and Adhiprajñā, in varying degrees; and the Vajrayāna tradition chiefly practices Adhicitta and Adhiprajñā.

### 3. *The Principles of Progress toward Enlightenment*

The principles of progress toward Enlightenment—other than the Middle Way, the Eightfold Path, and the Threefold Training to which they may be related—are stated in various Pāli, Sanskrit, Buddhist Hybrid Sanskrit, and other texts as sets of training rules which become self-imposed vows and disciplines for the Saṅgha and valued guidances for the laity. They are the four Pārajikas (in the Pāli *Pāṭimokkha*), the ten Sikkhāpadas and related ten Sīlas, and the ten Pāramīs (principally derived doctrinally from the Buddhist Hybrid Sanskrit Pāramitās) in the Theravāda tradition; the thirty-seven Bodhipakkhiya dhammās/Bodhipakṣyā dharmās in the so-called Hīnayāna tradition; and the ten Pārājikās (first four identical with the Pāli Pārajikas; in the Buddhist Hybrid Sanskrit *Prāṭimokṣa*) and the six or (later) ten Pāramitās in the Mahāsāṅghika and Sarvāstivāda Schools and the Mahāyāna and Vajrayāna traditions.

In the *Brahmajāla-sutta* of the Pāli Dīgha-Nikāya following the passage quoted in Chapter I, Section 1, the Buddha continues:

> If a worldling [Puthujjanā] desires to praise the Tathāgata, he would speak only things of small value, of mere morality. And what are those qualities of Morality that are of insignificant value and that he speaks of a little?
>
> [1] "Having abstained from taking the life of any living being, the monk Gotama refrains from the destruction of life. He has laid the stick and the weapon aside; he has moral shame and dread; shows kindness toward all beings; and is full of solicitude for the welfare of all sentient beings." It is thus the worldling, when speaking in praise of the Tathāgata, might speak.
>
> [2] Or he might say: "Having abstained from the taking of what is not given, the monk Gotama refrains from taking what is not given to him. He takes only what is given to him; appreciates the giving by others; and lives in honesty and purity of heart."
>
> [3] Or he might say: "Having abstained from unchastity, the monk Gotama practises chastity. He refrains from the

vulgar practice and also from the sexual act which is the practice of the country folk."

[4] Or he might say: "Getting rid of lying words, the monk Gotama refrains from falsehood. He speaks truth, and nothing but the truth; faithful and trustworthy, he does not break his word to the world."

[5] Or he might say: "Getting rid of slander, the monk Gotama refrains from calumny. What he hears here he does not repeat elsewhere to raise a quarrel against the people here; what he hears elsewhere he does not repeat here to raise a quarrel against the people there. Thus he binds together those who are divided, encourages those who are friends, makes peace, loves peace, is impassioned for peace, a speaker of words leading to peace."

[6] Or he might say: "Getting rid of rudeness of speech, the monk Gotama refrains from using harsh language. He speaks only those words that are blameless, pleasant to the ear, lovely, reaching to the heart, polite, pleasing to the people and beloved of the people."

[7] Or he might say: "Getting rid of frivolous talk, the monk Gotama refrains from vain conversation. At appropriate times he speaks, in accordance with the facts, words full of meaning, on the Doctrine, on the Vinaya. And at the right time he speaks words worthy to be noted in one's mind, fitly illustrated and divided according to the relevancy of facts."

[8] Or he might say: "The monk Gotama refrains from causing injury to seeds and plants.

[9] "He takes only one meal a day, not eating at night, and refrains from taking food after midday.

[10] "He refrains from dancing, singing, playing music and witnessing shows with dances, singing and music.

[11] "He refrains from wearing, adorning, ornamenting himself with garlands, scents, and ointments.

[12] "He refrains from the use of lofty and spacious resting places.

[13] "He refrains from accepting gold and silver. . . ."[11]

The first four of these "aversions, abstinences, moral practices" comprise the four Pārājikas in the *Pāli Pāṭi-*

*mokkha* (thus beginning the Suttavibhaṅga of the Vinaya Piṭaka; cf. the four Pārājikas in the Buddhist Hybrid Sanskrit *Prāṭimokṣa*) which are the prime requisites for the monastic life and, ideally regarded, for the lay life as well. The whole set of thirteen principles (disregarding here the remaining thirteen given in the text) constitutes the exemplary, doctrinal basis for the Uposatha ceremony, held by the Saṅgha at new moon and full moon days to observe the Vinaya. They are formulated variously in the Pāli Aṅguttara-Nikāya of the Sutta Piṭaka as eight rules (nos. 1-4 as 1-4 with 5-7 evidently as 4 and 8 as 1, 9 as 6, 10-11 as 7, and 12 as 8; with abstinence from "spirituous liquors that cause sloth" inserted as 5), later as nine rules (no. 7 originally combining 10-11 is divided to form 7 and 8), and finally as ten rules (adding no. 13 as 10) which thus constitute the Dasa-sikkhāpadāni or ten Sikkhāpadas.

The Dasa-sikkhāpadāni are ten training rules or precepts (but *not* "commandments") for the monks (cf. Dasa-sikkhāpadikā for the nuns). They are stated as the Dasa-sikkhāpada in the Khuddaka-pāṭha of the Pāli Khuddaka-Nikāya of the Sutta Piṭaka as follows:

1. *Pāṇātipatā veramaṇī-sikkhāpadaṁ samādiyāmi* (The training in aversion/abstinence from destroying life, I undertake).
2. *Adinnādānā veramaṇī-sikkhāpadaṁ samādiyāmi* (The training in aversion/abstinence from taking what is not given to me, I undertake).
3. *Abrahmacariyā veramaṇī-sikkhāpadaṁ samādiyāmi* (The training in aversion/abstinence from sexually immoral conduct [chastity for the monk or nun, non-adultery for the laity], I undertake).
4. *Musāvādā veramaṇī-sikkhāpadaṁ samādiyāmi* (The

training in aversion/abstinence from false speech, I undertake).

5. *Surā-merayamajja-pamāda-ṭṭhānā veramaṇī samādiyāmi* (The training in aversion/abstinence from occasions for the [wanton?] use of intoxicating liquor, I undertake).

6. *Vikāla-bhojanā veramaṇī samādiyāmi* (The training in aversion/abstinence from eating at the wrong hour [after mid-day], I undertake).

7. *Nacca-gīta-vādita-visūka-dassanā veramaṇī samādiyāmi* (The training in aversion/abstinence from dancing with singing and instrumental accompaniment and travelling shows or fairs [worldly amusements], I undertake).

8. *Mālā-gandha-vilepana-dhāraṇa-maṇḍana-vibhūsana-ṭṭhānā veramaṇī samādiyāmi* (The training in aversion/abstinence from occasions for adorning myself with garlands, perfumes, and unguents, I undertake).

9. *Uccā-sayana-mahā-sayanā veramaṇī samādiyāmi* (The training in aversion/abstinence from the use of high, large [comfortable] beds, I undertake).

10. *Jātarūpa-rajata-paṭiggahaṇā veramaṇī samādiyāmi* (The training in aversion/abstinence from accepting gold and silver [money], I undertake).[12]

When eight Sikkhāpadas are considered, they are together called Aṭṭhangika-uposatha or Aṭṭhanga-samannāgata-uposatha and thus mean the Uposatha Day with its eight constituents.

The so-called Dasa-sīla (ten requisites of good behavior) are of more concern to the laity. They are undoubtedly influenced by the Dasa-sikkhāpadāni: 1-4 are the same, but thereafter, (5) *Pisuna-vācāya veramaṇī* (abstinence from slander [cf. no. 5 in the *Brahmajāla-sutta* list]), (6) *Pharusa-vācāya veramaṇī* (abstinence from harsh or impolite talk [cf. no. 6 in the *Brahmajāla-sutta* list]), (7) *Samphapalāpā veramaṇī* (abstinence from frivolous and senseless talk [cf. no. 7 in the *Brahmajāla-*

*sutta* list]), (8) *Abhijjhāya veramaṇī* (abstinence from covetousness), (9) *Byāpāda veramaṇī* (abstinence from malevolence), (10) *Micchādiṭṭhiyā veramaṇī* (abstinence from heretical views).[13] The first five Sīlas are regarded the most important for the Saṅgha and laity alike and are commonly called the Pañca-sīla which are recited in ceremonies as the "Pansil" by the Saṅgha and laity, either separately or together in assembly.

Elsewhere, a formula of thirty-seven principles conducive to Enlightenment for the Pacceka/Pratyeka-buddha, called Bodhipakkhiyā-dhammā in noncanonical Pāli works and Bodhipakṣyā-dharmā in Buddhist Hybrid Sanskrit texts, was devised and developed as a principal so-called Hīnayāna way. It has been well described by Har Dayal in *The Bodhisattva Doctrine in Buddhist Sanskrit Literature.*

Another set of principles, the Pāramitās (perfections, virtues, requisites), for the training of the Bodhisattva toward Enlightenment arose with the Mahāyāna, possibly as an attempt to combine monastic and lay Buddhist practices, and provided its characteristic approach. They are restated as Pāramīs or Pāramitās in later Pāli works, such as the *Buddhavaṃsa* and *Cariyā-piṭaka* (nos. 14 and 15 of the Pāli Khuddaka-Nikāya of the Sutta Piṭaka) and the *Visuddhimagga* by Buddhaghosa (fifth century AD.), and, in their customary Mahāyāna form, are profoundly expounded in Vajrayāna doctrine and practice.

The Six Pāramitās (*ṣaṭ-pāramitā*) are stated in their usual Buddhist Hybrid Sanskrit form elementally in the *Mahāvastu* of the Mahāsāṅghikas and *Lalitavistara* of the Sarvāstivādins and more fully and authoritatively in various Mahāyāna texts. They may be summarized as follows:

1. *Dāna-pāramitā* (Perfection, etc. of Giving) according to which a Bodhisattva must know and practice (a) whom to give, (b) what to give, (c) how to give, (d) why to give, (e) Karuṇā (Universal Compassion), and (f) transfer his Puṇya (Merit) to others.

2. *Śīla-pāramitā* (Perfection, etc. of Virtuous Conduct), which is comparable to the Dasa-sīla of the Theravāda Pāli tradition listed above, the Sanskrit names being: (i) Prāṇ-ātipātād viratiḥ, (ii) Adatt-ādānād viratiḥ or Adatta-haraṇam viratiḥ, (iii) Kāma-mithy-ācāraḥ or Kāma-mithyā-vādaḥ (cf. Abrahmacarya), (iv) Mṛṣā-vādād viratiḥ or Anṛta-vacanad viratiḥ, (v) Paiśunyād viratiḥ or Piśuna-vacanād viratiḥ, (vi) Pāruṣyād viratiḥ or Paruṣa-vacanād viratiḥ, (vii) Sambhinna-pralāpād viratiḥ, (viii) Abhidhyāyā viratiḥ, (ix) Vyāpādād viratih, (x) Mithyā-dṛṣṭer viratih or Mithyā-darśanam.

3. *Kṣānti-pāramitā* (Perfection, etc. of Forbearance, Endurance, and Acceptance of the Truth).

4. *Vīrya-pāramitā* (Perfection, etc. of "Energy") in which there is (i) the *vīrya* of practice and activity (*prayoga-vīryam*), and hence a threefold activity of moral development, textual study and general education, and altruism.

5. *Dhyāna-pāramitā* (Perfection, etc. of Meditative Concentration) by which, generally speaking in the Theravāda, Mahāyāna, and Vajrayāna traditions, the Bodhisattva undertakes and develops (i.e., trains in Adhicitta-sikkhā/Adhicitta): (i) Mindfulness (Sati/Smṛti; cf. Sammā-sati/Samyak-smṛti, Right Mindfulness, no. 7 of the Eightfold Path); (ii) Concentrative Absorption (Samādhi; cf. Sammā-samādhi/Samyak-samādhi, Right Concentration, no. 8 of the Eightfold Path); and (iii) Attentive Concentration (Bhāvanā, in two aspects, *samatha/śamatha-bhāvanā*, tranquillity and fixedness of mind = concentration, and *vipassanā/vipaśyanā-bhāvanā*, introspection and intuition = insight).

6. *Prajñā-pāramitā* (Perfection, etc. of Transcendent Comprehension and Understanding for Enlightenment), in which Prajñā "depends on hearing the teaching from another person and on the study of Scripture [*śrutamayī*]; that which arises from reflexion [*cintāmayī*]; and that which is developed by cultivation and realisation [*bhāvanāmayī*]."[14]

To these Six Pāramitās four more have been added to make Ten Pāramitās (*daśa-pāramitā*), as mentioned in the *Mahāyāna-sūtrālaṃkāra, Daśabhūmika-sūtra, Bodhisattva-bhūmi,* and listed in the *Mahāvyutpatti* (Section 34):

7. *Upāya(-kauśalya)-pāramitā* or *Upāya-kauśala* (Perfection, etc. of Beneficial Expediency), according to which the Bodhisattva exercises "skilfulness or wisdom in the choice and adoption of the means or expedients for converting others or helping them"[15] and so uses (i) the four *saṅgaha-vatthūni/saṅgraha-vastūni* (requisite virtues for propagating the Dhamma/Dharma, (ii) the four *praṭisambhidā/pratisaṃvid* (requisite detailed and thorough knowledge for propagating the Dhamma/Dharma), and (iii) various *dhāraṇī* (esoteric, oral "protective" formulas).
8. *Praṇidhāna-pāramitā* (Perfection, etc. of the Profound Resolution to Produce the Thought of Enlightenment, Bodhicitt-otpāda).
9. *Bala-pāramitā* (Perfection, etc. of the Ten Powers, which are differently listed in the *Dharma-saṅgraha* and the *Mahāvyutpatti*).
10. *Jñāna-pāramitā* (Perfection, etc. of Transcendent Understanding and Knowledge).[16]

In the Theravāda tradition, ten Pāramīs (cf. Pāramitās) are attributed to the Buddha in the *Buddhavaṃsa*, seven Pāramīs (lacking nos. 4, 5, 6) are narrated in the *Cariyā-piṭaka*, and ten Pāramitās are briefly described in the *Visuddhimagga* by Buddhaghosa (fifth century A.D.) as follows:

When he has understood thus that the special efficacy of each resides respectively in "Having beauty as the highest," etc., he should besides understand how they bring to perfection all the good states beginning with giving. For the Great beings' minds retain their balance by [the Four Brahma-vihāras:] giving preference to beings' welfare [*mettā*], by dislike of beings' suffering [*karuṇā*], by desire for the various successes achieved by beings to last [*muditā*], and by impartiality towards all beings [*upekkhā*]. And to all beings they give *gifts* [1. *dāna-pāramitā*], which are a source of pleasure without discriminating thus: "It must be given to this one; it must not be given to this one." And in order to avoid doing harm to beings they undertake the precepts of *virtue* [2. *sīla-pāramitā*]. They practise *renunciation* [3. *nekkhamma-pāramitā*] for the purpose [of] perfecting their virtue. They cleanse their *understanding* [4. *paññā-pāramitā*] for the purpose of non-confusion about what is good and bad for beings. They constantly arouse *energy* [5. *viriya-pāramitā*], having beings' welfare and happiness at heart. When they have acquired heroic fortitude through supreme energy, they become *patient* [6. *khanti-pāramitā*] with beings' many kinds of faults. They *do not deceive* [7. *sacca-pāramitā*] when promising "We shall give you this; We shall do this for you." They are unshakably *resolute* [8. *adhiṭṭhāna-pāramitā*] upon beings' welfare and happiness. Through unshakable *lovingkindness* [9. *mettā-pāramitā*] they place them first [before themselves]. Through *equanimity* [10. *upekkhā-pāramitā*] they expect no reward. Having thus fulfilled the [Ten] Perfections, these [divine abidings] then perfect all the good states classes as the Ten Powers, the Four Kinds of Fearlessness, the Six Kinds of Knowledge Not Shared [by Disciples] and the Eighteen States of the Enlightened One. This is how they bring to perfection all the good states beginning with giving.[17]

With regard to the conception and practice of the Six Pāramitās in the Vajrayāna tradition, an authoritative exposition is presented by the Tibetan sGam.po.pa (1079–1153 A.D.) in his "Jewel Ornament of Liberation." He correlates the Six Pāramitās with the Threefold Training (Trīṇi Śikṣāṇi) and generally follows the earlier views of Vasubandhu (*ca.* 320–400 A.D.) in his commentary in the *Mahāyāna-sūtrālaṅkāra*:

The training in forming an enlightened attitude of perseverance is threefold: (i) in higher ethics [*adhiśīla*], (ii) higher thoughts [*adhicitta*] and (iii) deeper understanding [*adhiprajñā*]. The "Byaṅ.chub.lam.sgron" ("Bodhipathapradīpa," 36) says:

When with an attitude of perseverance one adheres to the discipline and trains oneself in the three ways in ethics and manners, a delight in this then grows.

(i) Training in higher ethics consists of the triad of liberality [*dāna-pāramitā*], ethics and manners [*śīla-pāramitā*], and patience [*kṣānti-pāramitā*].

(ii) That in higher thoughts involves meditative concentration [*dhyāna-pāramitā*]; and

(iii) That in deeper understanding is discriminating awareness born from wisdom [*prajñā-pāramitā*].

Strenuousness [*vīrya-pāramitā*] partakes of all three types. . . .

(i) The three perfections [*pāramitās*] which refer to higher forms of life are: liberality leading to great enjoyment, ethics and manners which adorn physical existence and patience which pleases those around us.

(ii) Those leading to ultimate good are: strenuousness which increases virtues, meditative concentration which produces tranquillity and discriminating awareness born from wisdom which gives mystic insight. . . .

It is called (i) liberality because it abolishes poverty (*dāridryam apanayatīti dānaṃ*), (ii) ethics because it leads to coolness (*śaityaṃ lambhayatīti śīlaṃ*), (iii) patience because it endures harshness (*kṣayaḥ kruddher iti kṣāntiḥ*), (iv) strenuousness because it applies itself to what is most sublime (*vareṇa yojayatīti vīryaṃ*), (v) meditative concentration because it holds mind in its own inner sphere (*dhārayaty adhyātmaṃ mana iti dhyānaṃ*) and (vi) discriminating awareness born from wisdom because by it the ultimately real is known (*paramārthaṃ jānāty anayeti prajñā*).

These six are known as perfections (*pāram-itā*) because they enable us to cross over to the other side of Saṃsāra.[18]

In commenting on sGam.po.pa's statement, Herbert V. Guenther, his English translator, summarizes the whole subject:

> The interrelation between attitude and act needs constant attention. Here the six "perfections" [*ṣaṭ-pāramitā*] strengthen an enlightened attitude which, in turn, makes the "perfections" more and more perfect. Five of them, liberality [*dāna-pāramitā*], ethics and manners [*śīla-pāramitā*], patience [*kṣānti-pāramitā*], strenuousness [*vīrya-pāramitā*], and meditative concentration [*dhyāna-pāramitā*], are overshadowed by and lead up to the sixth perfection: discriminating awareness born from wisdom [*prajñā-pāramitā*].
>
> This last perfection makes us see Reality as it is. It abolishes the formidable superstitions in existence and non-existence, it liberates us from the philosophical systems of realism and mentalism (usually confused with and presented as idealism), and leads us beyond monism and pluralism. It is in the discussion of the perfection of discriminating awareness born from wisdom (*śes.rab, Skt. prajñā*) that sGam.po.pa blends the Sūtra and Tantra conceptions.
>
> However, discriminating awareness is only the beginning, not the climax of our striving for enlightenment, because it makes us see Reality so that we can follow it with open eyes. With this seeing the Buddhist Path starts, and every step we take leads to wider horizons termed spiritual levels, until it terminates in Buddhahood: potentiality has become actuality. As such, Buddhahood is no soporific state, but stretches out into all sentient beings as motive and goal.[19]

### 4. *The Stages of Progress toward Enlightenment*

In following the principles of progress toward Enlightenment, irrespective of their particular formulation in the Theravāda, Mahāyāna, and Vajrayāna traditions and various Schools, the Buddhist must be mindful of the Threefold Training (Ti-sikkhā/Tri-śikṣā)—that virtuous conduct (*sīla/śīla*), concentrative absorption (*samādhi*), and transcendent comprehension and understanding (*paññā/prajñā*) for Enlightenment (Bodhi) are interrelated and interdependent. He should objectively know and subjectively experience that he is in the process of development toward Enlightenment.

Such process is conceived and described in all major Buddhist traditions as "stages of progress toward Enlightenment" in categories of the Four Brahma-vihāras, the Four Caryās, and the Seven, Ten, or Thirteen Bhūmis (cf. Vihāras).

The Four Brahma-vihāras (Sublime States) are: (1) *mettā* (cf. Sanskrit *maitrī*), loving-kindness or benevolence; (2) *karuṇā* (cf. Sanskrit *karuṇā*), compassion; (3) *muditā* (cf. Sanskrit *mudita*), joyous sympathy or gladness in others' well-being; (4) *upekkhā* (cf. Sanskrit *upekṣā*), equanimity. In Pāli works they are mentioned in the Dīgha-Nikāya (III.220), stated in the Saṃyutta-Nikāya (V.326), and expounded notably by Buddhaghosa (fifth century A.D.) in his *Visuddhimagga* (chap. 13). These Brahma-vihāras may be regarded in three ways: (1) as virtues to be exemplified (cf. *sīla*), (2) as objects of meditation (cf. *samādhi*), and (3) as states of mind or being (cf. *paññā*). Buddhaghosa gives various instructions for effecting or realizing them and then explains:

Now as to the meaning firstly of lovingkindness, compassion, gladness and equanimity: it is melting (*mejjati*), thus it is lovingkindness (*mettā*); it is solvent (*siniyhati*) is the meaning. Also: it comes about with respect to a friend (*mitta*), or it is behaviour towards a friend, thus it is lovingkindness (*mettā*).

When there is suffering in others it causes (*karoti*) good people's hearts to be moved (*kampana*), thus it is compassion (*karuṇā*). Or alternatively, it combats (*kiṇāti*) others' suffering, attacks and demolishes it, thus it is compassion. Or alternatively, it is scattered (*kiriyati*) upon those who suffer, it is extended to them by pervasion, thus it is compassion (*karuṇā*).

Those endowed with it are glad (*modanti*), or it itself is glad (*modati*), or it is the mere act of being glad (*modana*), thus it is gladness (*muditā*).

It looks on at (*upekkhati*), abandoning such interestedness as thinking "May they be free from enmity" and having recourse to neutrality, thus it is equanimity (*upekkhā*).

As to the characteristic, etc. *lovingkindness* is characterized here as promoting the aspect of welfare. Its function is to prefer welfare. It is manifested as the removal of annoyance. Its proximate cause is seeing lovableness in beings. It succeeds when it makes ill will subside, and it fails when it produces [selfish] affection.

*Compassion* is characterized as promoting the aspect of suffering. Its function resides in not bearing others' suffering. It is manifested as non-cruelty. Its proximate cause is to see helplessness in those overwhelmed by suffering. It succeeds when it makes cruelty subside and it fails when it produces sorrow.

*Gladness* is characterized as gladdening [produced by others' success]. Its function resides in being unenvious. It is manifested as the elimination of aversion (boredom). Its proximate cause is seeing beings' success. It succeeds when it makes aversion (boredom) subside, and it fails when it produces merriment.

*Equanimity* is characterized as promoting the aspect of neutrality toward beings. Its function is to see equality in beings. It is manifested as the quieting of resentment and approval. Its proximate cause is seeing ownership of deeds (kamma) thus: "Beings are owners of their deeds. Whose [if not theirs] is the choice by which they will become happy, or will get free from suffering, or will not fall away from the success they have reached?" It succeeds when it makes resentment and approval subside, and it fails when it produces the equanimity of unknowing, which is that [worldly-minded indifference of ignorance] based on the house life.

The general purpose of these four divine abidings [Brahmavihāras] is the bliss of insight and an excellent [form of future] existence.[20]

As already mentioned in Chapter II, Section 5, when the Śrāvaka has made a profound resolution (Praṇidhāna), which becomes a prediction (Vyākaraṇa) of his success, and undertakes the production of the thought of Enlightenment (Bodhi-citt-otpāda), then he is ready to train as a Bodhisattva. According to the *Mahāvastu* of the Mahāsāṅghika School, his career will be in four stages (*caryās*):

Here, Mahā-Maudgalyāyana, are the four stages in the careers of Bodhisattvas. What are the four? They are these: the "natural" career [*Prakṛti-caryā*], the "resolving" career [*Praṇidhāna-caryā*], the "conforming" career [*Anuloma-caryā*] and the "persevering" career [*Anivartana-caryā*].

And what, Mahā-Maudgalyāyana, is the "natural" career? It is the nature of Bodhisattvas in this world to respect mother and father, to be well-disposed to recluses and brāhmans, to honour their elders, to practise the ten right ways of behaviour, to exhort others to give alms and acquire merit, and to honour contemporary Buddhas and their disciples, But as yet they do not conceive the thought of winning the unsurpassed perfect enlightenment. . . .

And what is the "resolving" career? . . . Apprehending the remorseless force of impermanence, (Śākyamuni) as soon as he had worshipped [a Buddha], resolutely exerted himself to destroy that power. . . . This, Mahā-Maudgalyāyana, is the "resolving" career.

And what is the "conforming" career? In this career, the great being, the Bodhisattva, is established in conformity with his (future) enlightenment. This, Mahā-Maudgalyāyana, is the "conforming" career.

And what is the "persevering" career? *Vivartacaryā* means that Bodhisattvas fall away and go again through the round of rebirths. *Avivartacaryā* means that they are unwaveringly set for enlightenment.[21]

This rudimentary scheme of sub-division was subsequently amplified in the list of the *bhūmis* (Stages), which a *bodhisattva* progressively occupies.

Another group of four *caryās* is mentioned in the *Bodhisattva-bhūmi* and the *Mahāyāna-sūtrālaṅkāra.*

(1) *Bodhi-pakṣya-caryā* (Practice of the *"bodhi-pakṣyā dharmāḥ",* i.e. principles conducive to Enlightenment).

(2) *Abhijñā-caryā* (Practice of the Super-knowledges).

(3) *Pāramitā-caryā* (Practice of the Perfections).

(4) *Sattva-paripāka-caryā* (Practice of maturing the living being, i.e. preaching and teaching).[22]

A *bodhisattva's* entire career has been divided into several parts and stages. He rises and advances from one stage to another till he attains Enlightenment. These stages have been called *bhūmis,* and also *vihāras.* . . . *Bhūmi* has thus become a philosophical term, meaning "Stage" (of spiritual progress). Almost all the [Sanskrit] Buddhist treatises divide a *bodhisattva's* career into *bhūmis,* but the *Bodhisattva-bhūmi* also discusses thirteen *vihāras* (states, stations). . . .

There are at least four different schemes of division in the principal Sanskrit treatises. The *Çata-sāhasrika Prajñāpāramitā,* the *Mahā-vastu* and the *Daça-bhūmika-sūtra* describe ten *bhūmis* in different ways, and the *Bodhisattva-bhūmi* speaks of seven *bhūmis* and thirteen *vihāras.* Candrakīrti's *Madhyamakāvatāra* [follows the *Daśabhūmika-sūtra* with minor variations]. . . .[23]

Other notable descriptions of the Ten Bhūmis are contained in the *Abhisamayālaṃkāra* (*kārikā*) or *Abhisamayālaṃkāra-nāma Prajñāparamita-upadeśaśastra* by

Ārya Maitreya(nātha) (*ca.* 270–350 A.D.) and the "Jewel Ornament of Liberation" by sGam.po.pa (1079–1153 A.D.). A useful summary of the previously mentioned Buddhist Hybrid Sanskrit texts concerning the Bhūmis is made by Har Dayal in his *The Bodhisattva Doctrine in Buddhist Sanskrit Literature;* a less detailed account is given by Edward J. Thomas in his *The History of Buddhist Thought*, which includes a translation of the *Cāryāmārgabhūmi-sūtra* contained in the *Daśabhūmika-sūtra.*

The titles of the Ten Bhūmis, commonly recognized by the Mahāyāna and Vajrayāna traditions, are as follows:

1. *Pramuditā* (The Joyful One)
2. *Vimalā* (The Pure, Immaculate One)
3. *Prabhākarī* (The Illuminating One)
4. *Arciṣmatī* (The Radiant, Flaming One)
5. *Sudurjaya* (The One Difficult to Conquer)
6. *Abhimukhī* (The One Which Is Present)
7. *Dūraṅgamā* (The One Which Goes Far)
8. *Acalā* (The Unmovable One)
9. *Sādhumatī* (The One Having Good Discrimination)
10. *Dharma-meghā* (The Cloud of Dharma)

To these sometimes are added:

11. *Tathāgata* (The Buddha) or *Samantaprabhā* (The Universally Luminous One)
12. *Nirupamā* (The Incomparable One)
13. *Jñānavatī* (The One Possessing Knowledge)

### 5. *Buddhist Ceremonies and Rituals*

Various explanations can be given for the presence, development, and function of Buddhist ceremonies and rituals which are elementary in the Theravāda, advanced in the Mahāyāna, and paramount in the Vajrayāna traditions.

Sociologically considered, there was the usual practice, if not actual need also, of Buddhism accommodating and adapting folk customs wherever it established itself in Asia. Furthermore, Buddhist court ceremonies were valued politically as sanctions and exaltations of kingship, especially when the king aspired to be recognized as a Cakkavattin/Cakravartin (Universal Ruler) or a Buddha-rājā/rāja. Paritta or Parittā/Parītta were, and still are on occasion, chanted by bhikkhus/bhikṣus as "protections" against all manner of individual and national calamities.

Doctrinally speaking, there is the practice of venerating the Buddha as described in Chapter II, Section 2, especially the Vesākha/Vaiśākha-pūjā (often called "Wesak" in South and Southeast Asia) for remembering his birth and various thūpa/stūpa-pūjā for remembering his demise. The Buddha Jayanti (2,500-year anniversary celebrations) of 1956 in Burma, Ceylon, India, and Nepal and 1957 in Cambodia, Laos, and Thailand may be regarded as an historic example of Buddhists venerating the Buddha nationally and internationally. Even the Buddha Dhamma/Dharma is revered by special ceremonies connected with texts, particularly in Mahāyāna and Vajrayāna traditions, in which case "remembering" means more than mere study.

Organizationally viewed, there has been the customary

practice, still well observed in the Theravāda tradition, of maintaining and managing the Saṅgha as a monastic institution by means of special ceremonies: the Pabbajjā/ Pravrajya (initiation ceremony for novices following their period of probation or Parivāsa), the Upasampadā (ordination ceremony for monks or nuns), the Parāvaṇā (ceremony concluding the Vassa or Vassāvāsa, monastic residence or "retreat" during the monsoon rainy season) and related Kaṭhina (annual ceremony in which the laity dedicates cotton cloth to the monks for the making of robes), and the important Uposatha (meetings at new moon and full moon to expound the Dhamma, observe the Vinaya, and recite the *Pāṭimokkha*).

Mention should also be made of pilgrimages as a form of veneration (*pūjā*) toward the Buddha by both laity and the Saṅgha, as well as the varied use of esoteric media (*mantra, mudrā, dhāraṇī, maṇḍala*) by the Mahāyāna and especially the Vajrayāna ceremonies and rituals.

The most universal and common ceremony or ritual for all Buddhists—Theravāda, Mahāyāna, Vajrayāna; Saṅgha and laity—is the Ti-saraṇa-gamana/Tri-śaraṇa-gamana or Saraṇattaya/Trīṇi-śaraṇāni, described and quoted in Chapter I, Section 5, which serves as the basic veneration of the Ti-ratana/Tri-ratna: the Buddha, the Dhamma/Dharma, the Saṅgha. It also forms the initial part of the Dasa-sikkhāpadāni, described and quoted above in Section 3, which together introduce the Pabbajjā and Upasampadā ceremonies initiating novices and ordaining monks.

The Ti-saraṇa-gamana, Dasa-sikkhāpadāni, Pabbajjā, and Upasampadā ceremonies in their Sinhalese practice have long been the traditional model for Theravāda countries. They have been recorded by J. F. Dickson as follows:

The chapter house (Sinhalese, Poya-ge) is an oblong hall, with rows of pillars forming an inner space and leaving broad aisles at the sides. At the top of this inner space sat the aged Abbot (Sinhalese, Maha Náyaka), as president of the chapter; on either side of him sat the elder priests, and down the sides sat the other priests in number between thirty and forty. The chapter or assembly thus formed three sides of an oblong. The president sat on cushions and a carpet; the other priests sat on mats covered with white calico. They all sat cross-legged. On the fourth side, at the foot, stood the candidates, behind the pillars on the right stood the deacons, the left was given up to the vistors, and behind the candidates at the bottom was a crowd of Buddhist laymen.

To form a chapter for this purpose not less than ten duly ordained priests are required, and the president must be not less than ten years' standing from his Upasampadá ordination. The priests attending the chapter are required to give their undivided, unremitting, and devout attention throughout the service. Every priest is instructed to join heart and mind in the exhortations, responses, formulas, etc., and to correct every error, lest the oversight of a single mistake should vitiate the efficacy of the rite. Previously to the ordination the candidates are subjected to a strict and searching examination as to their knowledge of the discourses of Buddha, the duties of a priest, etc. An examination and ordination is [*sic*] held on the full-moon day in Wesak, and on the three succeeding Poya days, or days of quarters of the moon. . . .

In the translation I have placed in italics the rubrical directions in the texts, and all explanations and amplifications of the text I have placed in square brackets. . . .

*Upasampadā-Kammavācā*

Namo tassa bhagavato arahato sammásambuddhassa. . . .

*The Ordination Service*

Praise be to the Blessed One, the Holy One, to him who has arrived at the knowledge of all Truth.

[The candidate, accompanied by his Tutor, in the dress of a layman, but having the yellow robes of a priest in his arms, makes the usual obeisance and offering to the President of the chapter, and standing says],

Grant me leave to speak. Lord, graciously grant me admission to deacon's orders. *Kneels down.* Lord, I pray for admission as a deacon. Again, lord, I pray for admission as a deacon. A third time, lord, I pray for admission as a deacon. In compassion for me, lord, take these yellow robes, and let me be ordained, in order to the destruction of all sorrow, and in order to the attainment of Nirváṇa. *To be repeated three times.* [The President takes the bundle of robes.] In compassion for me, lord, give me those yellow robes, and let me be ordained, in order to the destruction of all sorrow, and in order to the attainment of Nirváṇa. *To be repeated three times.* [And the President then gives the bundles of robes, the yellow band of which he ties round the neck of the candidate, reciting the while the tacapañcakaṁ, or formula of meditation on the perishable nature of the human body, as follows: kesá lomá nakhá dantá taco—taco dantá nakhá lomá kesá. Hair of the head, hair of the body, nails, teeth, skin—skin, teeth, nails, hair of the body, hair of the head. The candidate then rises up, and retires to throw off the dress of a layman, and to put on his yellow robes. While changing his dress he recites the following:—Paṭisankhá yoniso cívaraṁ paṭisevámi yávad eva sítassa paṭighátáya uṇhassa paṭighátáya ḍamsamakasavátátapasiriṁsapasamphassánaṁ paṭighátáya yávad eva hirikopínapaṭicchádanattham. In wisdom I put on the robes, as a protection against cold, as a protection against heat, as protection against gadflies and musquitoes [*sic*], wind and sun, and the touch of serpents, and to cover nakedness, *i.e.* I wear them in all humility, for use only, and not for ornament or show. Having put on the yellow robes, he returns to the side of his tutor, and says], Grant me leave to speak. I make obeisance to my lord. Lord, forgive me all my faults. Let the merit that I have gained be shared by my lord. It is fitting to give me to share in the merit gained by my lord. It is good, it is good. I share in it. Grant me leave to speak. Graciously give me, lord, the three refuges and the precepts.

[He kneels down.] Lord, I pray for the refuges and the precepts.

[The tutor gives the three refuges and the ten precepts as follows, the candidate still kneeling, and repeating them after him sentence by sentence.

1. [For the Saraṇattaya omitted here in quotation, see above, Chapter I, Section 5.]

2. [For the Dasa-sikkhāpada omitted here in quotation, see above, Section 3.]

[The candidate says],

I have received these ten precepts. Permit me. [He rises up, and makes obeisance to his Tutor.] Lord, I make obeisance. Forgive me all my faults. May the merit I have gained be shared by my lord. Give me to share in the merit of my lord. It is good, it is good. I share in it.

[This completes the ordination of a deacon, and the candidate retires.]

The foregoing ceremony [Pabbajjā] is gone through previous to the ordination of a priest [Upasampadā] in all cases, even where the candidate has already been admitted as a deacon [sāmaṇera = novice]. If the candidate is duly qualified for the priestly office [bhikkhu = monk], he can proceed at once from deacon's to priest's orders; otherwise he must pass a term of instruction [parivāsa = probation period] as a deacon: but a candidate who has received deacon's orders must solicit them again, and go through the above ceremony when presented for priest's orders.

[The candidate, being duly qualified, returns with his tutor, and goes up to the President of the chapter, presenting an offering, and makes obeisance, saying],

Permit me to speak. Lord, graciously grant me your sanction and support [note: *Nissayo.* Without the consent and promise of assistance of a priest of ten years' standing, the candidate cannot obtain ordination. *Nissayo* involves mutual assistance and association for at least five years. The elder who gives *nissa* becomes the spiritual superior or preceptor (*upajjháyo*), and the one who receives *nissa* becomes his co-resident or pupil (*nissantevásiko*). The relative duties of the two are laid down in detail in the *Vinayapiṭaka*. Briefly the superior is to advise him and instruct his co-resident, and to perform towards him all the duties of a parent in sickness and in health. The co-resident is to treat his superior with all the respect due a father, and to perform for him all the duties of a personal attendant. Buddha directs that fluent-speaking and well-informed priests shall remain as pupils for five years. They who are not fluent-speaking shall remain as pupils as long as they live.] *He kneels down.* Lord, I pray for your sanction and support; a second time, lord, I pray for your sanction and support; a third time, lord, I pray for your sanction and support. Lord, be my superior. *This is repeated three times.* [The President says,] It is well. [And the candidate replies,] I am content. *This is repeated three times.* From this day forth my lord is my charge. I am charge to my lord. [This vow of mutual assistance] *is repeated three times.*

[The candidate rises up, makes obeisance, and retires alone to the foot of the assembly, where his alms-bowl is strapped on to his back. His tutor then goes down, takes him by the hand, and brings him back, placing him in front of the President. One of the assembled priests stands up, and places himself on the other side of the candidate, who thus stands between two tutors [note: *Kammavácáriṇo.* The tutors represent the assembly, and conduct the examinations on its behalf. Compare the relation of the proctors at Oxford to Convocation.] The tutors say to the assembly,] With your permission, [and then proceed to examine the candidate as to his fitness to be admitted to priest's orders]. Your name is Nága? It is so, lord. Your superior is the venerable Tissa? It is so, lord. [The two tutors together say,] Praise be to the Blessed One, the Holy one, to him who has arrived at the knowledge of all Truth. [They then recite the following commands of Buddha.] First it is right to appoint a superior. When the superior has been appointed, it is right to inquire whether the candidate has alms-bowl and robes [which they do as follows]. Is this your alms-bowl? It is so, lord. Is this the stole? [note: *Saṅgháṭi.* This part of the dress is a large double robe folded to about five inches in breadth, which is thrown over the left shoulder, and fastened close to the body by a waist-belt. This robe is used by a priest when travelling as a cloak.] It is so, lord. Is this the upper robe? It is so, lord. Is this the under robe? It is so, lord. Go and stand there. [The candidate here retires, going backwards in a reverential posture, and stands at the lower corner of the assembly. The tutors remain in front of the President, and one of them says,] Priests, hear me. The candidate desires ordination under the venerable Tissa. Now is the time of the assembly of priests. I will instruct the candidate. [The tutors make obeisance to the President, and go down to the foot of the assembly, and join the candidate, whom they instruct and examine as follows.] Listen, Nága. This is the time for you to speak the truth, to state what has occurred. When asked concerning anything in the midst of the assembly, if it be true, it is meet to say so; if it be not true, it is meet to say that it is not. Do not hesitate. Conceal nothing. *They inquire of the candidate as follows.* Have you any such diseases as these? Leprosy? No, lord. Boils? No, lord. Itch? No, lord. Asthma? No, lord. Epilepsy? No, lord. Are you a human being? Yes, lord. Are you a male? Yes, lord. Are you a free man? Yes, lord. Are you free from debt? Yes, lord. Are you exempt from military service? Yes, lord. Have you come with the permission of your parent? Yes, lord. Are your alms-bowl and robes complete? Yes, lord. What is your name? Lord, I am called Nága. What is the name of your superior? Lord, my superior is called the venerable Tissa. [The two tutors here go to the top of the assembly, and make obeisance to the President, and one of them says,] Priests, hear me. The candidate desires ordination under the venerable Tissa. He has been duly instructed by me. Now is the time of the assembly of priests. If the candidate is here, it is right to tell him to approach. [One of the tutors says,] Come hither. [The candidate comes up, and stands between the tutors, makes obeisance to the assembly, and kneels down [and says,]] Priests, I ask the assembly for ordination. Priests, have compassion on me, and lift me up. [note: *ullumpatu*. The meaning of this is explained in the commentary to be, lift me up from the slough of demerit (*akusala*) to the dry land of merit (*kusala*), *or* lift me up from the lower order of a deacon (*sámaṇéra*) to the higher order of a fully ordained priest (*upasampadá*).] A second time, lords, I ask the assembly for ordination; lords, have compassion on me, and lift me up. A third time, lords, I ask the assembly for ordination. Lords, have compassion on me, and lift me up. [The candidate rises up, and makes obeisance. The tutors say,] Priests, hear me. This candidate desires ordination under the venerable Tissa. Now is the time of the assembly of priests. I will examine the candidate respecting the disqualifications for the priestly office. Listen, Nága, This is the time for you to speak the truth, to state what has occurred. I will inquire of you concerning facts. If a thing is, it is right to say it is; if a thing is not, it is right to say it is not. Have you any such diseases as these? Leprosy? No, lord. Boils? No, lord. Itch? No, lord. Asthma? No, lord. Epilepsy? No, lord. Are you a human being? Yes, lord. Are you a male? Yes, lord. Are you free from debt? Yes, lord. Are you exempt from military service? Yes, lord. Have you come with the permission of your parents? Yes, lord. Are you of the full age of twenty years? Yes, lord. Are your alms-bowl and robes complete? Yes, lord. What is your name? Lord, I am called Nága. What is the name of your superior? My superior, lord, is called the venerable Tissa. [Here ends the examination in the midst of the assembly, and one of the tutors reports the result as follows.] This candidate desires ordination under the venerable Tissa. He is free from disqualifications. He has his alms-bowl and robes complete. The candidate asks the assembly for ordination under his superior the venerable Tissa. The assembly gives the candidate ordination under his superior the venerable Tissa. If any of the venerable assembly approves the ordination of the candidate under the venerable Tissa, let him be silent; if any objects, let him speak. A second time I state this matter. Priests, hear me. This candidate desires ordination under the venerable Tissa. He is free from disqualifications for the priestly office. His alms-bowl and robes are complete. The candidate asks the priesthood for ordination under his superior the venerable Tissa. The assembly gives the candidate ordination under his superior the venerable Tissa. If any of the venerable assembly approve the ordination of the candidate under his superior the venerable Tissa, let him be silent; if any objects, let him speak. A third time I state this matter. Priests, listen. This candidate desires ordination under the venerable Tissa. He is free from disqualifications for the priestly office. His alms-bowl and robes are complete. The candidate asks the priesthood for ordination under his superior the venerable Tissa. If any of the venerable assembly approves the ordination of the candidate under his superior the venerable Tissa, let him be silent; if any objects, let him speak. [The two tutors here again make obeisance to the President, and say,] The candidate has received ordination from the priesthood under his superior the venerable Tissa. The assembly approves the resolution: therefore it keeps silence. So I understand your wish.

[The ordination is here ended, and the candidate retires to the foot of the assembly, in which the tutors now resume their seats. The ceremony is repeated with each candidate, and when all the candidates have been ordained, one of the assembly (generally one of the tutors) rises up, and addresses the following exhortation to the recently ordained priests, who stand in a reverential attitude.]

It is meet to measure the shadow of the sun [note: The hour, day and month are carefully recorded, to settle the order of seniority among the newly ordained priests]. It is meet to tell the season. It is meet to tell the division of the day. It is meet to tell all these together. It is meet to tell the four requisites for a priest. It is meet to tell the four sins forbidden to priests to commit. Food collected in the alms-bowl is a requisite of a priest. So fed, it is good for you to strive so long as life shall last. The following exceptions are allowed: rice offered to the whole body of the priests; rice offered to a certain number of priests; rice offered on special invitation to a particular priest; rice offered by lot; rice offered once in fifteen days; rice offered on the full-moon days; rice offered on the day following full-moon day. Yes, lord.

Robes made of pieces of rag are a requisite of a priest. So clad, it is good for you to strive so long as life shall last. The following exceptions are allowed: robes made of linen, of cotton, of silk, of wool, of hemp, or of these five materials together. Yes, lord. Lodging at the foot of a tree is a requisite for a priest. So lodged, it is good of you to strive so long as life shall last. The following exceptions are allowed: monasteries; large halls; houses of more than one story; houses surrounded by walls; rock caves. Yes, lord. Cow's urine as medicine is a requisite for a priest. Thus provided, it is good for you to strive so long as life shall last. The following exceptions are allowed: cow's butter; cream; rape oil; honey; sugar. Yes, lord.

A priest must not indulge in sexual intercourse, in short not even with a female of any kind. If any priest indulges in sexual intercourse, he ceases to be a priest, and is no longer a son of Sakya. Just as a man whose head is cut off is unable to live, so does a priest who has indulged in sexual intercourse cease to be a priest, or to be a son of Sakya. This is to be avoided by you as long as life shall last. Yes, lord.

A priest must not take, with dishonest intent, anything which is not given to him, not even a blade of grass. If any priest takes, with dishonest intent, either a quarter of a pagoda [monetary unit], or anything worth as much or more, he ceases to be a priest, and is no longer a son of Sakya. Just as a sere leaf loosed from its stalk can never again become green, so a priest who, with dishonest intent, has taken anything which has not been given to him, ceases to be a priest, or to be a son of Sakya. This is to be avoided by you as long as life shall last. Yes, lord.

A priest must not knowingly destroy human life, in short not even the life of an ant. If any priest destroys human life even by causing abortion, he ceases to be a priest, or to be a son of Sakya. Just as a large rock once cleft in two can never be re-united, so does a priest who has knowingly destroyed human life, cease to be a priest, or to be a son of Sakya. This is to be avoided by you as long as life shall last. Yes, lord.

A priest must not lay claim to more than human perfection, even by saying, "I delight in a solitary hut." If any priest with evil intent and for sake of gain untruly and falsely lays claim to more than human perfection, whether a state of mystic meditation [Jhānaṁ], or freedom from passion [Viṁokkho], or perfect tranquillity [Samádhi], or a state of absorption removed from all worldly influence [Samápatti], or attainment of the four paths, or of the fruition of those paths [Phala], he ceases to be a priest, and is no longer a son of Sakya. Just as a palmyra tree, the top of which has been cut off, can never sprout again, so a priest who, with evil intent and for sake of gain, untruly and falsely has laid claim to more than human perfection, ceases to be a priest, or to be a son of Sakya. This is to be avoided so long as life shall last. Yes, lord.[24]

CHAPTER FIVE

# The Saṅgha: Buddhist Monasticism

As the third part of the Three Valued Components of Buddhism (Pāli/Sanskrit: Ti-ratana/Tri-ratna), the Saṅgha is the Buddhist assembly, community, or collective body which authoritatively studies, experiences, and expounds the Dhamma/Dharma in various Schools and the Theravāda, Mahāyāna, and Vajrayāna traditions. It is spelled the same in Pāli and Sanskrit (Saṅgha), although sometimes rendered Saṃgha and often Sangha, and is usually translated into English as the Buddhist Order.

Previously, the Saṅgha in all Buddhist countries accepted political authority in principle, usually in the form of kingship, and sanctioned its exercise when conducted on behalf of the people. Today, the Theravāda Saṅgha still enjoys official status in Burma, Cambodia, Laos, and Thailand and a favored position in Ceylon; whereas the Mahāyāna Saṅgha is less valued politically in Japan, Korea, Taiwan, and Việt-Nam and is governmentally exploited in Communist areas. The fate of the Vajrayāna Saṅgha in Mongolia and Tibet is in grave doubt, but it may carry on in Bhutan, Ladakh, and Sikkim.

Throughout Buddhist history, the laity as individuals and communities has supported the Saṅgha in return for its instruction and guidance in the fundamental meaning of life. In recent times, however, the laity in all Buddhist areas except Laos has established lay Buddhist organizations in order to meet relatively new situations arising from the notable increase of technological changes, secular values, and ideological conflicts in society. These groups tend to supplant the social services of the Saṅgha which has been heretofore traditionally regarded as "the guardian of the national culture."

In most cases in the past, Buddhist monasteries have actually been "this-worldly" in maintaining their favored political status and exercising their social-cultural role. But societal problems and needs are changing rapidly, and in reaction some Saṅgha leaders have become conservative minded, while others attempt to comprehend and use new ways of preparing for their future; both groups wish to preserve the Dhamma/Dharma and present it more meaningfully to the new generation.

In short, Buddhism has provided a meaning and way of life for both Saṅgha and laity through the centuries in which monasticism has been the primary example, source of authority, and stabilizing influence. Today, however, Buddhist monasticism is subject to change.

### 1. *The Organization of the Monastic Order: The Saṅgha*

In the Theravāda, Mahāyāna, and Vajrayāna traditions and in times past in the Sarvāstivāda and other major Schools, the Saṅgha has consisted of bhikkhus/bhikṣus (monks; thus, *bhikkhu-saṅgha* = assembly of monks), bhikkhunīs/bhikṣunīs (nuns), and sāvakas/śrāvakas (disciples) as sāmaṇeras/śrāmaṇeras (male novices) and sāmaṇerīs/śrāmaṇerīs (female novices). In a wider sense and often in modern lay usage, the Saṅgha may also include upāsikas/upāsakas (male lay devotees) and upāsikās/upāsikās (female lay devotees; now the customary status of bhikkhunīs in Theravāda areas).

Generally speaking, four types of Saṅgha organization may be distinguished: (1) a national Saṅgha identified with the function and exercise of political authority (cf. theocracy) as formerly in Vajrayāna Mongolia and Tibet;[1] (2) a national Saṅgha supervised by leaders and aided by the government as in Theravāda Cambodia, Laos, and Thailand today where the King is traditionally the Protector of the Buddha Sāsana, and formerly at times in Theravāda Burma and Ceylon, and Mahāyāna China; (3) within a country, influential monastic groups as in present-day Burma (nikāyas) and Ceylon (nikāyas) where they receive governmental aid or special interest, and customarily in Mahāyāna China and Chinese communities elsewhere (-tsung), Japan (-shū), Korea (-jong), and Việt-Nam (-tông); and (4) within a country, important monasteries as in all areas.[2]

As an example of type (2) Saṅgha organization—a national Saṅgha supervised by its leaders and aided by the government—the following excerpts from the *Ordonnance Royale N° 160 du 25 Mai 1959, Statut du Clergé Bouddhique du Royaume du Laos*, are quoted in translation.

[*Objects*]

*Article* 1. The Saṅgha in the Kingdom of Laos is governed by the present regulation which has for its object:

1°—to reorganize the Statut du Clergé [Bouddhique du Royaume: Ordonnance Royale N° 62 du 8 Mars 1951] in order to assure the preservation of the Religion, the maintenance and restoration of monasteries [*wats*] and monuments of a religious and Buddhist nature;

2°—to develop religious education in order to promote higher intellectual and moral culture of the people and of the Saṅgha;

3°—to renovate Buddhist institutions and work and to broaden the scope of Buddhist activities.

Title I. *Hierarchy of Monks and Religious Leaders*

*Article* 2. The religious grades of the Saṅgha in the Kingdom, six in number, are established as follows [in ascending order]: *Nhotkèo, Loukkhèo, Lakkham, Khrou, Sa* and *Somdet*. Their conditions of conferment will be the object of a special Ordinance.

*Article* 3. All members of the Saṅgha in the Kingdom, monks and novices, are placed under the spiritual authority of a Superior (*Phra Sang Kharath* [the Venerable Saṅgha-rājā)] residing in the capital of the Kingdom [actually in Luang Prabang instead of Vientiane. Ordonnance Royale N° 62 significantly added here: For the administration of the Saṅgha in the Kingdom, the *Phra Sang Kharath* is assisted by a Religious Council composed of five high monks (*Chao Rajakhana*)].

*Article* 4. Each province (Khouèng) of the Kingdom constitutes a diocese. The monasteries and all members of the Saṅgha, monks and novices, are placed under the authority of a Head (*Chao Khana Khouèng*) residing in a monastery in the capital of the province in order to be in permanent contact with the Chao Khouèng (governor). The Heads of the Dioceses are amenable to the spiritual authority of the *Phra Sang Kharath*. [This sentence replaces the following from Ordonnance Royale N° 62: The Heads of the Dioceses are directly subordinate to the *Phra Sang Kharath* whom they represent to the head of each province.]

*Article* 5. All monasteries located within a Muong (district) constitute a *Khana Muong*, placed under the authority of a religious Head of the Muong (*Chao Khana Muong*) directly subordinate to the Head of the Diocese and residing in a monastery in the capital of the Muong in order to be in permanent contact with the Chao Muong.

*Article* 6. All the monasteries located within a Tassèng (subdivision of a Muong) constitute a *Khana Tassèng* placed under the authority of the *Chao Khana Tassèng* directly subordinate to the *Chao Khana Muong* and residing in a principal monastery in the Tassèng.

*Article* 7. Each monastery with resident monks and novices is placed under the authority of a Head of the monastery (*Chao Athikane Vat* [or *Wat*]) who is immediately under the orders of the *Chao Khana Tassèng.*

Title II. *Article* 21. The religious authorities above-mentioned: *Phra Sang Kharath, Chao Khana Khouèng, Chao Khana Muong, Chao Khana Tassèng* and *Chao Athikane Vat* are chosen respectively among the members of the Saṅgha of the following grades: *Nhotkèo, Loukkèo, Lakkham, Khrou, Sa* and *Somdet* [the order should be reversed!]. In the absence of monks of the higher grades, the functions of authority may be exercised by monks of a grade immediately lower and titulars with at least diplomas and certificates of religious education according to the conditions determined here:

1°—Diploma of Higher Studies (Diplôme d'Études Supérieures) for the first two grades (*Phra Sang Kharath* and *Chao Khana Khouèng*);

2°—Diploma of Secondary Studies (Diplôme d'Études Secondaires) and Certificate of Primary Studies (Certificat d'Études Primaires) for the last three grades (*Chao Khana Muong, Chao Khana Tassèng* and *Chao Athikane Vat*).

An example of type (3) Saṅgha organization—influential monastic groups—may be cited here in the case of present-day Ceylon:

The highest dignitaries in the hierarchy [Saṅgha] are, in Ceylon, the heads of the sects, the *mahānāyaka.* Below them come the *anunāyaka,* charged with representing them in certain circumstances, next the *nāyaka,* who guide each group of monks of their sect residing in a given province. It is also necessary to mention the *adhikaraṇanāyaka,* charged with assuring good order in the community and of rendering justice when necessary, and whose jurisdiction is exercised over a province, sometimes over two or three.

Outside and paralleling this hierarchy stand the *upādhyāya,* who correspond approximately to the Christian bishops. They are the preceptors of the novices and introduce the candidates to the monastic life at the time of the ordination ceremony or *upasaṃpadā* which is held in the capitulary hall (*uposathāgāra*). The term *upādhyāya* designates a title and not a function. The *upādhyāya,* less numerous than the *nāyaka* and considered as being their superiors, are appointed by the chapter of the sect of which they belong. The *ācārya* are the professors of the monastic colleges. . . .

The monastery is directed by a head today called *vihārādhipati* and formerly *mahāthera,* who is responsible for the administration and discipline. He is chosen on the seventh day after the cremation of his predecessor by the community assembled in the presence of the laity. The latter have no voice, and their presence, by no means necessary, is only traditional. Generally, it is the steward (*vinayādhikārin*) of the monastery who is thus chosen. . . .[3]

### 2. *The Regulations of the Saṅgha: The Vinaya*

The Vinaya (Pāli and Sanskrit) comprised, and still constitutes for the Saṅgha, the established "code of ethics, monastic discipline, rule, rules of morality or of canon law. In this sense [it is] applied to the large collection of rules which grew up in the monastic life and habits of the bhikkhus and which form the ecclesiastical introduction to the 'Dhamma,' the 'doctrine,' or theoretical, philosophical part of the Buddhist Canon."[4]

The Vinaya Piṭaka in Pāli of the Theravāda tradition is arranged in three parts: (1) *Suttavibhaṅgha* (analysis of the principal disciplinary rules concerning monastic offenses: the *Pāṭimokkha*), (2) *Khandakas* (chapters dealing with monastic regulations, divided into Mahāvagga or major section and Cullavagga or minor section), and (3) *Parivāra* ("appendix": summaries and classifications of the rules). The *Suttavibhaṅga* is organized into two divisions: a Mahā-vibhaṅga or Bhikkhu-vibhaṅga for monks, and a corresponding Bhikkhunī-vibhaṅga or Bhikkunī-vinaya for nuns. The Mahā-vibhaṅga states the basic monastic discipline in 227 rules: *Pāṭimokkha* ("that which should be made binding") which consists of 4 Pārājikas (offenses requiring permanent expulsion), 13 Saṅghādisesas (serious offenses decided by a formal meeting, *saṅgha-kamma*), 2 Aniyatas (concerning undetermined cases), 30 Nissaggiyas (what ought to be forgone as personal property), 92 Pācittiyas (faults requiring expiation), 4 Pāṭidesanīyas (faults to be confessed), 75 Sekhiyas (rules of training), and 7 Adhikaraṇasamathas (how to settle questions raised).

A comparable Vinaya Piṭaka in Buddhist Hybrid Sanskrit of the Sarvāstivāda tradition is similarly arranged: (1) *Vinayavibhaṅga* (cf. *Suttavibhaṅga;* including the *Prāṭimokṣa* in 250 rules), (2) *Vinayavastu* (cf. the Mahāvagga and portions of the Cullavagga of the *Khandakas*), and (3) *Vinayakṣudraka* (cf. Cullavagga) and *Vinaya-uttaragrantha* (cf. *Parivāra*). The original Buddhist Hybrid Sanskrit texts have largely been lost but are now being recovered and restored; otherwise they are available in Chinese, Tibetan, and other translated versions and adaptations which became the basis of the Vinaya in the Mahāyāna and Vajrayāna traditions.

As mentioned in Chapter IV, Section 5, important Buddhist ceremonies and practices are held periodically, especially in Theravāda areas, to observe the Vinaya as stated in the Vinaya Piṭaka. They are notably the Uposatha (meetings at new moon and full moon to expound the Dhamma and observe the Vinaya, including recitation of the *Pāṭimokkha*), the Vassa or Vassāvāsa (monastic residence or "retreat" during the rainy season), the Parāvaṇā (ceremony concluding the Vassa) and the related Kaṭhina (annual ceremony in which the laity dedicates cotton cloth to the bhikkhus for the making of robes).

Within monasteries special regulations have also long been established for their government. Such rules naturally vary according to the conditions and requirements of each institution, but a certain uniformity among them is also present due to the traditional routine of Buddhist monastic life. In some cases, however, special rules may be required; for example, the following regulations were established about 1300 A.D. for the famed Temple of the Tooth in Kandy, Ceylon, called in Pāli Dāṭhādhātughara (House of the Tooth-relic) and in Sinhalese Daḷadāmāligāva (Palace of the Tooth-relic).

(1) No one except those who lay out the couches may go in by the third golden door of the perfumed chamber of the three doors of the house of the Tooth-relic.

(2) No one else except the elders of the Church, the King, those who enter the crown room, those who look after the house of the Tooth-relic, and those versed in the Doctrine may go in by the second golden door.

(3) The company of ministers may go in by the third golden door.

(4) Any other spectator may stand outside the golden door and worship.

(5) When offerings are brought they should be brought to the accompaniment of such pomp as sky canopies, head-

dresses, a veil over the mouth, *sakpañca* and *vaḍḍāru* drums, trumpets, drums, and so forth, and on a festival day with the white parasol and the great ceremonial.

(6) When the vessels are brought for presentation every one should remain standing.

(7) When the food is brought the cooks should have a veil over the mouth, get the tooth-stick water strained, pour the spittoon water, remove the spittoon, spread a cloth . . . , arrange the row of dishes, offer the rice, and complete the offering with the ceremonial within eight (Sinhalese hours).

(8) The cloth and rice should be distributed among the servants and drummers.

(9) When great kings endowed with righteousness go to the Tooth-relic house once a day for worship they should leave all their retinue outside, cleanse themselves, enter the house with devotion and respect, take a broom and sweep the house, wash their hands, offer gold, flowers, &c., worship by meditating on the nine virtues of the Buddha, such as sainthood, make obeisance, and take upon themselves the five commandments.

(10) On every quarter-moon day a sabbath bowl of rice should be offered by the King.

(11) The King's ministers should, according to their rank, one each day, offer rice, including the district bowl.

(12) A bowl of rice should be offered daily to the Lord Mahākāśyapa and the relic.

(13) For every time a *nānu* service is prepared for the house of the Tooth-relic an assembly for the worship of Mahākāśyapa should be held twice a month.

(14) When the King enters the palace (for the first time), first the Tooth and the Bowl relics should be brought, should be protected by causing the priests to hold the protection [*Pirit*] ceremony and by sprinkling protection water, then he should enter after making an offering to the Three Gems [Ti-ratana].

(15) The monastic servants who are engaged in the guard of the Tooth-relic house, the acolytes, supervisors of the house, should attend with jackets and *mayilakaṭṭu*.

(16) Further, after purifying the Tooth-relic house under an auspicious constellation, setting up canopies, decorating with various kinds of silk cloth of varied hues, the King with the harem, the ministers, the people of the city should for seven days hold an offering of rice, flowers, lamps, with great pomp. On the seventh day after an offering of flowers, lamps, &c., has been made in the forenoon, the city should in the afternoon be decorated like the city of the gods, and, in the presence of him who holds the office of president in the Uttaromūḷa [an important monastery] and fit persons from the two families of Gaṇaväsi and Kiliṁ, the casket in which it (the relic) abides should be brought forth from the perfumed chamber and placed on an auspicious couch on a chariot adorned in the variegated fashion. Two fit persons of the Gaṇväsi and Kiliṁ families should mount the chariot to carry the casket.

(17) An auspicious elephant bearing favourable marks should be yoked to the car. Monks of seemly conduct should follow the car in order, bearing protection threads tied to the car and performing the protection rites.

(18) The protection water should be sprinkled on the city from a silver pitcher by a suitable person of the Doranāväsi family.

(19) On both sides of the car white parasols and fly-whisks should be waved.

(20) The officials and drummers of the Tooth-relic house should walk beside and in front of the chariot.

(21) After that the officials and drummers of the royal household should walk in attendance.

(22) After that the company of ministers should walk, escorted by the fourfold army for protection.

(23) After circumambulating the city in this fashion they should take it to the (King's?) house, then, in presence of the King, the one who has attained the presidency of the Uttaromūḷa, the two members of the Gaṇaväsi and Kiliṁ families, and the supervisors of the house, the seals of the casket should be broken, its Lordship the Tooth-relic should be taken out and shown by the president of the Uttaromūḷa to the reverend priests, and then its Lordship the Tooth-relic

should be placed in the King's hands, and with feelings of devotion and worship and with great pomp of fly-whisks, white parasols, chanks, &c., with an escort of the president of the Uttaromūḷa, the reverend priests, the two families of Gaṇaväsi and Kiliṁ, the company of ministers, it should be displayed from a lofty place to the multitude.

(24) To strangers it should be shown from afar under good guard.

(25) Then it should be taken to the Tooth-relic house, and with the King standing in the middle they should place the Lord in the casket and seal it with the three seals, *taṭu-kassa, pāmulpeṭṭiya,* and *gaṇa.*

(26) Grace should be given to those who have brought offerings.

(27) Revenue and gifts should be taken to the Tooth-relic house under a guard.

(28) Protection ceremonies should be held incessantly by seven or five monks.

(29) In this manner worship should be carried out annually.

(30) When rain does not fall the Tooth-relic should be worshipped in this manner.

(31) When the Lord Mahākāśyapa is exhibited he should be exhibited at a suitable place after erecting an arch.

(32) On the festival of the King's birthday and the festival of the (New) Year a grant should be made to the Tooth-relic house.

(33) At the (New) Year and the Kārtika [October-November], when presents are given to the King by the different office-bearers, presents should be offered to the Tooth-relic, afterwards presents should be given to the King.

(34) If a dispute arises concerning the Tooth-relic house, ministers appointed by the King and the president of the Uttaromūḷa should meet and decide; if anything is left undecided, the priests [*Mahasaṅgana*] should meet and decide it.

(35) Not even a *kahāpaṇa* coin from the Tooth-relic house should be taken to the King's house.

(36) If anything is taken innocently, the double should be returned within six months.

(37) Any one coming to the Tooth-relic house in fear of something should not be molested.

(38) Gifts should be given by those holding grants of freeholds in Ceylon, oil and wicks from villages holding service lands, from others monthly dues, poll tax, daily dues.[5]

## 3. *Life in a Thai Theravāda Monastery*

Life in the Theravāda Saṅgha today in many respects continues essentially in its traditional form in the monasteries of Burma (*pongyi-kyaungs*), Cambodia (*wats*), Ceylon (*vihāras* or *sanghārāmas*), Laos (*wats*), Penang (*wats* and *vihāras*), and Thailand (*wats*). In spite of certain ethnic and societal differences and increasing non-Buddhist, secular, and urban influences, the pattern of monastic life in all these institutions is fairly uniform. Thus a bhikkhu from one area will feel at home in the Saṅgha when visiting a monastery in another area. As the textual language of the Theravāda tradition, Pāli may be spoken on doctrinal matters with slight differences in pronunciation between the various countries.

The following account of monastic life in Wat Mahādhātu, Bangkok, was specially written for this book by the Venerable Phra Kaveevorayan, a Pāli scholar of the Ninth (highest) Grade and Secretary-General of Mahāchulalongkorn Rājavidyālaya, a Buddhist university located within its compound.

In most areas of Thailand it is the cultural expectation that all adult males will spend at least a few months in Buddhist monastic life. The length of time a monk [Thai: *phigsu*/Pāli: *bhikkhu*/Sanskrit: *bhikṣu*] wishes to remain a monk is determined by him alone, the monastic rules permit him to request disrobement at any time. In actual practice, however, a monk would not leave the Sangha during the Phansaa (Vassa), about three months which coincide with the season of heaviest moonsoon rain. Since religious activities are most strict and intense during this period, the following description of monastic life in the Thai Theravāda Sangha will concern the Phansaa.

During the Phansaa the monks are required to spend every night inside their own *wat* (monastery), except in certain authorized cases which are rare. Even in such instances, they must return to their own wat within seven days (cf. Sattāha-karaṇīya, that which should be done within seven days); approval for each case must be given by the Sangha (at least four monks). Therefore the Phansaa is the period of the year when there is the largest number of monks living in the same wat. Afterwards, many of them leave their wat and travel about visiting other wats, preaching or making pilgrimages to holy Buddhist places or returning to lay life.

The daily routine varies somewhat from wat to wat, but the following description of monastic life during the Phansaa at Wat Mahādhātu in Bangkok may be considered as generally typical. Since the beginning of the Bangkok Period (1782 A.D.), Wat Mahādhātu has been one of the most important centers of Buddhist education and meditation in Thailand. At the present time it accommodates Mahāchulalongkorn Rājavidyālaya, one of the two Buddhist universities in Thailand, the other being Mahāmakuta Rājavidyālaya located in Wat Bovoranives, Bangkok. During the Phansaa, about six hundred monks and novices live in Wat Mahādhātu, whereas at other times the number is usually three or four hundred.

At 4 A.M. a bell is rung for several minutes by the Phaanroong (caretaker of the wat) who is responsible for awakening the monks. The monks rise and wash their faces, clean their teeth, and sometimes take a bath. Then they put on three yellow robes: (1) the Sabong [cf. Pāli: Antaravāsaka] or lower garment which is fastened around the waist; (2) the Ciiwaun (Pāli: Cīvara [Uttarāsanga in other Theravāda areas, Cīvara being the term for robes or garments in general]) or upper garment which covers the shoulders, but only the left shoulder when the monk is inside the wat; and (3) the Sangkhaati (Pāli: Sanghāṭī) or another folded Ciiwaun which is placed over the Ciiwaun on the left shoulder.

Then the monks kneel on the floor and light candles and joss-sticks at the Phra Prathaan (an altar on which a Buddha-image has been placed; every *kuti* or residence of the monk has such an altar). Thereupon they *kraab* (make a bow from kneeling position to floor with joined palms to forehead) three times before the Phra Prathaan. Then they change their posture from kneeling to *phabphiab* (a polite, sideways sitting position in which both legs are flexed backwards on the same side with the soles of the feet everted behind). Next the monks chant the salutation to the Phra-Radtana-Traj: the Buddha, the Dhamma, the Sangha [the venerated Ti-ratana; cf. Ti-saraṇa-gamana or Saraṇattaya]. Portions of Buddhist texts, particularly the popular *Kauraniya-meeta-suud* (*Karanīya-metta-sutta*), are also chanted [after the Ti-saraṇa-gamana]. When the chanting has ended, the monks ritually transfer their merit to all kinds of living beings. Then they change their position from *phabphiab* to a cross-legged posture and begin to meditate for a few minutes. After meditation, they leave their kuti and walk around for a while in the compound of the wat. They customarily group together in twos, each monk ritually acknowledges to the other in comprehensive manner any and all infraction of the Vinaya which he may have made since his last confession. All this takes place just before sunrise. Then the monks return to their kuti, remove their Ciiwaun and Sangkhaati, and rest.

After resting for a while, the monks put on their Ciiwaun again, this time covering both shoulders, and, carrying their alms-bowls, leave the wat to receive food-offerings from the laity who are waiting along the roadsides. About 7:00–7:30 A.M., the monks return to the wat and take their breakfast in their own kuti. (In most wats outside Bangkok where there are only a few monks, they usually take their meals together.) After eating, they give a ritual blessing to their alms-givers, whether present or not.

At 8:15 A.M., the bell is rung again. This is a notice for all monks and novices to enter the Bood (Pāli: Uposatha [Uposathaggaṁ or Uposathāgāraṁ]), or sanctuary, for the Tham Wad Chaaw (morning chanting ceremony). This building is surrounded by the Siima [eight stone boundary markers] which have been specially given to the Sangha by the King. The Bood is the most important place in the wat since Sangha ceremonies, such as the ordination (Upasampadā) and Kathin (Kaṭhina), are held there. After entering the Bood, the monks take their seats in rows according to seniority, the elder monks sitting in front of the younger ones and the novices behind. About 8:30 A.M., the Caw-aawaad (head of the wat) enters the Bood and lights the candles and joss-sticks at the Buddha-altar. As this is being done, all monks and novices kneel and raise their hands to their forehead with palms joined together. After lighting the candles and joss-sticks, the Caw-aawaad sits kneeling in front of the assembly and leads them in chanting the salutation to the Phra-Radtana-Traj, followed by recitation of some suttas. All chanting is in Pāli.

After this, about 9:00 A.M., the Caw-aawaad gives basic instruction to the new monks, called Nawaka-phigsu (Navaka-bhikkhu), about the Winaj (Vinaya) and general Dhamma for half an hour or so each day. When the instruction is finished, the monks *kraab* three times toward the Buddha-image on the Phra Prathaan. Then they leave the Bood for their kuti, except that each day on a rotating basis two or three of them will go to the preceptor's residence to serve as his attendants according to the rules observed by the newly initiated. Those who return directly to their kuti now busily prepare themselves for the lesson which will be taught that evening.

At 11:00–11:30 A.M., the monks begin to take their main meal which must be finished by twelve o'clock. The food may be part of that received earlier in the morning from the laity, or it may be newly prepared by the Luug-sid (helper-boy in the wat).

After the noon meal, the monks rest for a while and then begin to read texts on the Winaj as well as other parts of the general Dhamma or an account of the Buddha's life. About 5:00 P.M., they stop their studies, take a bath and rest.

At 6:00 P.M., the bell is rung for another meeting in the Bood. For this occasion the monks wear the same three robes as in the morning ceremony. They customarily group together in twos, each monk ritually confesses to the other his Aabad (Āpatti) or infraction of the Vinaya, if any, committed since the morning confession. Then all join in the evening chanting of the suttas (Tham Wad Jen); everything is done as in the morning ceremony (Tham Wad Chaaw), the only difference being that the evening session lasts longer and more suttas are customarily chanted (each day on a rotating basis so as to include as many texts as possible over a period of time). The evening ceremony is concluded by the transferring of merit to all kinds of living beings; the whole service lasts about forty-five minutes. Then all monks and novices return to their respective kuti.

The newly ordained monks (Nawaka-phigsu) must attend the evening Dhamma classes which usually begin at 7:30 P.M. and end about 9:00 or 9:30. Four subjects are taught alternately each day: (1) Riang-Khwaam-Kae-Krathuu-Tham, or essays giving an explanation of the general Dhamma; (2) the Dhamma; (3) the story of the Buddha's life; and (4) the Winaj (Vinaya). Before the class ends, the monk-teachers give the assignment for the next meeting. Customarily before and after class, the new monks show their respect to their teachers by standing with heads slightly bowed and joined palms to forehead in salutation.

After their evening classes, the new monks may visit elder monks and ask them about the lessons they have been studying. Then they return to their kuti and prepare their lesson for tomorrow. Before retiring about 10:00–12:00 P.M., they *kraab* three times before the Buddha-image on the altar in their kuti, sometimes chant suttas, and then perhaps sit meditatively for a few minutes (Samaathi; cf. Samādhi).

Such is the daily routine of the newly ordained monks during the three months of Phansaa (Vassa).

With respect to educational matters, the new monks will study the third, or lowest, grade of Dhamma studies (Nag Tham Trii). Thereafter when they have passed their examinations in Nag Tham Trii, they are permitted to prepare for higher examinations which are in two graded series: (a) the Nag Tham (Dhamma) series taught in vernacular Thai, in progression Third Grade (Nuk Thum Trii), Second Grade

(Nuk Thum Thoo), First Grade (Nuk Thum Eek); and (b) the Paarian (Pāli language) series, which proceeds from the Third to the Ninth Grade.

Monks attend classes according to their Nag Tham and/or Paarian Grades. The time schedules of the classes vary according to the convenience of the teachers and classroom space. It is generally expected that all new monks, and senior monks intending to take the Dhamma examinations, will attend these classes without interruption from May to December, when the Nag Tham examinations are given. Those who intend to take the Paarian examinations in February will also begin their studies in May. Some monks study both subjects, Dhamma and Paarian, simultaneously and will sit for both examinations.

Mention should be made of special ceremonies which are held during Wan Phra, or Buddhist holidays on the eighth and fifteenth days of the waxing moon and on the eighth and fourteenth or fifteenth days of the waning moon. On these occasions, many people come to the wat to take the five or eight vows, called Siin (Sīla), and listen to sermons. This particular ceremony begins in the Bood at 9:00 A.M. with the monks and novices, seated on a raised carpeted part of the floor, chanting the salutation to the Phra-Radtana-Traj. This is followed by the laity similarly chanting the salutation. Then a prominent representative of the laity requests a monk to give them the Uposatha-sīla and a sermon. Usually, the head of the wat (Caw-aawaad) ascends the pulpit (*thammaad*) and expounds the Uposatha-sīla, consisting of eight vows of abstention from (1) killing, (2) stealing, (3) incelibacy, (4) lying, (5) drinking liquor, (6) taking food after 12 o'clock noon, (7) dancing, singing, music, inappropriate shows, and the use of garlands, perfumes, unguents and other things which would beautify and adorn the body, and (8) using high and luxurious seats and beds. Some of the laity take the first five vows listed above. The head monk then preaches to both monks and laity assembled for some thirty or forty minutes and concludes with a ritual blessing. Following this, the entire assembly *kraab* three times before the Buddha-image and leave the Bood.

In the afternoon, sermons will be given in the Bood by a monk other than the Caw-aawaad. These will continue until evening, when the time arrives for the monks' evening chanting ceremony (Tham Wad Jen) as previously described for ordinary days.

On every alternate Uposatha-day, there is a special Patimoog (Pāṭimokkha) ceremony held in the Bood for the monks only, excluding both novices and laity. This evening ceremony is conducted on the day of the fully waxing moon and of the fully waning moon. All monks are required to attend. At the beginning of the ceremony, all monks perform the first part of the evening chanting ceremony (Tham Wad Jen) by chanting the salutation to the Phra-Radtana-Traj. The chanting of suttas and the transferring of merit are deferred until after the Patimoog ritual is finished. One specially trained monk now recites the lengthy *Pāṭimokkha* in Pāli. This monk must recite the 227 rules clearly and fluently from memory, while another monk checks the recitation by aid of a printed text. Thus a monk who can recite the entire *Pāṭimokkha* is highly respected by all monks regardless of his age or rank. During this part of the ceremony he ascends the *thammaad* (pulpit), which physically and ritually elevates him above all the other monks including the Caw-aawaad. The recitation usually lasts about 30–45 minutes. At its conclusion, all monks acknowledge the rendering by intoning in unison the word "sādhu," an exclamation of approval. Then the reciter-monk descends from the thammaad and resumes chanting with the other monks.

Two important ceremonies begin and conclude the three months of Phansaa, the Wan Khaw Phansaa and the Wan Aug Phansaa respectively, which all monks are required to attend without exception. In the Wan Khaw Phansaa, which is held on the first day of the waning moon of the eighth lunar month, all monks pledge that they will not spend the night outside the Siima (boundary) of the wat during the Phansaa.

On the full moon day of the eleventh lunar month which ends the Phansaa, in the Wan Aug Phansaa ceremony there is a Parāvaṇā ritual which takes the place of the usual fortnightly Patimoog (Pāṭimokkha) ritual. In it every monk is expected to announce his willingness for any one in the Sangha to offer him guidance whenever it is believed that he has behaved in an improper manner. All monks are expected to give such consent regardless of their rank; even a sick monk who cannot attend the ceremony is expected to convey his consent by proxy.

Sometime during the month following the end of the Phansaa, another important ceremony is held: the Kathin (Kaṭhina) in which new yellow robes are presented by the laity to the monks in the wats. This ceremony is for monks only.

Within a few weeks after the Kathin ceremony, perhaps a third of those in the yellow robes will decide to leave the Sangha. Most of them in Wat Mahādhātu will be government officials who have been granted special leave with pay, not exceeding 120 days, in order to serve in the Sangha as male Thai according to the cultural tradition.

## 4. *Life in a Japanese Mahāyāna Monastery*

Life in the Mahāyāna Saṅgha today is undergoing marked changes in almost all areas. Economic, political, and social factors are notably affecting monastic institutions in Japan (*o-tera, -ji*), Korea (*-sa*), Taiwan (*-ssü*), Việt-Nam (*chùa-*), and Chinese communities in Hong Kong, Malacca, Manila, Penang, Singapore, and elsewhere. Nevertheless, the Buddhist monastic ideal and routine are followed with the least deviation from traditional practices whenever possible.

In Japan, for example, such life may still be observed in certain Shingon, Tendai, Zen and other monasteries. Dr. Daisetz Teitaro Suzuki has described "The Training of the Zen Buddhist Monk" according to the routine at the Engaku-ji in Kamakura. The following passages are selected from his account.

[In Zendō life there is] a spirit of grim earnestness, with which higher truths are sought; there is determined devotion to the attainment of superior wisdom, which will help to put an end to all the woes and ailments of human life, and also to the acquirement of the fundamental social virtues, which quietly pave the way to world-peace and the promotion of the general welfare of all humankind. The Zen life thus aims, besides maturing the monk's spiritual development, at turning out good citizens as social members as well as individuals.

The Zendo life may be roughly analysed into (1) life of humility, (2) life of labour, (3) life of service, (4) life of prayer and gratitude, and (5) life of meditation. After his initiation to the Brotherhood, the monk is to be trained along these lines.[6]

### (1) *Life of humility*

While there is no doubt that the chief means of supporting the Zendo life is begging, as was in the ancient days of the Buddha, begging has, besides its economic value, a two-fold moral signification: the one is to teach the beggar humility and the other is to make the donor accumulate the merit of self-denial. Both have a great social value when they are understood in their proper bearings, and what is most strongly emphasised in the monk's life is this social meaning, and not necessarily its economic importance. For if it were necessary to support themselves by some other means, the monastery authorities would soon have found the way for it. But on account of its educative value begging has been selected for the monks to be the chief method of maintaining themselves physically. On certain days the monks all go out forming a long line and walk slowly in the streets, crying "Hō." Each of them carries a bowl, in which he receives money or rice. The offering is thanked for with a short recitation. Generally, however, the monks go out in a small company of four or five. They all wear deep broad hats which permit the wearer to see only three or four feet ahead. They cannot even notice the face of the donor who may drop a cent in their bowl. This is purposely done. The donor is not to know who the beggar is, nor does the beggar observe who the donor is. The deed of charity is to be practised altogether free from personal relationships. When the latter are present, the deed is apt to lose its spiritual sense. It is just an act of favouritism, that is, it harbours in it on the one side the feeling of personal superiority and on the other the degrading consciousness of subserviency. . . .

Attached to a Zendo there are generally many householders who regularly contribute so much rice towards the maintenance of the institution. To collect such offerings, the monks are detailed to go out once a month. Each carries a bag over his shoulders, and visits the donors' houses one after another; when the bag is filled with rice, it proves to be quite a heavy load, especially when he has to walk along the muddy or pebbly country road in a storm back to his monastery. . . .

In the autumn the monks go out in the country when the farmers are ready to gather up pumpkins, daikons, potatoes, turnips, and other vegetables. They ask for such as are rejected by the farmers as unfit for the market. When they have enough collected they pile them on a hand-cart which is pulled by them as far as the foot of the hill where the monastery is situated. After that, the load will be carried on their backs up to the kitchen, and then some will be made ready for immediate consumption while others will be used for pickles or preserved for winter supply.[7]

### (2) *Life of labour*

"A day of no work is a day of no eating" is the literal rendering of the first rule of the monastery life. Pai-chang (720-814), who was the founder of the Zendo institution, was always found together with his monks engaged in some manual work. The monks wanted to keep him away because they did not wish to see their old master working as hard as themselves. But he insisted, "I have accumulated no merit to deserve service by others; if I do not work, I have no right to take my meal." His motive of work evidently came from his feeling of humility, but in fact manual labour forms one of the most essential features of the Zen life. . . .

However high and soaring to the sky our ideas may be, we

are firmly fixed to the earth; there is no way of escaping this physical existence. Whatever thoughts we may have, they must definitely be related to our body, if they are to have the power to influence life in any way. The Zen monk is asked to solve highly abstract metaphysical problems; and to do this he devotes himself to meditation. But as long as this meditation remains identified with abstractions, there will be no practical solution of the problems. The Yogin may think he has clearly seen into this meaning. But when this does not go beyond his hours of meditation, that is, when it is not actually put to experiments in his daily life, the solution is merely ideational, it bears no fruits, and therefore it dies out before long. Zen masters have, therefore, always been anxious to see their monks work hard on the farm, in the woods, or in the mountains. In fact, they themselves would lead the labouring party, taking up the spade, and scissors, or the axe, or carrying water, or pulling the cart.

There was also a democratic spirit here in action. The term *pu-ch'ing*, "all-invited", means to have every member of the Brotherhood on the field. No distinctions are made, no exemptions are allowed; for the high as well as the low in the hierarchy are engaged in the same kind of work. There is a division of labour, naturally, but no social class-idea inimical to the general welfare of the community.[8]

### (3) *Life of service*

The government of the Zendo life is entrusted to the hands of the senior members of the Brotherhood. Their offices are generally: Tenzo-ryō which looks after food supplies and prepares them for the monks: Densu-ryō which attends to all the affairs connected with the Buddha shrine; Shika-ryō which is a kind of general directing office; Fūsu-ryō which keeps accounts; Yinji-ryō which attends on the master known as Rōshi; Jisha-ryō which looks after the Holy Monk as well as the Zendo; etc. Generally the offices change twice a year. . . .

Eating is a solemn affair in the Zendo life, though there is not much to eat. The best meal called *saiza* or *otoki* which takes place about ten o'clock in the morning consists of rice mixed with barley, *miso* soup, and pickles. The breakfast is gruel and pickles, while the supper is what is left of the *saiza*. Properly speaking, the Zen monks are supposed to eat only twice a day after the fashion set up by the Buddha in India. The evening meal is, therefore, called *yaku-seki*, "medicinal food." The modes of living are to be adjusted to climatic conditions.

When they are all seated, the *Prajñāpāramitā-hṛidaya-sūtra* (*Shingyō*) is recited, the ten Buddha-names are invoked: Vairochana Buddha as the Dharmakāya pure and undefiled; Lochana Buddha as the perfected Sambhogakāya; Śākyamuni Buddha as one of the innumerable Nirmāṇakāyas; Maitreya Buddha who will descend among us in the time to come; all the Buddhas of the past, present, and future, in all the ten quarters; Mañjuśrī the Bodhisattva of Great Wisdom; Samantabhadra the Bodhisattva of Great Deed; Avalokiteśvara the Bodhisattva of Great Love; all the venerable Bodhisattva-Mahāsattvas; and Mahāprajñāpāramitā. After this, if it is breakfast, the virtues of rice gruel are recounted; if it is dinner, the prayer is offered that the meal be equally shared by all sentient beings including the denizens of the spiritual worlds. The five subjects of meditation are then repeated: (1) Do we really merit this offering? (2) We are seriously made to think about our own virtues; (3) The object is to detach ourselves from the fault of greed and other defects; (4) Meal is to be taken as medicine in order to keep the body health and strong; (5) We accept this meal so as to make ourselves fit receptacles for the truth. The Five Meditations are followed by these vows: The first morsel is for destroying all evils; the second morsel is for practising all deeds of goodness; the third morsel is for delivering all beings so that we all finally attain Buddhahood.

No words are uttered during the course of eating, everything goes on silently and in the most orderly sequence. The waiters are monks themselves taking their turn. When finished, the head-monk claps the wooden blocks. The bowls are quietly washed at the table and wiped and put up in a piece of cloth which is carried by each monk. While this is going on, some verses are recited. When the hand-bell is struck, the diners all stand and walk back to their Hall in perfect order.

When a monk is sick and cannot stand the Zendo life, he is taken into a separate room called *Enjudo* ("life-prolonging room") where he is nursed by a fellow-monk. It is thus that the young novitiate begins to learn how to serve his fellow-monks. In graver cases the patient will of course be sent to a hospital where he is with due care looked after.

Even while sick, the monk is not to release himself from spiritual exertion; he is always made to think of the masters and their ways of dealing with the problem—the problem of human ills which befall us most annoyingly in multitude of forms. . . .

The Brotherhood is a community of men pursuing one common object, and the spirit of mutual help and service is everywhere evident in its life. Democracy is also made, as was already stated, one of the principles governing this social body. Each monk, therefore, endeavours, on the one hand, to give others the least trouble for his own sake, while on the other he will do his utmost to do the most good he can for the general welfare of the community. This is known technically as "accumulating a stock of merit." It is natural that those who have successfully graduated from the Zendo life are some of the most efficiently trained and the most thoroughly equipped members of society.

To do service does not always mean to do something for others. If it is done with the thought of a reward or without the sense of gratitude and humility, it is not at all service, it is a deed of mean commercialism. The Zen monk ought to be above that. A life of service is closely related to that of humility and gratitude.[9]

### (4) *Life of prayer and gratitude*

In Zen Buddhism prayers are offered to all the Buddhas and Bodhisattvas of the past, present, and future in the ten quarters and also to Mahāprajñāpāramitā. . . . With Zen Buddhists prayer is more in the form of self-reflection and vow or determined will than asking for an outside help in the execution of desires. . . .

Besides . . . prayers and admonitions, the sutras are also daily recited in the early morning and in the afternoon. In Japanese and Chinese Buddhism sutra-reading performs a double function; primarily as getting in touch with the thought of the founder, and secondarily as creating spiritual merit. The first may better be called sutra-study whereas the latter is properly sutra-reading or reciting, for the object is just to recite it, not necessarily accompanied by an intellectual understanding of its content. The recitation itself is regarded as meritorious as it is so stated in the sutras. Not only reciting or reading but copying is also merit-producing. The sutra-reading in the Buddhist monasteries can thus be reckoned as a sort of prayer. The reading, even when its full meaning is not grasped, detaches one's mind from worldly concern and self-centered interests. Though negative, the merit herewith gained tends to direct the mind towards the attainment of Sarvajñatā.

The sutra-reading is also an expression of gratitude towards one's teachers, ancestors, and other beings generally. To be grateful in Buddhism means that Sarvajñatā has gained so much towards its realisation in the world. In this feeling there is nothing personal, that is, egotistic. The monks, therefore, in their daily exercises which consist in sutra-reading, prayer-recitation, incense-offering, bowing, and so on, express their appreciation of what the Buddhas, Bodhisattvas, patriarchs, teachers, and other personages have done for the Buddhist cause.

The sutras most commonly used in the Zen monastery are (1) The *Prajñāpāramitā-hṛidaya Sūtra,* known as *Shingyō,* (2) The *Samantamukha-parivarta* known as *Kwannongyō,* which forms a chapter of the *Puṇḍarīka Sūtra,* and (3) The *Vajracchedikā Sūtra* or *Kongōkyō* in Japanese. Of these three, the *Shingyō* being the simplest is recited almost on all occasions. Besides these Chinese translations, the original Sanskrit texts in Chinese transliteration which is pronounced in the Japanese way are also used; they belong more or less to the Dhārani class of Buddhist literature and are altogether unintelligible, even when they are translated.

On some special occasions the *Mahā-prajñā-pāramitā*

*Sūtras* in six hundred fascicules are read in the way known as *ten-doku* (*chuan-tu* in Chinese). *Ten-doku* means "to read revolving." As the sutras are of such a bulk, they cannot be finished within a prescribed period. The six hundred volumes are divided among the monks and each monk reads two or three pages in the beginning and at the end of each volume while the middle part is read by turning over the entire volume for a few times; hence the phrase "read by revolving." Each volume consisting of one long sheet of strong paper is folded up to so many folios, and when the monks read them "by revolving" the sutras look as if they were so many long narrow pieces of yellow cloth flying in the air. And especially because they recite them at the top of their voices, the whole scene is quite a lively one. The reading of the sutras is full of spiritual benefits not only for readers themselves but for all to whom the merit is dedicated. The first three early mornings of the New Year are devoted to this ceremony at all the Zen monasteries, when not only the welfare of the nation but the peace of the entire world is most earnestly prayed for.[10]

### (5) *Life of meditation*

The interior of the [Meditation] Hall [*zendō/ch'an-t'ang*] is furnished with raised platforms called *tan* which runs along the longer sides of the Hall. The *tan* is about eight feet wide and about three feet high. At one end of the empty floor oblong in shape, which occupies the centre of the building between the *tan*, there stands the shrine for Mañjuśrī the Bodhisattva, which opens towards the front entrance. This centre-floor is used for an exercise called *kinhin* (*ching-hsing* in Chinese), which consists in circulating in Indian file along the *tan*. This is practised at definite intervals during the meditation hours. This walking helps to keep the monks' minds from falling into a state of torpidity.

The *tan* has a *tatami* floor, and a space of one *tatami*, about three by six feet, is allowed to each monk. This little space is for each monk his "heaven and earth," for here he sleeps, sits, meditates, and does all other things permitted in the Hall. Whatever little belongings he has are kept at the window-end of the *tan*, where a low closet-like arrangement is provided along the whole length of the *tan*. The bedding is put away on the spacious shelf constructed overhead and concealed with a curtain.

When the hour to sleep comes which is ordinarily about 9 p.m., the monks recite the *Shingyō* (*Prajñāpāramitā-hṛidaya-sūtra*) and bow three times to Mañjuśrī. They lie down in one row. The *jikijitsu* (*chih-jih* in Chinese), who directs every movement of the monks in the Hall—the most important office in the Zendo, seeing them all quiet under the *futon*, offers his last incense to the Bodhisattva and puts away his *keisaku* ("staff of admonition," *ching-ts'e* in Chinese). When this is all done, he himself goes under a scanty *futon*. The one who sits on the opposite *tan* is called *tantō*, meaning the "head of the tan." His office is nowadays more or less honorary.

The bedding given to each monk is one broad *futon* or quilt wadded with cotton-wool, which is about six feet square in size. He wraps himself in this only, even in the midst of the cold winter, and sleeps from 9 p.m. till about 3:30 in the morning. For the pillow he uses a pair of small cushions, each about two feet square, on which during the daytime he sits and keeps up his meditation. As soon as he wakes, the bedding is put up to the common shelf overhead. He then goes out from the rear door to what may be called a general wash-stand. The stand holds one big basin filled with fresh water and supplied with a number of small bamboo dippers. The dipper does not hold much water. This is purposive, for, according to Zen philosophy, as was stated before, it is an act of impiety to use the gifts of nature too lavishly or more than is actually needed. . . .

What properly constitutes the study of Zen in the Zendo life is to study on the one hand the writings or sayings or in some cases the doings of the ancient masters and on the other to practise meditation. This practising is called in Japanese to do *zazen*, while the studying of the masters consists in attending the discourses given by the teacher of the Zendo known as *rōshi*. *Rōshi* means literally "an old teacher," but in this case "old" means "venerable," and has no reference to the age of the master. The discoursing is technically called *teishō* or *kōza*. To give a *teishō* or *kōza* does not mean "lecturing on the textbook," it means to manifest the inner meaning of it. The master (*rōshi*) does not explain anything, for he refuses to appeal to the intellect of his audience in his discourse; what he tries to do is rather to re-awaken in the minds of his monks the psychology of the ancient master that directed the course of the Zen interview in question. This being the case, the monks whose Prajñā-eye still remains closed will not be any wiser after attending so many discourses given by the Rōshi. . . .

The monk, therefore, must by all means . . . [resort to] his *koan*, which is a kind of question given him for solution. When one *koan* is successfully solved, another is given until the master is thoroughly satisfied with the understanding of his monk. There is a large number of such questions available for the purpose. But in fact when one *koan* is grasped in a most penetrating fashion, all the remaining ones present no substantial hindrances to the final Zen realisation. The *koan* exercise is the most important feature in the Zendo life.

A special posture is recommended, though the *koan* exercise can be carried on in whatever work one may be engaged and in whatever bodily position one may assume; for Zen has nothing to do with the form the body may take, sitting or lying, walking or standing still. . . .

In the Zendo [of the Rinzai School] all the monks sit facing one another along the *tan*. The practice of the Sōtō School, however, is just the opposite: instead of facing one another the monks of one *tan* sit with their backs turned against those of the opposite *tan*. When they are not actually engaged in outdoor work, or when they are permitted to look after their personal affairs, they are invariably found sitting in meditation in their Zendo.

There is a special period generally once a month during the "stay-at-home" season, which is May-August and November-February. The period called "Great Sesshin" lasts one week. *Sesshin* means "to collect thoughts," and during this period the monks are exempt from work and practise *zazen* from early morning (3:30 a.m.) till evening (9:30 or 10 p.m.), except when they eat and when they attend the *kōza* which now takes place once every day.

Without doing what is known as *sanzen, zazen* does not bear fruit. *Sanzen* means the monk's seeing the master and presenting his views on the *koan*. Ordinarily, this takes place as a rule twice a day, but during the great *sesshin* the monks have to see the master at least four times a day. But if they have no special views to present for the master's examination it is not necessary for them to do *sanzen*. This kind of *sanzen* is called *dokusan*, individual or voluntary *sanzen*. At the *sōsan*, however, no monks are allowed to stay away from seeing the master. *Sōsan* means "general *sanzen*." This is enforced three times while the *sesshin* is going on. . . .

At the end of each sojourn, the summer and the winter, each monk is taken to task to render account for his behaviour during the term. He is then free to leave the monastery where he has spent his term and go somewhere else. Each is summoned before the chief monk-official and asked what he is going to do now that the *angya* [*hsing-chiao* in Chinese, "going on foot"] season has set in and he is at liberty to take advantage of it. If he expresses the desire to leave for one reason or another, he is so registered in the book. But if he wishes to continue his Zendo life here, the chief monk may have something to say about his conduct during the period that has just past. If the monk behaved properly, he will pass without much comment. When otherwise, he will quite severely be reprimanded for his misdemeanour, and in some extreme cases even a refusal to renew his term will be the verdict. This is fatal to the career of the monk, because the stain clings to him wherever he goes, and all the Zendo doors may be found closed to him.[11]

## 5. *Life in a Tibetan Vajrayāna Monastery*

Life in the Vajrayāna Saṅgha today apparently continues in its traditional form in Bhutan, Ladakh, and Sikkim. On the other hand, Buddhist monasticism has been declining in Nepal for some centuries, and in the case of Mongolia and Tibet is subject to Communist exploitation and persecution.

The following description of monastic life in the Barbong Monastery (dPal.sPuṅs.) of the Ghagyupa School (*b*Kah.*r*Gyud.Pa = Ka-gyü-pa) in Dege, Kham (Eastern Tibet), was specially written for this book by the Chinese upāsaka Chang Chen-chi, now residing in New York City.

I first met my Guru, His Holiness Kong Ka Lama, in Hankow, China, in 1936 when I was seventeen years old. He initiated me into the Vajrayāna, and imparted to me the essential teachings of Mahāmudrā (Phyag. *r*Gya.Chen.Po.) and the Six Yogas of Nāropa (Naro.Chos.Drug.) of the Whispered Succession or the Ghagyupa School *b*Kah.rGyud. Pa.). I studied with him for six months through an interpreter. He then strongly urged me to go to Tibet because, as he rightly pointed out, one cannot understand Tibetan Buddhism thoroughly without having the direct experience of living in a Tibetan monastery.

Following his advice, I went to Dege, Kham (Eastern Tibet) in 1937, and spent my first year in the Barbong Monastery (*d*Pal.*s*Puṅs.), the center of the Karma Ghaygu, a subsect of the Ghagyupa School in Kham. I was treated as a special student in the Monastery because I was a Chinese and a layman, and also because I had quite different interests and background from those of the average Tibetan Lama. My experiences in the Barbong Monastery, as well as in other Tibetan monasteries were, therefore, not quite the same as those of the Tibetan Lamas, for I participated only in some, but not in all, of the activities and programs required and sponsored by the monasteries.

The Abbot of Barbong, Situ Rimpoche, assigned a private instructor to teach me elementary Tibetan for a few months. Then I joined the regular Seminary (*s*Lob.Grwa.) which was one of the four main organizations of the Monastery.

At that time this greatest learning center of the Ghagyudpa School in Kham consisted of four main organizations: the Temple (*d*Gon.Pa.), the Seminary (*s*Lob.Grwa.), the Meditation House (*s*Grub.Khaṅ.), and the Hermitages (Ri.-

Khrod.). Generally speaking, the Temple is the ecclesiastical center responsible for general administrative and supervisory duties; the Seminary is a school for both basic and advanced training in Buddhist studies; the Meditation House is specially designed for the very strict training in Yoga practice of the Vajrayāna; and the Hermitages are small huts and caves for those devoted yogis who have found even the monastic life too worldly for their practices.

It is indeed a very strange fact that the Seminary of a predominantly Vajrayāna monastery like Barbong did not offer any course in Buddhist Tantrism. The spirit of a seminary in most Tibetan monasteries is, I believe, to keep to the Śrāvaka tradition as closely as possible.

The main curriculum offered in the School contained four major studies: Vinaya, Abhidharma, Yogācāra, and Mādhyamika. Buddhist logic, poetry, Sanskrit, and the history of the Dharma were also taught. We had only one Chief Professor (*m*Khan.Chen.) in the Seminary, a few assistant lecturers, and about 50 students; the faculty was quite sufficient to meet the teaching demand. No tuition fee was required for enrollment in the class; one might offer the Professor as much or as little as one wished. Some form of oral examination was required for admission to the School, but otherwise the requirements were rather simple: a basic knowledge of the Dharma, a fairly good reading proficiency in Tibetan, and a letter of recommendation from a well-known Guru or monastery would ensure one's acceptance by the Seminary.

After five months of intensive training in basic Tibetan, I enrolled in the Seminary as a special student—which meant that I was exempt from many duties and attendance at many services (Tshogs.Pa.).

We arose when we heard the first gong, which was a little before sunrise. Then, after half an hour, the second gong sounded. All the monks came out of their private cells and joined in the "mass," which took place in the congregation hall. (I am not certain what ritual and prayers were used in this service, for I never attended this early morning service in the Seminary. I presume they recited the Tri-śaraṇa-gamana (*s*Kybs.*h*Gro.), the Bodhisattvas' Vows, Praises to the Buddha, repentance, dedication, etc.). This service lasted about 45 minutes; then everyone returned to his own cell to prepare his own breakfast. Except on very rare occasions, meals were not provided or prepared by the School. However, the Seminary did provide one "butter-tea" a day, in the evening. Tea and Tsampa (cooked barley flour) are the two most important items of a Tibetan meal; together with dry cottage cheese and dried meat, tea and Tsampa comprise the mainstay of the average Tibetan diet.

Preparations for a Tibetan meal in a monastery are extremely simple: just brew a pot of hot tea, add some butter and salt, and mix them well. Tibetans drink butter-tea in frightening quantities, and I often wondered how my fellow Lamas could take gulp after gulp during tea hours. The evening tea prepared and offered by the Seminary was much appreciated by everyone; one need bring only Tsampa and dry cheese and the meal was ready.

When the sun emerged from behind a mountain peak in the distance, about eight o'clock in the morning, the third gong sounded. This was also the time for the class to begin. Our classroom was rather spacious, large enough to accommodate at least fifty persons. No benches or desks were needed; we all sat on the floor cross-legged and placed our folio-scriptures, contained in a specially made bamboo folder, on our knees and waited for the instruction. But before we took our seats, we all made three obeisances to our professor, and then sat down quietly in our assigned places.

Before the professor opened his book, he usually gave a five-minute sermon to the students, such as on the importance of observing the Vinaya, tolerance, compassion, or the Bodhisattvas' Vows. Then he took up a large bowl containing many "lots" made by rolling slips of paper into little balls. On each of these lots was written the name of a student. The professor then shook the bowl with a rapid, revolving motion until one ball jumped out. He opened this lot and called out the name. The "selected student of the day" then began to "re-lecture" the lesson of the previous day. The professor would interrupt him at any time and challenge his interpretation or understanding. Although the classmates were supposed to join the professor in questioning the "selected student of the day," usually no one did so for often it was obvious that the poor student was having a difficult time. The grade or mark the student received for his re-lecture was not written down on paper but was noted in the professor's memory.

When the professor was about to begin the lesson, he first led the class in a prayer to Mañjuśrī—for Mañjuśrī is the great Bodhisattva of Wisdom who would guide us to a sound and deep understanding of the Dharma through the lesson.

The textbooks used in most Tibetan seminaries are śāstras, not sūtras. Strangely enough, no sūtra is taught in Tibetan monasteries but is used only as a reference book or for daily prayer. Since the majority of Buddhist śāstras are written in stanzas or gāthās, students are urged, if not also required as in the Gelukpa School (*d*Ge.Lugs.Pa.), to memorize the basic stanzas of the important śāstras. This practice not only helps the student to absorb fully the basic part of the text but also facilitates his quoting freely and extemporaneously during the philosophical debate (Chos. *r*Tsod.), an absolutely necessary discipline and training in many Tibetan seminaries.

The lecture by the professor usually took an hour and a half or two hours. If the lesson was extremely difficult, such as the *Abhidharmakośa* (*m*Ṅon.Pa.*m*Dsod.) or the *Abhisamayālaṃkāra* (*m*Ṅon.*r*Tog.*r*Gyan.), the teaching period was often longer. I recall the first time when I studied the *Abhidharmakośa* in Kong Ka Monastery, we spent two whole weeks on the first stanza of the book!

After the morning class, it was nearly noon. The students all returned to their quarters for the noon meal and rest. In the early afternoon, about two o'clock, the assistant lecturer (whose position was intermediary between the faculty and the students) led the class and reviewed the morning's lesson. If the weather was good, we usually went to the woods or meadows nearby to enjoy an open-air class. This time the professor was not present. And this was also the most enjoyable time of the day! Free discussions and debates, jokes and laughter filled the air. Thus the assistant lecturer played a very important role in the class: the morale and spirit of the class depended upon him.

The afternoon class began about four o'clock, with the professor reviewing the morning lesson and answering all questions from the students. This class period was a rather short one, usually lasting less than an hour. Afterwards, the students were free to spend their time as they liked, except during the half-hour evening service which they were required to attend. After the evening meal, the students could visit their classmates and talk into the night, provided they did not disturb the others. Most students spent an hour or so in meditation or prayer before retiring. This ended the day in the Seminary.

I have already mentioned that no curriculum of Tantra is offered in the seminary of a predominantly Vajrayāna monastery. Then where and when do the monks learn the teaching of Tantra? The fact is that they learn Tantra from the very first day they enter the monastery. Every monk is required to memorize thoroughly, and thus be able to recite at will without the slightest hesitation, all the basic rituals (Chos. Ga.) of the Vajrayāna practices. Initiations and Tantric studies are given frequently in the general monastery by individual gurus. A seminary, on the other hand, is the place where one learns the basic and advanced Buddhist philosophies of the Sūtra Schools (*m*Do.Lugs.). A graduate of the seminary is expected to have mastered the general philosophy of Hīnayāna and Mahāyāna Buddhism. He is then equipped with the necessary background for studying Tantra under a particular guru of his own choice. The tradition of a Tibetan seminary is strictly "Sūtra-ic" (*m*Do.Lugs.), and the atmosphere of learning there is most inspiring. When one visits such a seminary in Tibet, he can feel the spirit of Nālandā still lingering in the air.

I stayed less than a year in the Barbong Monastery and then returned to Mei Nya Kong Ka to join my Guru's School, where I remained for more than six years. During my rather brief stay in Barbong, my experience and observation of the life and organization of the Monastery naturally could not be very thorough. But because of my personal interest, I learned a great deal about the life in the Meditation House (*s*Grub.-Khaṅ.) which is, I believe, the most important and vital part of this Monastery. Applications for entering the Meditation

House were always piled high on the Abbot's desk. One must complete the training in the Meditation House before he can be called a full-fledged "Lama." The position of such a Lama is high in the monastery as well as in the community.

The training period in the Meditation House lasts three years, three months, and three days. Anyone who enters the Meditation House must be prepared to be a "voluntary prisoner," observing silence most of the time, and meditating continuously for 16 hours a day—for three years, three months, and three days—without a single day's leave! He is permitted to doze, but not to sleep lying down, for only three or four hours a day.

The House at Barbong occupied an area smaller than half an acre. It contained a small courtyard, 36 tiny cells for 36 residents, one assembly hall, a general kitchen, large lavatory, a large room for Heat Yoga (*m*Tum.Mo.) practice, and a small chamber for the Guru who leads and supervises the group. All the windows of the 36 cells faced inward on the court, so no one could see anything happening outside. One liaison officer and one servant were assigned by the Abbot to maintain contact with the outside. The training in the Meditation House was indeed most vigorous and exacting, almost incredible to witness!

The yogis awake from their doze about three o'clock in the morning and immediately begin the so-called "Four Preparatory Practices" for the day, which include: (1) One-hundred full prostrations, (2) one-hundred Mantra recitations of the Vajrasattva, (3) one-hundred Guru Yoga prayers, and (4) one-hundred Maṇḍala offerings. Two hours of silent meditation (Mahāmudrā practice) follow, and then a half-hour leave for the first meal. Upon its conclusion, the so-called regular Tantric meditation begins. It starts with the Arising Yoga (*s*Kyed.Rim.) of *r*Do.*r*Je.Phag.Mo. the main Patron Buddha of the School. This training contains two major stages: (1) a six months' practice of the "Outer Visualization Practice," i.e., the visualization of the bodily form of the Patron Buddha, and (2) an eighteen months' training in the "Inner Visualization Practice," which includes the Prāṇa and Chakra Yogas, together with the practice of the

Six Yogas of Nāropa. The regular Arising Yoga Practice (*s*Kyed.Rim.) in the House occupied four periods a day, each period lasting about two hours. When the four periods are completed, it is evening. Then all the yogis pray to the Guards of Dharma (Chos.*s*Kyoṅ.); in this case it was to Mahākalā-with-Two-Arms, the special Guard of the Karma Ghagyu Sect.

It should be mentioned here that in spite of his rigorous schedule, the yogi does have two or three hours of rest after the noon meal every day. Then, in the late afternoon, there follows a period of Heat Yoga (*m*Tum.Mo.) practice in which all the yogis join. They go to the Heat-Yoga room, take off their robes, and practice the Prāṇaāma and Bodily Movement (*h*Khrul.*h*Khor.). At night, the "Cutting Yoga" (*g*Cod.) is conducted, which is a form of Prajñāpāramitā practice most ingeniously devised by the outstanding Tibetan woman philosopher and yoginī, the great Magi Lodrun (Ma. *g*Cig.Labs.*s*Gron.) of the 11th century. The chanting and music of this Cutting Yoga are very beautiful and touching—down in the valley men and women of distant villages listen half attentively and half unmindfully to this great Song of Wisdom, as their forefathers did, from the 36 forgotten yogis whose minds are imbued in the Great Voidness as they chant in the Meditation House high on the mountain.

After repeated petitions to the Abbot, I finally received permission to visit the Meditation House twice a month. Thereby I met several most remarkable Lamas in the House, who convinced me with their living examples that true Buddhism can only be found in persistent, profound, and uncompromising meditation. Without actual meditation there is no realization, without realization there is no enlightenment, without enlightenment there is no Buddhism. In looking back upon the long years I spent in Kham—the most wonderful, adventurous, and rewarding years of my life—the deepest impression left in my mind is the spirit and tradition of the unforgettable Meditation House of Barbong.

CHAPTER SIX

# The Saṅgha: Buddhist Society and the Laity

The nature of Buddhism in society, or the lay aspects of the Buddha Sāsana, may be described in several ways.

According to the Dhamma/Dharma (Pāli/Sanskrit) all existence, individual and collective, is imperfect (*dukkha-sacca/duḥkha-satya*). Thus any society or group, including the Saṅgha itself, is subject to change (*anicca/anitya*), interrelated and composite (*anattā/anātman*), and conditioned (*dukkha/duḥkha*) by many interdependent factors (*samudaya* = *paṭicca-samuppāda/pratītya-samutpāda*). Such metaphysical views may provide the basis for a Buddhist conception of change in society and the Saṅgha, and a potential Buddhist interpretation of history.

The canonical view of the Buddha as a World Ruler (Cakkavattin/Cakravartin), usually in the role of a previous Bodhisattva, and a corresponding theory of the virtuous king as a benign Bodhisattva or even a Buddha (hence, Buddha-rāja) together with the practical recognition that the Buddha Sāsana and kingship, as institutionalized political authority, are interdependent may be the beginnings of traditional Buddhist political thought.

The Buddha's knowledge of and concern about societal matters, as reported in the Pāli Sutta-Piṭaka of the Theravāda tradition, and the Bodhisattva ideal of the

Mahāyāna tradition, which inspires and assists the laity as well as the Saṅgha, may be regarded as formative elements in Buddhist social thought.

And lastly, the responses of the laity to these teachings in relation to particular social environmental problems, and the expression of essentially all Buddhist ideas and practices in the cultural arts may be indicative of the viable nature of Buddhism in society.

### 1. *Buddhist Conceptions of Change in Society and the Saṅgha*

Various Pāli and Sanskrit, or Buddhist Hybrid Sanskrit, texts describe the nature and causes of change in the universe, in society and its government, and in the Buddha Sāsana and its Saṅgha. These views could have been supported doctrinally by the general Buddhist principle of *anicca/anitya* (impermanence, rise and decline) but evidently were more influenced by the unstable, changing state of societal affairs during the advent and development of Buddhist thought and institutions.

Changes in the cosmic order are noted in the *Pāṭika-sutta* of the Pāli Dīgha-Nikāya, but more attention is given elsewhere to the dissolution of the universe (significantly, not initial creation) and then its gradual evolution including the formation of beings and humans, the rise of the social order and attendant immorality, and hence the need for society to be governed justly by a chosen leader among men—as related in the *Aggañña-sutta* of the Dīgha-Nikāya and restated in the Buddhist Hybrid Sanskrit *Mahāvastu* of the Mahāsāṅghika School and Pāli *Visuddhimagga* by Buddhaghosa (fifth century A.D.).

A slightly different view, presented in the *Cakkavatti-Sīhanāda-sutta* of the Dīgha-Nikāya, envisages a former, ideal state of society with just government which gradually deteriorates, due largely to the inept administration and lack of consideration for public welfare by subsequent kings; hence anarchy follows, and then gradual restoration of order through a moral social compact by the people, and a new, righteous King Sankha arises coincidentally with the appearance of the Future Buddha, Metteyya (Sanskrit: Maitreya).

In any case, the texts advise kings to be mindful of their personal conduct and of their subjects' welfare and to reign by aid of the Dhamma/Dharma as taught by the Buddha and proffered by the Saṅgha. Henceforth the status and welfare of the king, of society, and of the Buddha Sāsana are correlated and interdependent: they need each other for stability.

But such a view or position also requires that the Saṅgha maintain high standards of conduct (Vinaya), based upon its knowledge and exemplification of the Dhamma/Dharma, as outlined by the Buddha and subsequently amplified and codified by the Saṅgha for monastic life. Alas! this is not easy or always done, and other, later Pāli and Buddhist Hybrid Sanskrit texts describe, prophesy, and lament such mishappenings. In the beginning, the Buddha reportedly advised the Saṅgha to be mindful of seven conditions of welfare (comparable to those similarly prescribed for the laity); later, the texts stress a necessary respect for the Dhamma/Dharma; and recently, at least in Ceylon, certain Buddhist leaders have warned the Buddhist society against the corruptive influence of "Western materialistic social and individual values"—as may be noted in the following selections.

Thus have I heard: Once the Exalted One dwelt near Vesāli at Sārandada shrine; and there a number of Licchavis visited him and saluted and sat down at one side. Then the Exalted One addressed them thus seated and said: "Licchavis, I will teach you seven things that cause not decline; listen, give heed, I will speak!"

"Yes, lord," they replied; and the Exalted One said:

"What seven things cause not decline? So long, O Licchavis, as the Vajjians shall be often assembled, much in assembly, growth for the Vajjians may be expected, not decline; so long as they shall sit down in concord, rise up in concord, do business in concord, growth may be expected, not decline; so long as they shall not decree the undecreed nor repeal the decreed, but conform to the ancient Vajjian laws as decreed, growth may be expected, not decline; so long as they shall honour, respect, venerate, revere the Vajjian elders, shall hold they ought to be listened to, growth may be expected, not decline; so long as they shall not forcibly kidnap and make live with them women and girls of their own clan, growth may be expected, not decline; so long as they shall honour, respect, venerate, revere the Vajjian shrines within and without (their borders), shall not fail to provide meet offerings as given of yore, made of yore, growth may be expected, not decline; so long as meet protection, refuge, shelter shall be provided for Vajjian arahants and it shall be known that arahants from abroad may come thither and that those here dwell in comfort, growth, O Licchavis, may be expected for the Vajjians, not decline.

"And so long as these seven things that cause not decline shall endure among the Vajjians and they shall live in conformity therewith, growth, O Licchavis, may be expected for the Vajjians and not decline."[1]

Thus have I heard: Once, while dwelling on Mount Vulture Peak, the Exalted One addressed the monks, saying: "Monks, I will teach you seven things that cause not decline; listen, pay heed, I will speak!"

"Yes, lord," the monks rejoined; and the Exalted One

said: "And what, monks, are these seven things that cause not decline?

"So long as the monks shall be often assembled, much in assembly, growth may be expected, not decline; so long as they shall sit down in concord, rise up in concord, do business in concord; shall not decree the undecreed, nor repeal the decreed, but conform to the decreed training; shall honour, respect, venerate, revere the elders, monks of experience, long gone forth, fathers of the Order, leaders of the Order, and deem them worthy to be heard; shall fall not into the power of craving's surge, the cause of renewed becoming; shall cleave to the forest bed and seat; shall each in himself make mindfulness stand up, and it shall be known that pious men in godly fellowship may come there from abroad and that those there dwell in comfort—growth may be expected for the monks, not decline.

"And so long as these seven things that cause not decline shall endure among the monks and they shall live in conformity therewith, growth may be expected, not decline."

[The Buddha then proceeds to teach the monks other sets of "seven things that cause not decline" concerning action, believing, awakening, thought, training, a lay-disciple's decline and not-decline, unprofitable and profitable matters, backslidings and progress.][2]

"If, Ānanda, women had not been allowed to go forth from the home to the homeless life into the discipline of Dhamma, declared by the tathāgata, then long would have lasted the godly life; for a thousand years would Saddhamma have lasted. But now, Ānanda, since women have gone forth . . . not for long will the godly life last; now, Ānanda, just for five hundred years will Saddhamma last."[3]

"How will it [the gradual decline of the Buddha Sāsana] occur? After my decease there will first be five disappearances. What five? The disappearances of attainment (in the Dispensation [Buddha Dhamma]), the disappearance of proper conduct [*paṭipatti*], the disappearance of learning [*pariyatti*], the disappearance of the outward form [*liṅga*], the disappearance of the relics [*dhātu*]. There will be these five disappearances.

"Here attainment means that for a thousand years only after the Lord's complete Nirvana [Pāli: Parinibbāna] will monks be able to practise analytical insights. As time goes on and on these disciples of mine are non-returners [Anāgāmins] and once-returners [Sakadāgāmins] and stream-winners [Sotaāpannas]. There will be no disappearance of attainment for these. But with the extinction of the last stream-winner's life, attainment will have disappeared. This, Sariputta, is the disappearance of attainment.

"The disappearance of proper conduct means that, being unable to practise jhana, insight, the Ways and the fruits, they will guard no more the four entire purities of moral habit. As time goes on and on they will only guard the four offences entailing defeat [Pārājikas]. While there are even a hundred or a thousand monks who guard and bear in mind the four offences entailing defeat, there will be no disappearance of proper conduct. With the breaking of moral habit by the last monk or the extinction of his life, proper conduct will have disappeared. This, Sariputta, is the disappearance of proper conduct.

"The disappearance of learning means that as long as there stand firm the texts with the commentaries pertaining to the word of the Buddha in the three Pitakas, for so long there will be no disappearance of learning. As times goes on and on there will be base-born kings, not Dhamma-men; their ministers and so on will not be Dhamma-men, and consequently the inhabitants of the kingdom and so on will not be Dhamma-men. *Because they are not Dhamma-men it will not rain properly*. Therefore the crops will not flourish well, and in consequence the donors of requisites to the community of monks will not be able to give them the requisites. Not receiving the requisites the monks will not receive pupils. As time goes on and on [Pāli] learning will decay. In this decay the Great Patthana [7th work of the Abhidhamma Piṭaka] will decay first. In this decay also (there will be) Yamaka, Kathavatthu, Puggalapannatti, Dhatukatha, Vibhanga and Dhammasangani [6th, 5th, 4th, 3rd, 2nd, 1st works of the

Abhidhamma Piṭaka]. When the Abhidhamma Piṭaka decays the Suttanta Piṭaka will decay. When the Suttantas decay the Anguttara [Nikāya of the Suttanta or Sutta Piṭaka] will decay first. When it decays the Samyutta Nikaya, the Majjhima Nikaya, the Digha Nikaya and the Khuddaka Nikaya [rest of the five collections of the Sutta Piṭaka] will decay. They will simply remember the Jataka together with the Vinaya-Pitaka. But only the conscientious (monks) will remember the Vinaya-Pitaka. As time goes on and on, being unable to remember even the Jataka, the Vessantara-jataka will decay first. When that decays the Apannaka-jataka will decay. When the Jatakas decay they will remember only the Vinaya-Pitaka. As time goes on and on the Vinaya-Pitaka will decay. While a four-line stanza still continues to exist among men, there will not be a disappearance of learning. When a king who has faith has had a pursc containing a thousand (coins) placed in a golden casket on an elephant's back, and has had the drum (of proclamation) sounded in the city up to the second or third time, to the effect that: 'Whoever knows a stanza uttered by the Buddhas, let him take these thousand coins together with the royal elephant'—but yet finding no one knowing a four-line stanza, the purse containing the thousand (coins) must be taken back into the palace again —then will be the disappearance of learning. This, Sariputta, is the disappearance of learning.

"As time goes on and on each of the last monks, carrying his robe, bowl and tooth-pick like Jain recluses, having taken a bottle-gourd and turned it into a bowl for almsfood, will wander about with it in his fore-arms or hands or hanging from a piece of string. As time goes on and on, thinking: 'What's the good of this yellow robe?' and cutting off a small piece of one and sticking it on his nose or ear or in his hair, he will wander about supporting wife and and children by agriculture, trade and the like. Then he will give a gift to the Southern community for those (of bad moral habit). I say that he will then acquire an incalculable fruit of the gift. As time goes on and on, thinking: 'What's the good of this to us?', having thrown away the piece of yellow robe, he will harry beasts and birds in the forest. At this time the outward form will have disappeared. This, Sariputta, is called the disappearance of the outward form.

"Then, when the Dispensation of the Perfect Buddha is 5000 years old, the relics, not receiving reverence and honour, will go to places where they can receive them. As time goes on and on there will not be reverence and honour for them in every place. At the time when the Dispensation is falling into (oblivion), all the relics, coming from every place: from the abode of serpents and the deva-world and the Brahma-world, having gathered together in the space round the great Bo-tree, having made a Buddha-image, and having performed a 'miracle' like the Twin-miracle, will teach Dhamma. No human being will be found at that place. All the devas of the ten-thousand world system, gathered together, will hear Dhamma and many thousands of them will attain to Dhamma. And these will cry aloud, saying: 'Behold, devatas, a week from today our One of the Ten Powers will attain complete Nirvana.' They will weep, saying: 'Henceforth there will be darkness for us.' Then the relics, producing the condition of heat, will burn up that image leaving no remainder. This, Sariputta, is called the disappearance of the relics."[4]

Such are the noble vows that I have observed during my career. But they, hearing this wondrous account, will find no pleasure in a single word. There will be laughter then, when they have heard this and this teaching. They are intent on food and sexual intercourse, always overcome by indolence, wicked crows, hating the Doctrine, always vulgar, spoiling the Doctrine, destitute of virtues. Having heard this tranquil Doctrine, they say:

"This is not the word of the Victorious One. I had a teacher, an ocean of learning, very learned, the best of narrators, and he has denied this: 'This is not at all the word of the Buddha.' Moreover he also had an old master, who had conquered the flood of virtues, and he too did not accept this: 'Do not apply yourselves to this; it is wrong.' Where there is no self and no life is taught and no individual at all, there the toil which consists of practice of good conduct and the observance of restraint is unprofitable. If there is a Mahāyāna, but no self, or being, or man in it, then my toil on it is unprofitable, as I do not find a self or a being there."

Fables, which people with wicked thoughts, heterodox thoughts, invented themselves! Never will the Victorious One say this word, which is only the discourse of [degenerate] bhikṣus. Deprived of shame and good conduct, impudent like crows, haughty and impetuous the bhikṣus of my Doctrine will be, aflame with jealousy, self-conceit and presumption. Waving their hands, swinging their legs, shaking the lappets of their robes, wearing their upper garment tightly around their throat, they go about the houses of the villages, intoxicated by liquor and presumption. Having seized the banner of Buddha they do services to the people of the householders; always they carry a scripture with them, having abandoned the mass of virtues, which gives teaching. As cattle, such as cows, asses and horses is given to them, they also get slaves, continually the mind of those vulgar men is intent on ploughing and the practices of trade. Nothing vulgar is blamable to them and there is nothing which (according to them) ought not to be done. Possessions of stūpas or of the Order and their own are the same to them. And, having seen bhikṣus who are rich in virtues, they speak ill even of them. And, having entered, those ill-behaved, crafty deceivers, those most hideous men, ruin the women.

A householder is not so desirous of delight as they are desirous after their entrance into the Order; with wives, sons and daughters they will be like householders. In the house where they are honoured with enjoyment of garments and gifts of good, there they desire the wife, as they obey the power of the kleśas, the mean. "Truly, in delights you must not indulge, they will cause you to fall into the states of animals, or pretas [ghosts], or into the hells," thus they always will speak to the householders, but they themselves are uncontrolled, and their heart is not tranquil. As they themselves are uncontrolled, the host of their pupils is not well controlled too; with talk about food and sexual intercourse days and nights will pass for them. For the sake of services, not for the sake of virtue they impart their favour to them: "Surrounded by hosts of my own pupils I always will obtain homage among men." And they tell the people: "This favour I grant them out of compassion; I never ask attendance from those hosts of pupils."

Greatly stricken with diseases, leprous, with stained limbs, very deformed, they will enter the hells, coming again and again, always abject. Without regulations and restraint, they always forsake the virtues of the bhikṣu; they are neither householders nor bhikṣus, they are shunned like a log of wood in a cemetery. They will have no respect for the teaching nor for the prātimokṣa and the discipline; they go unbound, at their own will, like kings of elephants escaped from the hook. Even when they live in the woods their mind will dwell in the villages; the mind of those men, who have been thrown down by the fire of the kleśas, is not firm. Having forgotten all buddha-virtues, the teachings, the moral precepts and the expedients, full of presumption, self-conceit and arrogance, they fall in the dreadful Avīcī [the lowest of the eight hot hells]. Always intent on the discussion of the king's affairs, on the telling of stories about thieves, devoted to promoting the interests of their relatives, they are worrying day and night.

Forsaking the meditation and study they are always occupied with the administration of the monastery, desirous of a dwelling, frowning and surrounded by unrestrained pupils. "I am no servant in the monastery: For me myself it is built. The monks who are well disposed towards me, for them there is room in the monastery." To those who are well-conducted and virtuous, supporters of the Doctrine, devoted to the interest of mankind, always applying themselves to self-control and restraint, to those they grant no favour. "This cell is designed for me and this for my fellow-monks, and this for my companion. Go away, there is not any dwelling-place for you. Seats and beds are all distributed, numerous monks are taken in here and there is no opportunity to get anything here; what will you have to eat here! Go way, bhikṣu." Never will they distribute seats or beds and like householders they will make stores, having numerous utensils and attendants.

And from all sides my true sons are threatened in the last

epoch. And then, remembering my word, they live in the woods of the border country. Ah, teaching of the excellent Victorious One, your destruction must be faced in a short time, when there will have appeared many bhikṣus who are overcome by desire of gain and hate the virtues. And always in the last epoch those who have good conduct and virtues will be despised and, abandoning the villages and the capital cities, they live in the jungle. Always honoured, destitute of virtues, disastrous slanderers, loving quarrels, the others will be considered teachers by the people and they will be aflame with self-conceit and presumption.

This, my most lovely teaching, store of virtues, mine of all virtues, will come to ruin by corruption of morality and the vices of jealousy and presumption. Like a ruined mine of jewels it will stand, like a dried up lotus-pond, like a sacrificial post of excellent jewels broken down, the teaching will be ruined in the last epoch. Thus in the most dreadful, last epoch the destruction of the Doctrine takes place and those unrestrained bhikṣus will be the destroyers of this, my teaching.[5]

Buddhist civilisation held up before all who came within its influence, a model of what a worthy human being should be, an ideal of character equally worthy of emulation by king or beggar. While this ideal found full expression in the charity, courage and wisdom of the Sangha, it was adopted by laymen and emulated by them as far as lay within their capacity. The production of wealth for social use instead of individual profit, the measuring of an individual in terms of his moral stature and true wisdom and not of his economic power, and of the nation's greatness in terms of the peace and prosperity of its inhabitants and not solely in terms of its balance of trade—these were some of the values embodied in the Buddhist ideal of character.

As we have said earlier, the prime necessity is to dethrone the false ideal which now reigns in our country as the desirable social reform, and to replace it with a more genuine and enduring ideal of public purpose and individual aspiration. In a society whose motive force is the acquisition of wealth by fair means or foul, the incidence of violence, crime, drunkenness and gambling is not a matter for surprise. Conversely, when the motive force of society is altered, the attendant evils will diminish and disappear. Till that major revolution in social thinking takes place, only piecemeal and temporary remedies for various particular ills can be suggested. The real and final remedy is the displacement of Western materialistic social and individual values and the establishment of genuine values founded on the Buddha Dhamma.[6]

## 2. *Buddhist Political Thought and Institutions*[7]

Historically speaking, in South and Southeast Asia, the Saṅgha and kingship were customarily interdependent: Saṅgha sanction and recognition of Buddhist kings were exchanged for their protection and promotion of the Buddha Sāsana. Occasionally, kings persecuted or utilized the Saṅgha for personal or non-Buddhist ends and its leaders endeavored to influence or even oppose rulers for the sake of monastic as well as public interest—thus inciting charges that both society and the Saṅgha were declining, as noted in Section 1. But in general, Buddhist sovereigns were religious-minded, enforced the Vinaya, and maintained Buddhist institutions, while Saṅgha leaders usually were moderately this-worldly-minded, served as political advisers, and organizationally helped to implement kingship at both court and provincial levels.

Thus in the development of Buddhist societies in South and Southeast Asia, Buddhism and political authority were correlated in prosperity and adversity: approval of the king by the Saṅgha ensured his public support and induced social stability, and the well-being of the Buddha Sāsana depended upon the king and nobility as well as the common people and required political recognition.

A similar situation prevailed elsewhere in Buddhist Central Asia until the advent of Islam, in Mongolia and Tibet where the Saṅgha became identified with political authority until the advent of Communism, and in China, Japan, and Korea except in periods and areas where Confucian or other beliefs predominated.

Former Buddhist contributions to political authority in Asian societies included notable expressions of political thought, proffered principles of political-social conduct, personnel assistance by bhikkhus/bhikṣus in effecting court and village administration and diplomatic missions between countries, and a cultural arts enhancement of the symbolic status of kingship. Through such means the king was customarily assured political stability and the people were provided social welfare and educational services.

Although rather unsystematic by Western models, Buddhist political thought, as found in Theravāda, Sarvāstivāda, and early Mahāyāna texts, expressed views on the origin, nature, location, objective, administration, and change of political authority which was customarily conceived in the form of kingship. Such theories evolved in Buddhist areas and periods of India from *ca.* fourth century B.C. to *ca.* tenth century A.D. or later and contributed—often with prescribed rituals and court ceremonies requiring the use of their texts—to the establishment of Buddhist kingdoms in Central Asia, China, Japan, Korea, Mongolia, Tibet, and, commingled with Hindu notions of kingship, also in Burma, Ceylon, and other countries in Southeast Asia. In more recent times in Buddhist Asia, with the advent of Western conceptions and institutions of political authority in the form of constitutional monarchies, parliamentary or presidential governments, and modern military regimes, traditional Buddhist political thought is being studied and reinterpreted for governmental guidance as in the case of Burma and for the formulation of new, non-Western political ideologies as in the case of Ceylon and, before 1945, in Japan.

In view of the varied nature of Buddhist political thought and the number of Asian societies to which it must be related in any reliable description, space here will permit only brief mention of some of the more important Buddhist texts as source materials for further study, and a few selected examples of relevant textual passages.

Regarding the origin, establishment, and location of political authority, a social-compact theory for society (establishing property rights) and a correlative governmental-contract theory for kingship (protecting property rights) were expressed principally in the *Aggañña-sutta* (cf. the *Cakkavatti-Sīhanāda-sutta*) of the Pāli Dīgha-Nikāya, and restated in the Buddhist Hybrid Sanskrit *Mahāvastu* and the Pāli *Visuddhimagga*. This latter work by Buddhaghosa (fifth century A.D.) identifies the elected king as the Buddha in the role of a Bodhisatta:

When beings had come to an agreement in this way in this aeon, firstly this Blessed One himself, who was then the Bodhisatta (Being Due to be Enlightened), was the handsomest, the most comely, the most honourable, and was clever and capable of exercising the effort of restraint. They approached him, asked him, and elected him. Since he was recognized (*sammata*) by the majority (*mahā-jana*) he was called Mahā-Sammata. Since he was lord of the fields (*khetta*) he was called Khattiya (warrior noble). Since he promoted others' good (*rañjeti*) righteously and equitably he was a king (*rājā*). This is how he came to be known by these names. For the Bodhisatta himself is the first man concerned in any wonderful innovation in the world. So after the Khattiya circle had been established by making the Bodhisatta the first in this way, the Brahmans and the other castes were founded in due succession.[8]

Elsewhere, as in the *Vajji-vagga* of the Pāli Aṅguttara-Nikāya (quoted in Section 1) and the *Mahā-parinibbāna-sutta* (cf. the *Mahā-parinirvāṇa-sūtra*), the principle of collective or representative political authority apparently lay dormant in Buddhist political theory but the practice of legislative procedure was preserved in meetings of the Saṅgha in various areas.

Regarding the nature of political authority, a juridical conception of kingship as a necessary political institution (established contractually because of the prevailing imperfect human conditions and consequent social requirements) was contained in the above-mentioned early texts. Later, however, this notion was replaced by the theory of kingship personified in the ideal Buddhist ruler who, as a Universal Ruler (Cakkavattin/Cakravartin), becomes identified as a Bodhisattva-rāja or even a Buddha-rāja (cf. Metteyya/Maitreya as a political concept) and governs more by virtue of his Buddhist merit than by divine right even though he may be recognized as the Devaputra (the Son of the Gods, the Divine Majesty).

Concerning the functions and exercise or administration of political authority, the theory prevailed among Buddhist writers that, in accordance with the contractual conditions of kingship, the purpose of a king's authority is to ensure individual and collective security and well-being. Later, a cosmological duty was added to this function by Mahāyānists, and especially Vajrayāna ritualists if not also by Theravādins in practice, of the king to co-ordinate the cosmic-natural order and the social-human order in society. Thus, the commonly recognized cosmic principle or natural law (*dhamma/dharma,* cf. Hindu *ṛta* or Chinese *tao*) was Buddhistically expressed, realized, and experienced in human affairs as "universal righteousness" through the personal and political conduct of the ideal (essentially chosen) ruler. In theory, "the science of politics" (Arthaśāstra) was regarded as subordinate to and governed by a universal and unitary ethics operative for both ruler and subjects alike. Subsequently, the interpretation developed that the king, when qualified and functioning as the temporal Protector of the Saṅgha, should serve the people through the Saṅgha and be guided by the Dhamma/Dharma, that bhikkhus/bhikṣus could serve the king like "civil servants," and that the country is "the land of the Buddha." As a result, the Saṅgha provided a monastic organization for the religious implementation of the king's administration of political authority and, as in the case of Ceylon, the Buddha Sāsana and ethnic culture became identified together as "Buddhist nationalism."

In these respects, various texts could be cited and quoted, such as the *Mahā-sudassana-sutta* of the Dīgha-Nikāya and other Pāli suttas in the Majjhima-Nikāya, Samyutta-Nikāya, Aṅguttara-Nikāya, and the Jātakas concerning kingly conduct and especially the *Suhṛllekha* attributed to Nāgārjuna (*ca.* 150–250 A.D.), the *Suvarṇaprabhāsa-(uttamarāja-)sūtra,* the *Catuḥśataka* by Āryadeva (*ca.* 170–270 A.D.), the *Rāṣṭrapālaparipṛcchā (pāla-sūtra),* the *Buddhacarita* and *Saundarānanda-kāvya* by Aśvaghoṣa (first century A.D.), the *Śikṣāsamuccaya* (which quotes other relevant texts) and *Bodhicaryāvatāra* by Śāntideva (*ca.* 691–743 A.D.), and other Buddhist

Hybrid Sanskrit works. As examples of Buddhist guidances to kings, the following passages are quoted from the *Mahāvastu*, the *Kāruṇikarāja-Prajñāpāramitā-sūtra* (from the Chinese translation *Jên-wang hu-kuo pan-chê po-lo-mi ching*), and the *Jātakamālā* by Āryaśura (sixth? century A.D.).

"O lord of men, a five-fold power is desirable for a king. Be attentive and hearken to my words.

"The first power is innate in him, the second power is the power of his sons, the third that of relations and friends, the fourth, O king, is that of his army, and regard as the fifth the matchless power of wisdom. Whosoever, O king, has this five-fold power, his kingdom is firm, prosperous, rich and populous.

"The force of wisdom is powerful above all the others. Through it a man accomplishes all he has to do, O lord of men. By it he shuns what is not to be done, and accomplishes what is to be done. It brings blessings to himself, to his relations and friends, and to the whole kingdom. A man who is deficient in wisdom in a king's affairs, even though he be of high birth, is not helpful to the king, nor dear to the kingdom. Soon, O king, such a realm is destroyed by rival kings. The subjects become alienated and seek another lord. Exceeding great honour has the king who is wise and sensible, who appoints as his ministers men who are good, courageous, brave and discerning. Glory will be his in this world and the heavenly way in the world beyond, if he has shunned unrighteousness and pursued righteousness.

"Do the right by your mother and father, O great king, for the king who has walked in righteousness in this world goes to heaven. Do the right by your son and wife, O great king, for the king who has walked in righteousness in this world goes to heaven. Do the right by your friend and minister, O great king, for the king who has walked in righteousness in this world goes to heaven. Do the right by recluse and brāhman, O great king, for the king who has walked in righteousness in this world goes to heaven. Do the right by town and country,

O great king, for the king who has walked in righteousness in this world goes to heaven. Do the right in this world and beyond, O great king, for the king who has walked in righteousness in this world goes to heaven.

"Such is my salutary counsel. Do you, O king, accept it fully, and act in accordance with it. If you will follow this, glory and renown will be yours, and your kingdom will be peaceful, prosperous, flourishing and populous."[9]

The good of his subjects is the first care of a king, and the way leading to it tends to the happiness of both (his subjects and himself). And this end will be attained, if the king loves righteousness; for people like to follow the conduct of their ruler.[10]

The Buddha said to the great kings:

"Listen attentively, listen attentively! Now I shall explain on your behalf the Law of Protecting the Country. In all countries, when riots are imminent, calamities are descending, or robbers are coming in order to destroy (the houses and possessions of the inhabitants), you, the Kings, ought to receive and keep and read this *Prajñā-pāramitā,* solemnly to adorn the place of worship (the altar), to place (there) a hundred Buddha images, a hundred images of Bodhisattvas, a hundred lion-seats, to invite a hundred Dharma-masters (priests) that they may explain this *sūtra.* And before the seats you must light all kinds of lamps, burn all kinds of incense, spread all kinds of flowers. You must liberally offer clothes, and beddings, food and medicine, houses, beds and seats, all offerings, and every day you must read this *sūtra* for two hours. If kings, great ministers, monks and nuns, male and female lay-members of the community, listen to it, receive and read it, and act according to the Law [Dharma], the calamities shall be extinguished. Great Kings, in the countries there are innumerable demons and spirits, each of whom has innumerable relatives (followers); if they hear this *sūtra,* they shall protect your countries. If riots are imminent, the demons and spirits are uproarious beforehand, and it is for this reason that the people revolt; then robbery arises, and the hundred families (the people) perish; the Kings and the Crown-princes, the princes and the hundred magistrates mutually do right and wrong. If unnatural things happen in heaven and on the earth: the sun, the moon and the stars lose their times and their courses, and great fires, inundations and storms are prevalent, if all these calamaties arise, all people must receive and keep and read this *prajñā-pāramitā.* If they receive and keep and read this *sūtra,* all their desires shall be fulfilled; they shall obtain rank and wealth, sons and daughters, wisdom and intelligence, success in their actions, human and heavenly rewards. The dangers of disease and pestilence shall be removed from them, and if fetters, the cangue or chains restrain and bind their bodies, they shall be released. Even if they have broken the four important commandments, committed the five evils and violated all the commandments, even immeasurable crimes shall all be wiped out."[11]

### 3. *Buddhist Social Thought and Practices*

As already mentioned, the Buddha taught the laity as well as the Saṅgha and was mindful of its mode of life in society; furthermore, the Saṅgha developed as a monastic institution within society and was supported by it. Consequently, the Dhamma/Dharma often presents guidances and cites examples for the laity which may be regarded here as Buddhist social thought and practices.

To a considerable extent the Eightfold Path can be followed by the layman as well as a member of the Saṅgha and the course of everyday life can be directed with a Buddhist meaning, purpose, and value. Much of the Dhamma/Dharma can be interpreted and expounded plurally as well as singularly, socially as well as metaphysically, since it basically concerns conditioned existence as a problem for all beings, individually and collectively.

On the other hand, Buddhist doctrine has also incorporated many social beliefs and customs from Indian and other Asian environments in which it has developed and been propagated. In this process, certain mores have been recognized, given Dhamma/Dharma viewpoints, and approval by the Saṅgha, and then followed anew by the laity as the Buddhist way of life. By such means Buddhism has established and maintained a living relationship with various peoples and their cultures wherever possible.

Among many Pāli texts which report the Buddha's guidance to the laity on daily conduct, the *Sigālovāda-sutta*, *Uggaka-sutta*, and *Mahā-maṅgala-sutta* will be quoted here in part as being representative of Theravāda social thought and practices still widely known and followed in South and Southeast Asia. They may be compared with the typical Mahāyāna description of the ideal householder in the *Vimalakīrti-nirdeśa-sūtra* which has been similarly influential in Chinese, Japanese, and other Buddhist societies.[12]

And how, O young householder, does the Ariyan disciple protect the six quarters? The following should be looked upon as the six quarters:—parents as the east, teachers as the south, wife and children as the west, friends and companions as the north, servants and work people as the nadir, religious teachers and brahmins as the zenith.

In five ways a child should minister to his parents as the eastern quarter:—Once supported by them I will now be their support; I will perform duties incumbent on them; I will keep up the lineage and tradition of my family; I will make myself worthy of my heritage.

In five ways parents thus ministered to, as the eastern quarter, by their child, show their love for him:—they restrain him from vice, they exhort him to virtue, they train him to a profession, they contract a suitable marriage for him, and in due time they hand over his inheritance.

Thus is this eastern quarter protected by him and made safe and secure.

In five ways should pupils minister to their teachers as the southern quarter:—by rising (from their seat, in salutation), by waiting upon them, by eagerness to learn, by personal service, and by attention when receiving their teaching.

And in five ways do teachers, thus ministered to as the southern quarter by their pupils, love their pupil:—they train him in that wherein he has been well trained; they make him hold fast that which is well held; they thoroughly instruct him in the lore of every art; they speak well of him among his friends and companions. They provide for his safety in every quarter.

Thus is this southern quarter protected by him and made safe and secure.

In five ways should a wife as western quarter be ministered to by her husband:—by respect, by courtesy, by faithfulness, by handing over authority to her, by providing her with adornment.

In these five ways does the wife, ministered to by her husband as the western quarter, love him:—her duties are well performed, by hospitality to the kin of both, by faithfulness, by watching over the goods he brings, and by skill and industry in discharging all her business.

This is this western quarter protected by him and made safe and secure.

In five ways should a clansman minister to his friends and familiars as the northern quarter:—by generosity, courtesy and benevolence, by treating them as he treats himself, and by being as good as his word.

In these five ways thus ministered to as the northern quarter, his friends and familiars love him:—they protect him when he is off his guard, and on such occasions guard his property; they become a refuge in danger, they do not forsake him in his troubles, and they show consideration for his family.

Thus is the northern quarter by him protected and made safe and secure.

In five ways does an Ariyan master minister to his servants and employees as the nadir:—by assigning them work according to their strength; by supplying them with food and wages; by tending them in sickness; by sharing with them unusual delicacies; by granting leave at times.

In these ways ministered to by their master, servants and employees love their master in five ways:—they rise before him, they lie down to rest after him; they are content with what is given to them; they do their work well; and they carry about his praise and good fame.

Thus is the nadir by him protected and made safe and secure.

In five ways should the clansman minister to recluses and brahmins as the zenith:—by affection in act and speech and mind; by keeping open house to them, by supplying their temporal needs.

Thus ministered to as the zenith, recluses and brahmins show their love for the clansman in six ways:—they restrain him from evil, they exhort him to good, they love him with kindly thoughts; they teach him what he has not heard, they correct and purify what he has heard, they reveal to him the way to heaven.

Thus by him is the zenith protected and made safe and secure.

Thus spake the Exalted One. . . .[13]

Now when the night was over, the Exalted One, robing himself in the morning, took bowl and cloak and went to Uggaha's house, and there sat down on the seat made ready. And Uggaha, Meṇḍaka's grandson, served and satisfied the Exalted One by hand with plenty of hard and soft food; and when the Exalted One had removed his hand from his bowl, he sat down at one side. Thus seated, he said:

"Lord, these girls of mine will be going to their husbands' families; lord, let the Exalted One counsel them, let the Exalted One advise them, for their good and happiness for many a day!" Then the Exalted One spoke to them and said:

"Wherefore, girls, train yourselves in this way: To whatsoever husband our parents shall give us—wishing our weal, seeking our happiness, compassionate, because of compassion—for him we will rise up early, be the last to retire, be willing workers, order all things sweetly and be gentle voiced. Train yourselves thus, girls.

"And in this way also, girls: We will honour, revere, esteem and respect all whom our husband reveres, whether mother or father, recluse or godly man, and on their arrival will offer them a seat and water. Train yourselves thus, girls.

"And in this way also, girls: We will be deft and nimble at our husband's home-crafts, whether they be of wool or cotton, making it our business to understand the work, so as to do and get it done. Train yourselves thus, girls.

And in this way also, girls: Whatever our husband's household consist of—slaves, messengers and workfolk—we will know the work of each by what has been done, their remissness by what has not been done; we will know the strength and the weakness of the sick; we will divide the hard and soft food, each according to his share. Train yourselves thus, girls.

"And in this way also girls: The money, corn, silver and gold that our husband brings home, we will keep safe watch and ward over it, and act as no robber, thief, carouser, wastrel therein. Train yourselves thus, girls.

"Indeed, girls, possessed of these five qualities, women, on the breaking up of the body after death, are reborn among the devas of lovely form."[14]

1. "Many gods and men have devised blessings, longing for happiness, tell thou (me) the highest blessing."

2. Buddha said: "Not cultivating (the society of) fools, but cultivating (the society of) wise men, worshipping those that are to be worshipped, this is the highest blessing.

3. "To live in a suitable country, to have done good deeds in a former (existence), and a thorough study of one's self, this is the highest blessing.

4. "Great learning and skill, well-learnt discipline, and well-spoken words, this is the highest blessing.

5. "Waiting on mother and father, protecting child and wife, and a quiet calling, this is the highest blessing.

6. "Giving alms, living religiously, protecting relatives, blameless deeds, this is the highest blessing.

7. "Ceasing and abstaining from sin, refraining from intoxicating drink, perseverance in the Dhammas, this is the highest blessing.

8. "Reverence and humility, contentment and gratitude, the hearing of the Dhamma at due seasons, this is the highest blessing.

9. "Patience and pleasant speech, intercourse with Sam*a*nas, religious conversation at due seasons, this is the highest blessing.

10. "Penance and chastity, discernment of the noble truths, and the realisation of Nibbâna, this is the highest blessing.

11. "He whose mind is not shaken (when he is) touched by the things of the world (lokadhamma), (but remains) free from sorrow, free from defilement, and secure, this is the highest blessing.

12. "Those who, having done such (things), are undefeated in every respect, walk in safety everywhere, this is the highest blessing."[15]

### 4. *Buddhist Lay Groups and Activities*

For centuries the Buddhist laity traditionally regarded the Saṅgha as the only Buddhist organization. But with the advent of modern technological changes, secular trends, and Western ideological challenges in society, Buddhist followers have established various Buddhist lay societies and associations. These groups had their precedent in the customary community support of the bhikkhu/bhikṣu as, for example, the *dāyakasabhā* in Ceylon, but they generally adopted the form and procedures of Western civic organizations. Thus, in the late nineteenth century the Young Men's Buddhist Association (YMBA) movement developed in Ceylon and spread to India and Burma, and subsequently Young Buddhists Associations (YBA's) were established in Japan, the United States (including Hawaii), Thailand, and Korea with comparable groups developing in China, Penang, Singapore, Việt-Nam and elsewhere.

At the present time, Buddhist social welfare work is being conducted by the Saṅgha especially in Burma (e.g., the Union Burma Social Service [= *parahita*] Sangha Association, founded in March, 1956), Hong Kong, Japan, Korea, Laos, Nepal, and Thailand and by the organized Buddhist laity, often in co-operation with the Saṅgha, in these areas (except Laos) as well as in Cambodia, Ceylon, India, Penang, Singapore, and Việt-Nam. Such welfare activities usually include education for children (at least at the elementary school level) and the provision of facilities in temples or other buildings for orphans and the poor, the aged, and sometimes for unfortunate animals, medical dispensaries and hospitals, vocational training centers, supplies for leper and refugee settlements, moral guidance for delinquents, and other assistance intended to further community spirit and well-being.

A good example of this activity is presented in the following translated summary of the Annual Report of the Young Buddhists Association of Thailand which reviewed its work for the year 1958.

The Fourth All Thailand Conference of the [National] Young Buddhists Association, convened by the Young Buddhists Association of Thailand [of Bangkok, the original group to be distinguished now from the national organization of the same name], was opened on March 13, 1959, at the Sala Santitham [in Bangkok]. The object of this Conference was to review the activities of the past year and to discuss plans for the future. A detailed record of the activities can be perused in the Annual Report of the Young Buddhists Association of Thailand for 1958 but we would like to give a short summary of it here. All the activities may be divided into eleven sections as follows:

1) *Propagation of the Dhamma and Buddha's Teachings.* On almost every Sunday of the year under review either a lecture or a discussion on the Dhamma or other aspects of Buddhism was organized at the Association's Headquarters [in Bangkok, at the office of the Young Buddhists Association of Thailand of Bangkok]. Many distinguished and learned men and women, both Thai and foreigners, were invited to give lectures, and on the second Sunday of every month there was a panel discussion and a session of answering religious questions. During the period from May to December [1958] twenty-one important lectures were given. Moreover, religious teachers were sent by the Association to many educational institutions including the Suan Sunanda Teachers Training College, Petchburi Vidyalongkorn School, Natasilpa School, The Secondary Demonstration School, and Thammasat University. Religious teachers were also sent to some of the provinces, namely to Surindr, Utaradit, Samudprakarn, and Rajburi. Twice a month the Association arranged a radio panel discussion on various aspects of Buddhism, including problems of the Dhamma, on the first Sunday of the month over the Thai TV Radio and on the last "Wan Phra" of the month over the Education Radio. Also on every Thursday a talk on some aspect of Buddhism was given on the Post Office Radio.

During the year under review the Association published several books on the Dhamma and Buddhism. Some of these books were sold and some were distributed free of charge. The most important and the most successful of the Association's publications of the year was the "Illustrated Story of the Buddha's Life for Young People." This book proved to be very popular among school children, teachers, and parents, and it went through several printings in a short time. The Association, moreover, was delighted to comply with the request from Laos for publication of this book in the Lao language. The other publications of the year 1958 were "The Buddhist Way" by Nai Sathien Bodhinanda; "Grown-ups Must Be Clever" by Major Pin Mutukanta, copies of which were distributed on Visakapuja Day [Wesak Day]; and "Jātaka Tales," copies of which were distributed on Children's Day.

The Association is at present in the process of producing a picture book about Onkuliman. For this undertaking the Association has the cooperation of Hem Vejakorn, a leading artist of Thailand.

2) *Social Services.* One of the Association's activities in this field during the year under review was the help given to the Tadindaeng Refuse Heap children. Every Sunday food, clothing, and medicine were taken to these children, regular Sunday classes were held for them by members of the Association, and trips to the Dusit Zoo and Pataya Beach were arranged. Besides, the Association managed to raise a fund of 20,000 baht [about US $1,000] which was spent on the construction of two classrooms for Vibulpracharungsan College, and in 1959 two hundred children from the Tadindaeng Refuse Heap will receive schooling in these two new classrooms.

The Association also cooperated with the Department of Public Welfare in establishing a children's club, within the Vibulpracharungsan College, with an aim to provide for these poor children a place where they could play, relax, and learn to use their spare time constructively.

During the year the Young Buddhists Welfare Unit was opened. Volunteers were invited to join the Unit and at the request of the Association the Department of Public Welfare sent officials to train the volunteers in social welfare techniques so that they might be well prepared to undertake the work of the Unit. There were 120 volunteers in all and almost half of the number were university undergraduates. The theoretical side of the training was given at the Association's Headquarters [in Bangkok] every Saturday afternoon and Sunday morning from August until the end of September. Apart from this the trainees also had a chance to do practical work and observe social workers give services at the Department of Public Welfare, at people's homes, and at other social welfare centers.

It may be said that this effort to establish the Young Buddhists Welfare Unit and to provide training in social welfare techniques, as the Association has done, is the first private enterprise of its kind in this country. It is also the first time in the history [of Thailand] that a Buddhist organization has made an attempt to organize voluntary social services which include proper training in social welfare techniques.

The Association joined the Department of Public Welfare and other social welfare organizations in establishing the Council of Social Welfare Agencies in Thailand. Its purpose is to act as a coordinator between Government organizations and private social welfare agencies in the country.

Other activities in the fields of relief and public welfare of the year under review include the rewarding of a grant of 1,500 baht [about US $75] to an undergraduate of the University of Agriculture, sending money and clothing to fire victims in Lopburi and Ubolrajdhani, collecting donations for the building fund for a Buddhist *wat* to be built in California, providing walking aids for the Public Health Center in Nondburi, and providing religious books and money for various *wats*.

3) *Voluntary Work Camp Activities.* Towards the end of 1957 the Association was invited by UNESCO to send a delegate to the International Voluntary Work Camp held in India from 1st December to 12th January 1958. Mr. Thavi Wongsratana, member of the Advisory Board of the Young Buddhists Association of Chacheongsao, was asked to represent the Association at this work camp. Upon his return, Mr. Thavi organized a camp for camp leaders at Wat Hua Suan, Tambol Smedtai, Amphur Bangkla, Chacheongsao; this effort was very successful. There were twenty-seven members in the camp and the activities included *klong*-digging, road-making, teaching health education to villagers, teaching and giving prizes to poor children, lectures, discussions, assessing the results of the camp activities, entertainment programs, and excursions.

With the view to promoting and encouraging work camps, the Young Buddhists Association of Thailand [of Bangkok], in the capacity of the head office of the Central Committee for the Young Buddhists Association, appointed a committee called "The Committee for Work Camps," comprised of members from the Young Buddhists Association of Thailand [of Bangkok] and the Young Buddhists Association of Chacheongsao. This Committee draws up work camp projects, encourages and helps the organizing of work camps all over the Kingdom, makes contact and cooperates with foreign countries in matters concerning work camp activities, and selects persons to represent Thailand at work camps abroad.

In September 1958, by invitation of the Indian Organizing Committee for Training Projects in Work Camp Methods and Techniques in Southeast Asia, the Association sent a delegation of two to the Conference on Work Camp Methods and Techniques, held in Bombay, India, from 1st to 23rd December 1958. The Association also accepted the invitation to join the Coordination Committee for International Voluntary Work Camps and this same Committee has approached the Association about the possibility of the Association being host to the International Work Camp in Thailand in 1959 or 1960.

In cooperation with the Department of Public Welfare and The Asia Foundation, the Association established five work camps, namely in Khonkaen, Ubolrajdhani, Surindr, Rayong, and Chacheongsao; these camps will be conducted by university undergraduates. So far about five hundred undergraduates have applied for admission to work camps but the Association will select about two hundred and fifty from that number and give them training in work camp techniques, social welfare work, rural development, and other useful branches of knowledge.

4) *Cooperation with Young Buddhists Associations in the Provinces.* At present there are twenty-one Associations belonging to the group [the (National) Young Buddhists Association of Thailand], namely the Young Buddhists Association of Thailand [of Bangkok, the original group], the Young

Buddhists Association of Chiengmai, YBA of Cholburi, YBA of Ubolrajdhani, YBA of Lampoon, YBA of Lampang, YBA of Nan, YBA of Chacheongsao, YBA of Nakorn Rajsima, YBA of Songkhla, YBA of Khonkaen, YBA of Uttaradit, YBA of Payao, YBA of Kamkuenkeo, YBA of Klaeng, YBA of Pibul Mangsaharn, YBA of Surindr, YBA of Nakorn Sawan, YBA of Puvieng, YBA of Lopburi, and YBA of Bangkeo.

In order to coordinate and control the activities and policies of these Associations a central committee was appointed. It was called the Central Committee for the Young Buddhists Association and was comprised of three members from each Association, from whom the chairman, vice-chairman, and secretary-general are appointed. The Central Committee has so far convened three All Thailand Conferences of the [National] Young Buddhists Association. The first conference took place in Chiengmai in January 1956, the second in Ubolrajdhani in December 1956, and the third in Cholburi in February 1958. At the third conference the Rules governing the Central Committee for the Young Buddhists Association were revised and a resolution was passed making the Young Buddhists Association of Thailand [of Bangkok] the office of the Central Committee.

5) *Activities on Important Days.* During 1958, three important days were observed by the Association, namely the Visakapuja Day [Wesak Day], the Khao Pansa (First Day of Phansaa or Vassa), and Children's Day. On Visakapuja Day, which fell this year on 2nd June, the Association organized celebrations in the Assembly Hall of the Ministry of Culture [in Bangkok] to commemorate the occasion which has much significance for all Buddhists, and at the same time to raise money for the Young Buddhists Welfare Fund for the Refuse Heap children.

On Khao Pansa Day which fell this year on 1st August, the Association made arrangements for members to gather together and present food and gifts to monks and novices and hear a sermon given by Phra Thera in accordance with the usual custom of observing this day.

On the eve of Children's Day, that is on 5th October, the Association broadcast a panel discussion on the importance of Children's Day and projects of organizations for children over the Thai TV Radio. On Children's Day itself the Association distributed books, presented food to monks at Wat Benjamabopitr, and attended a sermon given by Phra Wanarat. A get-together of members was held at the Sangha Hospital and the Association also put up a pavilion in the Dusit Zoo to provide refreshments and first aid for children who visited the Zoo on that day. A party was given for seventy Refuse Heap children at Nai Lek Kiengsiri's house.

6) *Excursions and Educational Tours.* In order to promote closer relationship between members of the Association and to enable members to get to know one another better, an excursion to Pataya Beach was organized on 24th June. Many Refuse Heap children were also taken along on this trip.

Many educational tours of places of archaeological and historical importance were arranged, namely a tour of Wat Jetupon on 14th September; a tour of several *wats* in Nakorn Pathom, including a Kathina ceremony at Wat Huay Jake, on 2nd November; and a tour around the ruins and excavations in Ayudhya on 21st December.

7) *Association Committee Meetings. . . .*

8) *Library Administration. . . .*

9) *The Fifth Conference of the World Fellowship of Buddhists. . . .*

10) *Publication of the Association News Bulletin. . . .*

11) *Size of Membership. . . .*

At the Fourth All Thailand Conference of the [National] Young Buddhists Association many items [of new business] were considered, including the amending of rules governing the Central Committee for the Young Buddhists Association, propagating Buddhism among young people, social welfare work, establishing the Young Buddhists School and Hostel, [aiding] rural development, improving the library, and encouraging more Young Buddhists Associations to be established. . . .[16]

### 5. *Buddhist Expressions in the Cultural Arts*

Consideration here of Buddhist expressions in the cultural arts may be a fitting conclusion to this exposition of the Budda Sāsana/Śāsana as a way of life for the individual and society.

For many centuries in Asia, various conceptions and venerations of the Buddha have been presented in sculpture and painting as well as in poetry and folk-literature. Interpretations and representations of the Dhamma/Dharma have been expressed in painting and architecture as well as in textual expositions. And all have been correlated and fused with life in ceremonies, rituals, and folk-drama. Indeed, the study of Buddhist thought and practice requires an understanding of the Buddhist arts which have brought the Buddha, the Dhamma/Dharma, and the Saṅgha more directly into the lives of many peoples.

Satisfactory description cannot be given here of Buddhist iconography, the meaning and use of the Mahāyāna-Vajrayāna esoteric media (*mantra, mudrā, maṇḍala, dhāraṇī*), or of Buddhist influences on Asian art and esthetics (such as that of Zen in Japanese painting, tea-ceremony, flower-arrangement, landscape gardening, poetry, and Nō-drama). The participation of Buddhist conceptions in the architectural symbolization of kingship in Buddhist Southeast Asia in former times is also a special study of twofold interest.

However, one example here may indicate the correlation of doctrine, iconography, architecture, and ritual in Buddhist thought and practice: the form, meaning, and veneration of the thūpa/stūpa. The following interpretation is given by the Anagārikā Brahmacāri Govinda (now

Lama Anagārikā Govinda) in his *Some Aspects of Stupa Symbolism*.

[In the *Mahā-parinibbāna-sutta* of the Pāli Dīgha-Nikāya] the Buddha gives a new meaning to the stūpas [Pāli: thūpas]. They are no longer intended to be the abodes of souls or spirits or mere receptacles of magic substances as in prehistoric times, but memorials which should remind later generations of the great pioneers of humanity and inspire them to follow their example, to encourage them in their own struggle for liberation and to make their hearts "calm and happy."

Thus the caitya [Pāli: ceitya] is elevated from the service of the dead to the service of the living. Its meaning does not remain centered in the particular relics, or the particular personality to whom those remains belonged, but in that higher actuality which was realized by the Holy Ones. The Buddha does not say "a stūpa should be erected for me or for my disciples" but "for the Awakened Ones and their disciples."

Thus the stūpas did not become objects of hero worship but symbols of nibbāna, of illumination.

In this connection it may be mentioned that some of the old stūpas were covered from top to bottom with small triangular recesses for oil lamps, so that the whole monument could be illuminated and appeared as one huge radiating dome of light.

The universality of the principle of enlightenment (bodhi) and the boundlessness of the Enlightened One who has surpassed the limits of individuality, who is deep and immeasurable like the ocean—this universality is expressed in the cosmic symbolism of the stūpa. Its main element, the cupola, in fact, imitates the infinite dome of the all embracing sky which includes both, destruction and creation, death and rebirth. The early Buddhists expressed these principles by comparing the cupola of the stūpa to the water bubble and the egg (aṇḍa) as the symbol of latent creative power (as such "aṇḍa" was also a synonym for the universe in the oldest Indian mythology), while the kiosk or altar-like structure (harmikā) which rose on the summit of the cupola, symbolised the sanctuary enthroned above the world, beyond death and rebirth. Nepalese stūpas, which in many respects have preserved archaic features, decorate the harmikā with painted human eyes, thus suggesting a human figure in the posture of meditation hidden in the stūpa: the crossed legs in the base, the body up to the shoulders in the hemisphere, the head in the harmikā. This also corresponds to the psycho-physiological doctrine of the cakras or centres of psychic force, which are located one above the other in the human body and through which consciousness develops in ascending order: from the experience of material sense-objects through that of the immaterial worlds of pure mental objects, up to the supramundane consciousness (lokuttara-cittaṁ) of enlightenment which has its base in the crown cakra of the head (sahasrara cakra). The latter would correspond to the harmikā.

The symbolism proceeds in two lines, the cosmic and the psychic; they find their synthesis in the psycho-cosmic image of Man, in which the physical elements and laws of nature and their spiritual counterparts, the different world planes (loka) and their corresponding stages of consciousness (lokiya cittāni) as well as that what transcends them (lokuttara-cittaṁ) have their place. . . .

The altar-shaped harmikā on the summit of the cupola was crowned by one or more honorific umbrellas of stone and served, in accordance with its symbolical importance, as a receptacle of relics; in pre-Buddhistic times these were buried most probably in or under the massive and more or less flattened stone hemisphere or its (round) terrace-like base if such a one existed. The resemblance of the harmikā to a sacrificial altar is perhaps not unintentional, because the Holy One, instead of sacrificing other beings, sacrifices himself to the world. As the Buddha teaches: There is only one sacrifice which is of real value, the sacrifice of our own desires, our own "self." The ultimate form of such a sacrifice is that of a Bodhisattva who renounces even nirvāṇa until he has helped his fellow-beings to find the path of liberation.

From the standpoint of the sacrificial altar also, the later idea, which compares the harmikā with the element of fire, gets a new significance. Even the eyes on the harmikā of

Nepalese stūpas fit into this symbolism, because according to the Tantras, fire (agni) corresponds to the eye (faculty of vision, also of inner vision).

The stūpas were surrounded by great stone fences (vedikā) originally made of wood, as their architectural character indicates, separating the sacred place from the profane world. Most of them were decorated with auspicious signs in order to ward off evil influences and to prepare the minds of the worshippers before entering the sanctuary. Four beautifully carved gates, (toraṇa), the climax of the decorations of the fence, opened towards the four quarters of the world, emphasizing the universal spirit of the Buddha Dharma, which invites all beings with the call: "come and see!" The inner space, between the fence and the stūpa, and the circular terrace (medhi) at the basis of the cupola were used as pradakṣinā patha for ritualistic circumambulation in the direction of the sun's course. The orientation of the gates equally corresponds to the sun's course, to sunrise, zenith, sunset and nadir. As the sun illuminates the physical world, so does the Buddha illuminate the spiritual world. The eastern toraṇa represents his birth (buddha-jati), the southern his enlightenment (sambodhi), the western his "setting in motion the wheel of the Law" (dhammacakkapavattana) or the proclamation of his doctrine, and the northern his final liberation (parinibbāna).

The entrances were built in such a way that they appear in the ground plan as the four arms of a svastika, which has its centre in the relic shrine on the top of the hemisphere in other words: in place of the cosmic centre, which according to ancient Indian ideas, was mount Meru with the tree of divine life and of knowledge (in Buddhism the Bodhi tree), there stood the Buddha, the Fully Enlightened One, who realized that knowledge in his own life. . . .

It is interesting to see how closely the architectural development follows the spiritual growth of the Buddha Dharma. . . . The original elements of the stūpa speak the same language if we analyse them from the psychological point of view. The ground-plan and starting principle of the stūpa is the circle, the symbol of concentration. As a three-dimensional form the stūpa is essentially a hemisphere, it represents the principle of concentration in a higher dimension which does not only co-ordinate the forces of one plane but creates an equilibrium of all the forces concerned, a complete relaxation of tension, the harmony of coming to rest within oneself. Every point of the surface is equally related to the centre, gets its meaning and its importance from there, immune against external influences or disturbances, combining concentration and restfulness. . . .

The symbolical meaning of the different parts of the stūpa according to the description of the [Tibetan] Tanjur [in terms of the orthodox Abhidhamma] is as follows . . . :

I. The first step of the four-sided basal structure, i.e., the foundation of the whole building corresponds to the Four Foundations of Mindfulness (cattāri satipaṭṭhānāni), namely: (1) mindfulness as regards the body (kāyānupassanā satipaṭṭhānaṃ); (2) mindfulness as regards sensation (vedanānupassanā satippaṭṭhānaṃ); (3) mindfulness as regards the mind (cittānupassanā satippaṭṭhānaṃ); (4) mindfulness as regards the phenomena (dhammānupassanā satippaṭṭhānaṃ).

II. The second step of the four-sided basal structure corresponds to the Four Efforts (cattāri sammappadhānāni): (1) the effort to destroy the evil which has arisen (uppannānaṃ pāpakānaṃ pahānāya vāyāmo); (2) the effort to prevent the evil which has not yet arisen (anuppannānaṃ pāpakānaṃ anuppādāya vāyāmo); (3) the effort to produce the good which has not yet arisen (anuppannānaṃ kusalānaṃ uppādāya vāyāmo); (4) the effort to cultivate the good that has arisen (uppannānaṃ kusalānaṃ bhīyobhāvāya vāyāmo).

III. The third step of the four-sided basal structure corresponds to the Four Psychic Powers (cattāro iddhipādā): (1) the desire to act (chandiddhipādo); (2) energy (viriyiddhipādo); (3) thought (cittiddhipādo); (4) investigation (vīmaṃsiddhipādo).

IV. The fourth step or the top of the four-sided basal structure corresponds to the Five Faculties (pañcindriyāni): (1) the faculty of faith (saddhindriyaṃ); (2) the faculty of energy (viriyindriyaṃ); (3) the faculty of mindfulness (satindriyaṃ); (4) the faculty of concentration (samādhindriyaṃ); (5) the faculty of reason (paññindriyaṃ).

V. The circular basis of the cupola corresponds to the Five Forces (pañca balāni) which are of the same kind as the Faculties, namely the forces of faith, energy, mindfulness, concentration and reason. These two groups represent the passive (latent) and the active side of the same properties and they can be regarded practically as one category. The same holds good of their architectural counterparts: they were originally one element, the mediator between the cubic substructure and the hemisphere, and were split into two according to the usual tendency of later periods to subdivide or to multiply the original elements. . . .

VI. The cupola (aṇḍa) represents the Seven Factors of Enlightenment (satta bojjhaṅgā): (1) mindfulness (satisambojjhaṅgo); (2) discerning the truth (dhammavicāya sambojjhaṅgo); (3) energy (viriya sambojjhaṅgo); (4) rapture (pīti sambojjhaṅgo); (5) serenity (passaddhi sambojjhaṅgo); (6) concentration (samādhi sambojjhaṅgo); (7) equanimity (upekkhā sambojjhaṅgo).

VII. The Harmikā corresponds to the Eightfold Path (aṭṭha maggaṅgāni): (1) right views (sammā diṭṭhi); (2) right aspirations (sammā saṃkappo); (3) right speech (sammā vācā); (4) right action (sammā kammanto); (5) right livelihood (sammā ājīvo); (6) right effort (sammā vāyāmo); (7) right mindfulness (sammā sati); (8) right concentration (sammā samādhi).

VIII. The stem of the tree of life corresponds to the Tenfold Knowledge (ñāṇaṃ): (1) knowledge of the law [Dhamma]; (2) knowledge of other persons' thoughts; (3) knowledge of relations; (4) empirical knowledge; (5) knowledge of suffering; (6) knowledge of the cause of suffering; (7) knowledge of the annihilation of suffering; (8) knowledge of the way that leads to the annihilation of suffering; (9) knowledge of the things connected with despair; (10) knowledge of the non-production of things.

Up to the Harmikā or the seventh element in the construction of the stūpa, the Tanjur follows word by word the enumerations of the Pāli-Abhidhamma as found for instance in the third paragraph of the seventh chapter (Samuccaya-Saṅgaha) of Anuruddha's Abhidhammattha-Saṅgaha. . . . it is characteristic that the categories representing the stūpa up to the Harmikā are identical with those of the orthodox canon while those which correspond to the tree of life show certain deviations. This indicates that the development of the more elaborate shape and symbolism of the crowning parts of the stūpa (htī) took place in later periods and under the influence of post-canonical ideas closely connected with the growth of Mahāyāna. . . .

IX. The thirteen discs or layers of the tree of life which correspond to the mystical powers of the Buddha. Ten of them are mentioned in Aṅguttara-Nikāya, Dasaka-Nipata XXII.

The 13 mystical powers according to the Tanjur: (1) The mystical power, consisting in the knowledge of the places which are suitable for the preaching and the activity of the Buddha; (2) the knowledge of the ripening of the different kinds of karma; (3) the knowledge of all the (states of) meditations, liberations, ecstasies, and unions with higher spheres; (4) the knowledge of the superior and inferior faculties; (5) the knowledge of the different inclinations of other beings; (6) the knowledge of the different spheres of existence; (7) the knowledge of those ways which lead to any desired end; (8) the knowledge and recollection of former existences; (9) the knowledge of the time of death and of rebirth; (10) the destruction of evil forces; (11 to 13) the three foundations of the particular mindfulness of the Buddhas (āveṇikasamṛtyupasthāna).

The 10 powers (dasa-tathāgata balāni) according to Aṅguttara-Nikāya: (1) The Enlightened One perceives what is possible as possible, what is impossible as impossible in accordance with reality; (2) he perceives the results of actions done in the past, the present, and the future according to circumstances and causes, etc.; (3) he perceives every result, etc.; (4) he perceives the world with its different elements, etc.; (5) he perceives the inclinations of other beings, etc.; (6) he perceives the superior or inferior faculties of other beings, etc.; (7) he perceives the purity or impurity of the states of trance and of liberation, of concentration and its attainments, etc.; (8) he remembers innumerable former existences, etc.; (9) he perceives with the celestial eye, the purified, the supra-human how the beings re-appear according to their deeds, etc.; (10) by conquering his passions he has attained, perceived and realized by himself the passionless liberation of heart and mind, etc.

At first sight this scholastic symbolism will appear rather arbitrary, but if we examine it more carefully we find that it is consistent with the constructive principles of the stūpa and their ideology. It represents the way to enlightenment, revealing the psychological structure of the Buddha-Dharma and the qualities of the Enlightened One in whom the Dharma is realized. The stūpa, accordingly, is as much a memorial for the Buddhas and saints of the past as a guide to the enlightenment of every individual and a pledge for the Buddhas to come.

As the stūpa consists of three main elements, socle, hemisphere and crowning parts, the spiritual development also proceeds in a threefold way. The first part (foundation) contains the preparatory, the second one (hemisphere) the essential conditions or psychic elements of enlightenment, the third one (harmikā and tree of life) consists in its realisation. Each of these main parts has again three subdivisions.

The first, preparatory step is mental and analytical. Just as the foundation of the monument rests on the natural ground, the foundation of the spiritual building of Buddhism rests on the experience and analysis of nature as far as it is accessible in the psycho-physical constitution of man.

The second preparatory step is moral: morality based on the insight into the nature of life.

The third preparatory step intensifies the mental and moral achievements and converts them into a psychic dynamism which arouses those latent forces which are the essential conditions or elements of enlightenment.

These elements from the static axis of the Buddhist system and occupy the central part of the stūpa: the hemisphere, its basis and the uppermost terrace on which it rests. The fact that the latter represents the same five psychic elements as the circular basis of the hemisphere justifies its combination with the central group, though from the standpoint of architecture it forms only the link between the original substructure and the hemisphere.

The first step of the upper triad (the harmikā) corresponds to the three steps of the substructure: it starts with right views and aspirations (sammā diṭṭhi and sammā saṃkappo) which are the outcome of the analytic knowledge (pañña) prepared in the first step; it continues with right speech, right action and right livelihood (sammā vācā, sammā kammanto, sammā ajīvo), which is the fulfillment of morality (sīlaṃ); it culminates in right energy, concentration and meditation (sammā vāyāmo, sammā sati, sammā samādhi) in which the dynamic forces of psyche reach their greatest potentiality.

Knowledge, morality, and concentration (paññā, sīlaṃ, samādhi) are the pillars of the Buddha-sāsanā. Morality has no meaning or value without knowledge. Therefore knowledge is placed before morality. Concentration on the other hand without morality is like a house without foundation. Morality is the discipline in the outer life on which concentration, the discipline of the inner life, is built up. Morality thus has to precede concentration. Concentration again is of no value in itself; it is an instrument for the attainment of insight (vipassanā) and wisdom (paññā), which in its turn produces a higher form of morality and concentration until by this spiral-like progression (in which the same elements re-appear on each higher stage in greater intensity) Bodhi or enlightenment is attained. On the first step Paññā is not more than an intellectual attitude, based on investigation and reflection (vitakkavicāra). On the corresponding step of the higher triad it is wisdom based on the experience of meditation (inner vision) and in the last two stages it is enlightenment as the true nature of a Tathāgata. These two highest stages (represented by the stem and the 13 Bhūmis of the tree of life) correspond to the factors of enlightenment (bojjhaṅga) and to those faculties and forces which form their basis.[17]

*Parting*

Studying the same doctrine,
Under one master,
You and I are friends.
See yonder white mists
Floating in the air
On the way back to the peaks.
This parting may be our last meeting
In this life.
Not just in a dream,
But in our deep thought,
Let us meet often
Hereafter.[18]

# References

## Chapter I


1. Sukumar Dutt, *The Buddha and Five After-Centuries* (London: Luzac & Co., Ltd., 1957), p. 123.
2. English Editorial Department (trans.), *Dīgha Nikāya: Sīlakkhandha. 1. Brahma-jāla Sutta (Discourses on the Supreme Net)* (Rangoon: Union Buddha Sāsana Council, n.d.), pp. 1–2: paragraphs 5–6.
3. F. L. Woodward (trans.), *The Book of the Gradual Sayings (Anguttara-Nikāya) or More-Numbered Suttas*, Vol. I (*Ones, Twos, Threes*) London: Published for the Pali Text Society by Luzac & Co., Ltd. (1932) 1951), pp. 171–173: Aṅguttara-Nikāya [Vol. 1], III. Tika-nipāta, 7. Mahā-vagga, 65 *Kālāma-sutta.*
4. Walpola Rahula, *What the Buddha Taught* (Bedford, England: Gordon Fraser, c1959), pp. 4–5.
5. Herbert V. Guenther (trans.), *Jewel Ornament of Liberation* . . . [by] sGam.po.pa (London: Rider & Co. (1959), Introduction, pp. x–xi.
6. See Bhikshu Sangharashita, "Ordination and Initiation in the Three Yānas," *The Middle Way* (London), XXXIV, No. 3 (November, 1959), 94–104.
7. Edward Conze, *The Prajñāpāramitā Literature* ('S-Gravenhage: Mouton & Co., 1960), p. 9.
8. E. Obermiller, "The Doctrine of Prajñā-pāramitā as Exposed in the Abhisamayālaṃkāra of Maitreya," *Acta Orientalia* (Leiden), XI (1933), 1.
9. *Ibid.*, pp. 14–17.
10. Franklin Edgerton, *Buddhist Hybrid Sanskrit Language and Literature* (Banaras: Banaras Hindu University, 1954), pp. 7, 61–62.
11. Lionel Giles, *Descriptive Catalogue of the Chinese Manuscripts from Tunhuang in the British Museum* (London: Published by The Trustees of the British Museum, 1957), Introduction, pp. ix–xiii.
12. T. W. Rhys Davids and William Stede (eds.), *The Pali Text Society's Pali-English Dictionary* (Chipstead, Surrey: The Pali Text Society, 1921–1925), Part VIII, p. 156b: "Saraṇa." Hereafter cited as *PTS-Dictionary*. See also Mrs. [C. A. F.] Rhys Davids (ed. & trans.), *The Minor Anthologies of the Pali Canon.* Part I: *Dhammapada:* Verses on Dhamma, and *Khuddaka-pātha:* The Text of the Minor Sayings (London: Humphrey Milford, Oxford University Press, 1931), Introduction to Khuddaka-pāṭha, pp. xliv–xlv.

13. *PTS-Dictionary*, III, 74b-75a: "Gamana."
14. Mrs. Rhys Davids, *op. cit., Khuddaka-pāṭha,* pp. 140–141: *Saraṇattayaṃ.*
15. T. W. Rhys Davids (trans.), *Dialogues of the Buddha* (London: Henry Frowde, Oxford University Press (1899) 1956), p. 94: Dīgha-Nikāya [Vol. I], 1. Sīlakkhandha-vagga, 2. *Sāmañña-phala-sutta.*
16. V. Fausböll (trans.), *The Sutta-Nipâta* (Oxford: Clarendon Press, 1881), pp. 39–40: Khuddaka-Nikāya, 5. Sutta-Nipāta [text 235–237], II. Culla-vagga, 1. *Ratana-sutta.*
17. E. Obermiller (trans.), "The Sublime Science of the Great Vehicle to Salvation, Being a Manual of Buddhist Monism. The Work of Ārya Maitreya with a Commentary by Āryāsanga," *Acta Orientalia* (Leiden), IX (1931), 143.
18. *Ibid.*, pp. 143–144.
19. Guenther, *op. cit.*, p. 144.
20. *Ibid.*, Introduction, p. xi; see chap. 8, "Taking Refuge," pp. 99–111.

Chapter II

1. E. M. Hare (trans.), *The Book of Gradual Sayings* (*Anguttara-Nikāya*) *or More-Numbered Suttas.* Vol. IV (*The Books of the Sevens, Eights and Nines*) (London: Published for the Pali Text Society by Luzac & Co., Ltd. (1935) 1955), pp. 237–238: Aṅguttara-Nikāya [Vol. IV], IX. Navaka-nipāta, 1. Sambodha-vagga, 4. *Nandaka-sutta.*
2. *PTS-Dictionary,* VI, 111b–112b: "Buddha."
3. G. P. Malalasekera, *Dictionary of Pāli Proper Names.* Vol. II, *N-H.* (London: Published for the Pali Text Society by Luzac & Co., Ltd. (in *Indian Text Series* 1938) 1960), pp. 294–295.
4. Har Dayal, *The Bodhisattva Doctrine in Buddhist Sanskrit Literature* (London: Kegan Paul, Trench, Trubner & Co., Ltd., 1932), pp. 19, 20, 23, 24, 25, 26, 27–28.
5. Nalinaksha Dutt, *Early Monastic Buddhism.* Vol. I (Calcutta: Calcutta Oriental Book Agency, 1941), chap. X, "Method of Preaching and Teaching," pp. 124–134.
6. Dutt, *The Buddha and Five After-Centuries*, pp. 82–88.
7. *Ibid.*, pp. 10–11.
8. Richard Robinson (trans.), *Chinese Buddhist Verse* (London: John Murray (1954), p. 48: In Praise of the Buddha, *Suvarṇa-prabhāsa Sūtra,* chap. 12; from the Chinese translation by I-ching, A.D. 703.
9. T. W. and C. A. F. Rhys Davids (trans.), *Dialogues of the Buddha.* Part III (London: Humphrey Milford, Oxford University Press (1921) 1957), p. 137: Dīgha-Nikāya [Vol. III], 3. Pātika-vagga, 30. *Lakkhaṇa-sutta.*

10. J. J. Jones (trans.), *The Mahāvastu*. Vol. III (London: Luzac & Co., Ltd., 1956), pp. 105–106 [text iii, 106–107].
11. T. W. Rhys Davids (trans.), *Buddhist Suttas* (Oxford: Clarendon Press, 1881), pp. 92–93: Dīgha-Nikāya [Vol. II], 2. Mahā-vagga, 16. *Mahā-parinibbāna-sutta*, chap. V, 25–26; cf. pp. 125–126.
12. J. S. Speyer (trans.), *The Gâtakamâlâ or Garland of Birth-stories by Ârya Sûra* (London: Henry Frowde, Oxford University Press, 1895), pp. 93–94; *Jātakamālā*, X; cf. pp. 55–56 and 114–115.
13. Rhys Davids, *Dialogues of the Buddha*, Part III, pp. 73–74: Dīgha-Nikāya [Vol. III], 3. Pāṭika-vagga, 26 *Cakkavatti-sīhanāda-sutta*.
14. Dayal, *The Bodhisattva Doctrine*, pp. 44–46.
15. Shashi Bhushan Dasgupta, *An Introduction to Tāntric Buddhism* (2d ed.; Calcutta: University of Calcutta, 1958), pp. 10–13.
16. Benoytosh Bhattacharyya, *The Indian Buddhist Iconography* (2d ed.; Calcutta: Firma K. L. Mukhopadhyay, 1958), pp. 42–56, 73–77, 79–80, 82–98, 100, 102, 124, 251.
17. T. W. Rhys Davids, *Buddhism: Its History and Literature* (2d ed.; New York and London: G. P. Putnam's Sons, 1904), pp. 108–112: Buddhaghosa, *Sumangala Vilāsinī* (Commentary on the Dīgha-Nikāya).
18. I. B. Horner (trans.), *The Book of the Discipline* (*Vinaya-Pitaka*). Vol. I (*Suttavibhaṅga*) (London: Published for the Pali Text Society by Luzac & Co., Ltd., 1949), Translator's Introduction, p. lii.
19. *PTS-Dictionary*, III, 85a: "Gotrabhū."
20. *Ibid.*, VIII, 184a: "Sota–"; cf. VIII, 134a: "Saddhā–," IV, 173b: "Dhamma–."
21. *Ibid.*, VIII, 119a: "Sakadāgāmin."
22. *Ibid.*, I, 31b: "Anāgāmin."
23. *Ibid.*, I, 77a: "Arahant."
24. Sir Monier Monier-Williams, *A Sanskṛit-English Dictionary* (new ed.; Oxford: Clarendon Press, 1899), p. 1097a: "Śrāvaka."
25. Horner, *The Book of the Discipline*, Vol. I, p. 42: Sutta-vibhaṅga [text iii, 23], Pārājika I.
26. Robinson, *Chinese Buddhist Verse*, p. 30: *Kāśyapa-parivarta-sūtra;* from the Chinese version by Dānapāla.
27. Daisetz Teitaro Suzuki, *The Training of the Zen Buddhist Monk* (Kyoto: The Eastern Buddhist Society, 1934), pp. 5–6: Shan-chao of Fên-yang (d. 1024 A.D.), "Song of Going on Foot," translated by Suzuki and adapted here.
28. Mrs. Rhys Davids (trans.), *Psalms of the Early Buddhists. I.—Psalms of the Sisters* (London: Published for the Pali Text Society by Geoffrey Cumberlege, Oxford University Press, 1909,

1932, 1948), p. 25: Khuddaka-Nikāya, 9. Therī-gāthā [text 23–24], Canto II: XXI. Sumangala's Mother.
29. *Ibid.*, p. 27: Khuddaka-Nikāya, 9. Therī-gāthā [text 27–28], Canto II: XXII. Cittā.
30. *Ibid.*, pp. 72–73: Khuddaka-Nikāya, 9. Therī-gāthā [text 112–116], Canto V: XLVII. Paṭācārā.

Chapter III

1. Th. Stcherbatsky, *The Central Conception of Buddhism and the Meaning of the Word "Dharma"* (London: Royal Asiatic Society, 1923), pp. 73–75, 96–97.
2. *Ibid.*, pp. 106–107.
3. Rahula, *What the Buddha Taught,* pp. 32–34.
4. Th. Stcherbatsky, *The Conception of Buddhist Nirvāṇa* (Leningrad: Publishing Office of the Academy of Sciences of the USSR, 1927), pp. 39–43.
5. I. B. Horner (trans.), *The Collection of the Middle Length Sayings (Majjhima-Nikāya)*. Vol. I. *The First Fifty Discourses (Mūlapaṇṇāsa)* (London: Published for the Pali Text Society by Luzac & Co., Ltd., 1954), p. 180: Majjhima-Nikāya [Vol. I], I. Mūlapaṇṇāsa, III. Tatiya-vagga, 23. *Vammīka-sutta.*
6. *Ibid.*, pp. 319–320: Majjhima-Nikāya [Vol. I], I. Mūlapaṇṇāsa, IV. Mahāyamaka-vagga, 38. *Mahā-taṇhāsaṅkhaya-sutta.*
7. Mrs. Rhys Davids and F. H. Woodward (trans.), *The Book of the Kindred Sayings (Saṃyutta-Nikāya) or Grouped Suttas.* Part II. *The Nidāna Book (Nidāna-vagga)* (London: Published for the Pali Text Society by Luzac & Co., Ltd. (1922) 1952), pp. 81–82: Saṃyutta-Nikāya [Vol. II], II. Nidāna-vagga, 12. Nidāna-saṃyutta, 7. Mahā-vagga, 68. *Kosambi-sutta.*
8. Bhikkhu Ñāṇamoli (trans.), *The Path of Purification (Visuddhimagga)* by Bhadantācariya Buddhaghosa (Colombo, Ceylon: R. Semage, 1956), p. 564: Part III, chap. XVI [B. Description of the Truths], 23.
9. Stcherbatsky, *The Conception of Buddhist Nirvāṇa*, pp. 60–62: [Section] XXI, Conclusion.

Chapter IV

1. F. L. Woodward (trans.), *The Book of the Kindred Sayings (Saṃyutta-Nikāya) or Grouped Suttas.* Part V *(Mahā-vagga)* (London: Published for the Pali Text Society by Luzac & Co., Ltd. (1930) 1956), pp. 356–357: Saṃyutta-Nikāya [Vol. V], V. Mahā-vagga, 12. Sacca-saṃyutta, II. *Dhamma-cakkappavattana-sutta.*
2. Th. Stcherbatsky (trans.), *Madhyānta-vibhaṅga.* Discourse on Discrimination between Middle and Extremes ascribed to Bodhi-

sattva Maitreya and commented by Vasubandhu and Sthiramati (Moscow and Leningrad: Academy of Sciences of USSR Press, 1936), Notes, p. 01 [= 107].

3. T. R. V. Murti, *The Central Philosophy of Buddhism.* A Study of the Mādhyamika System (London: George Allen & Unwin, Ltd. (1955), pp. 209–210.
4. Stcherbatsky, *Madhyānta-vibhaṅga,* pp. 24–26. A few typographical errors have been corrected.
5. T. W. and C. A. F. Rhys Davids (trans.), *Dialogues of the Buddha.* Part II (London: Published for the Pali Text Society by Luzac & Co., Ltd., 1910; 2d ed., 1938; 3d ed., 1951), pp. 343–345: Dīgha-Nikāya [Vol. II], 2. Mahā-vagga, 22. *Mahā-satipaṭṭhāna-sutta.* Cf. similar statement by Sāriputta in Majjhima-Nikāya [Vol. III], III. Uparipaṇṇāsa, IV. Vibhaṅga-vagga, 141. *Saccavibhaṅga-sutta.*
6. *PTS-Dictionary*, III, 61b: "Khandha."
7. *Ibid.*, VIII, 149b: "Sampadā."
8. Woodward, *The Book of the Gradual Sayings*, 214–215: Aṅguttara-Nikāya [Vol. I], III. Tika-nipāta, 9. Samaṇa-vagga: 88.
9. Horner, *The Collection of the Middle Length Sayings,* Vol. I, pp. 362–363: Majjhima-Nikāya [Vol. I], I. Mūlapaṇṇāsa, V. Cuḷayamaka-vagga, 44. *Cūḷavedalla-sutta.*
10. Ñāṇamoli, *The Path of Purification*, pp. 1, 3–5: Part I, chap. I [I. Introductory], 1, 7–10. The braces are mine to be distinguished from the parentheses and brackets used by the translator.
11. Union Buddha Sāsana Council, *Dīgha Nikāya: Sīlakkhandha,* 1, p. 2: paragraphs 7–10. The bracketed numbers are my own, inserted for reference purposes.
12. Cf. Rhys Davids, *The Minor Anthologies of the Pali Canon.* Part I. *Khuddaka-pāṭha,* pp. 140–141: *Dasasikkhāpadaṃ.*
13. See *PTS-Dictionary*, VIII, 171b–172b: "Sīla."
14. Dayal, *The Bodhisattva Doctrine*, p. 236; for the Six Pāramitās see pp. 165–248. On *prajñā* (Tibetan: *śes.rab*) see Guenther, *Jewel Ornament of Liberation*, Introduction, pp. xiii–xiv, note 3.
15. Dayal, *op. cit.*, p. 248; for the Seventh Pāramitā see pp. 248–269.
16. On *jñāna* (Tibetan: *ye.śes*) see Guenther, *op. cit.*, Introduction, p. xiv, note 3.
17. Ñāṇamoli, *op. cit.*, pp. 352–353: Part II, chap. IX, 124. The braces are mine.
18. Guenther, *op. cit.*, pp. 148, 149, 150.
19. *Ibid.*, Introduction, pp. xii–xiii.
20. Ñāṇamoli, *op. cit.*, pp. 343–344: Part II, chap. IX, 92–97. The brackets are the translator's.
21. J. J. Jones (trans.), *The Mahāvastu.* Vol. I (London: Luzac & Co., Ltd., 1949), pp. 39, 40, 52 [text i, 46, 48, 62, 63].

22. Dayal *op. cit.*, pp. 75–76.
23. *Ibid.*, p. 270.
24. J. F. Dickson (ed. & trans.) "The *Upasampadá-Kammavácá*, being the Buddhist Manual of the Form and Manner of Ordering of Priests and Deacons. The Pāli Text, with a Translation and Notes," *Journal of the Royal Asiatic Society of Great Britain and Ireland*, New Series (London), VII (1875), Article I, 1–16. The account quoted here is from pp.1–2, 6–7, 9–13 and omits part of the author's introductory remarks and some notes as well as the romanized Pāli text and translation given on pp. 3–6 and 7–9. The braces are mine to be distinguished from the parentheses and brackets used by the editor-translator.

Chapter V

1. For example, see William Frederick Mayers, *The Chinese Government*, rev. by G. M. H. Playfair (3d ed.; Shanghai: Kelly and Walsh, Ltd., 1896), Part XII, "Tibet and the Lamaist Hierarchy," pp. 105–122. Cf. Part X, "Buddhism and Taoism," pp. 84–86.
2. For example, see J. Prip-Møller, *Chinese Buddhist Monasteries* (Copenhagen: G. E. C. Gads Forlag; London: Oxford University Press, c1937), esp. pp. 358–369. This work has long been out of print and deserves republication; unfortunately, permission to quote from it in this book was not granted.
3. André Bareau, *La vie et l'organisation des communautés bouddhiques modernes de Ceylan* (Pondichéry: Institut Français d'Indologie, 1957), pp. 71, 72 translated here.
4. *PTS-Dictionary*, VII, 81b: "Vinaya."
5. A. M. Hocart, *The Temple of the Tooth in Kandy*. Memoirs of the Archaeological Survey of Ceylon, Vol. IV (London: Published for the Government of Ceylon by Luzac & Co., 1931), Chap. VI, pp. 34–37.
6. Suzuki, *The Training of the Zen Buddhist Monk,* p. 4.
7. *Ibid.*, pp. 17, 19, 20.
8. *Ibid.*, pp. 23-24.
9. *Ibid.*, pp. 31, 33–35, 37.
10. *Ibid.*, pp. 47, 51–52.
11. *Ibid.*, pp. 62–63, 68–69, 73–74, 75–76, 89.

Chapter VI

1. Hare, *The Book of the Gradual Sayings,* Vol. IV, pp. 10-11; Aṅguttara-Nikāya [Vol. IV], VII. Sattaka-nipāta, 3. Vajjī-vagga: 19.
2. *Ibid.*, Vol. IV, p. 13: Aṅguttara-Nikāya [Vol. IV], VII. Sattaka-nipāta, 3. Vajjī-vagga: 21; cf. 22-30.

3. *Ibid.*, Vol. IV, pp. 184–185: Aṅguttara-Nikāya [Vol. IV], VIII. Aṭṭhakanipāta, 15. Sa-ādhāna-vagga: 51.
4. Edward Conze (ed.), *Buddhist Texts through the Ages* (Oxford: Bruno Cassirer, 1953, pp. 47–50: *Anāgatavamsa,* trans. I. B. Horner. Brackets and italics are mine.
5. Jacob Ensink (trans.), *The Question of Rāṣṭrapāla* (Zwolle: N. V. Drukkerij en Uitgeverij van de Erven J. J. Tijl, n.d.), pp. 28–31 [texts 28–32].
6. *The Betrayal of Buddhism.* An abridged version of the Report of The Buddhist Committee of Inquiry [of the All-Ceylon Buddhist Congress] (Printed at Dharmavijaya Press, Balangoda; first pub. February 4, 1956), 2499/1956, pp. 100–101.
7. This section is adapted from my paper "Buddhism and Political Authority" prepared for the Sixteenth Conference on Science, Philosophy and Religion in Their Relation to the Democratic Way of Life, New York City, August 29–September 1, 1960. The Proceedings will be edited by Harold D. Lasswell and Harlan Cleveland and published by the Conference on Science, Philosophy and Religion as *Challenges to Traditional Ethics: Government, Politics, and Administration.*
8. Ñāṇamoli, *The Path of Purification,* p. 460: Part II, chap. XIII, 54.
9. Jones, *The Mahāvastu,* Vol. I, pp. 232–234 [text i, 280–281].
10. Speyer, *The Gâtakamâlâ,* p. 198: chap. XXII, 98; for amplification see p. 198: chap. XXII, 93–97.
11. M. W. de Visser, *Ancient Buddhism in Japan* (Leiden: E. J. Brill, 1935), Vol. I, pp. 132–133; trans. from the Chinese trans. by Kumārajīva, during 402–412 A.D., chap. 5, the main part of the text dealing with its principal object: protecting the country.
12. See Ryusaku Tsunoda, Wm. Theodore de Bary, Donald Keene (comps.), *Sources of the Japanese Tradition* (New York: Columbia University Press, 1958), pp. 101–106: adapted from Hokei Idumi, "Vimalakīrti's Discourse," *The Eastern Buddhist* (Kyōto), III, No. 2, 138–141. Cf. Robinson, *Chinese Buddhist Verse,* pp. 22–27: chap. 8, "The Bodhisattva's Household."
13. Rhys Davids, *Dialogues of the Buddha,* Part III, pp. 180–183: Dīgha-Nikāya [Vol. III], 3. Pāṭika-vagga, 31. *Sigālovāda-sutta,* 27–33.
14. E. M. Hare (trans.), *The Book of the Gradual Sayings* (*Anguttara-Nikāya*) *or More-Numbered Suttas.* Vol. III (*The Books of the Fives and Sixes*) (London: Published for the Pali Text Society by Luzac & Co., Ltd. (1934) 1952), pp. 29–30: Aṅguttara-Nikāya [Vol. III], V. Pañcaka-nipāta, 4. Sumana-vagga, 33. *Uggaka-sutta.*
15. Fausböll, *The Sutta-Nipâta,* pp. 43–44: Khuddaka-Nikāya, 5. Sutta-nipāta [text 257–268], II. Cūḷa-vagga, 4. *Mahāḷmaṅgala-sutta.*

16. Translated by Miss Napa Bhongbhibhat from the article published in the *Sapada Sarn* (Bangkok) for April 4, 1959.
17. Anagarika B. Govinda, *Some Aspects of Stupa Symbolism* (Allahabad and London: Kitabistan, 1940), [Part I] pp. 2–4, 5; [Part II] pp. 11–18.
18. Beatrice Lane Suzuki, *Impressions of Mahayana Buddhism* (Kyōto: The Eastern Buddhist Society; London: Luzac and Co., 1940), p. 120: trans. from "Parting" by Kōbō Daishi (774–835 A.D.).

# Index

TO IMPORTANT BUDDHIST CONCEPTIONS AND PRACTICES